THE CHILD AND THE WORLD

STUDIES IN SECURITY AND INTERNATIONAL AFFAIRS

The Child and the World

Child-Soldiers and the Claim for Progress

Jana Tabak

The University of Georgia Press
Athens

© 2020 by the University of Georgia Press
Athens, Georgia 30602
www.ugapress.org
All rights reserved
Set in Minion Pro by BookComp, Inc.

Most University of Georgia Press titles are
available from popular e-book vendors.

Printed digitally

Library of Congress Cataloging-in-Publication Data in process

ISBN: 9780820356396 (hardcover : alk. paper)
ISBN: 9780820356402 (pbk. : alk. paper)
ISBN: 9780820356389 (ebook)

To my parents, the best adults I've ever met

*To Theo, for disordering my ideas and, in doing so,
teaching me so much about who I am and who I can be*

To Yaniv, for being my home when everything seems to fall apart

CONTENTS

ACKNOWLEDGMENTS

This book began a long time ago, when I was a master's student at the Institute of International Relations at Pontifical Catholic University of Rio de Janeiro (PUC-Rio), and my mom gave me Ishmael Beah's autobiographical book, *A Long Way Gone: Memoirs of a Boy Soldier*. Having the opportunity to learn about his childhood through his own words was a life-changing experience for me. A lot has happened since then, and being able to thank the individuals who were important to the writing of this book is a great privilege. First, I would like to express my most sincere gratitude to my dear friend, dissertation adviser, and mentor, Monica Herz, who has taught me so much throughout my entire academic life, not only about international politics, but also about being a critical researcher and human being without silencing my own values and beliefs. This book is infinitely better for her insightful and sensitive thoughts. Additionally, I was fortunate to have the advice and guidance of two other esteemed professors: Daniel Thomas Cook, who generously agreed to have me as a visiting scholar at the Department of Childhood Studies at Rutgers University and who patiently guided my research project while I was there. It was a great honor for me to be advised by a scholar who through questions—and not necessarily answers—was able to teach me so much about the child (or children) and childhood(s) and, consequently, about myself. And my friend and thesis adviser, Nizar Messari, who introduced me to academic life in his uniquely generous and elegant way and who kept on attentively advising me whenever I turned to him for guidance or assistance. Also, I would not have been able to complete this process without the support of other esteemed professors at the Institute of International Relations at PUC-Rio: Anna Leander, Carolina Moulin, João Pontes Nogueira, and R. B. J. Walker. Also, I am very lucky to have had the opportunity to engage in inspiring conversations with Professor Paulo Esteves, who contributed so much to my writing process with his difficult questions, his expressions of discomfort regarding my approach toward child-soldiers, and his brilliant inputs, and Professor David Rosen, whose work I have admired since the beginning of my studies of children in armed conflict situations.

Additionally, I am very thankful to the nongovernmental organizations (NGOs), UNICEF, and UN representatives and diplomats who took time out from their busy schedules to meet with me and share their experiences. Our conversations gave me so much to think about that it is difficult to imagine what the result of this work would have been without their enlightening and challenging narratives. I must also express my gratitude to both the Brazilian graduate funding agency, Coordenação de Aperfeiçoamento de Pessoal de Nível Superior-Brasil (CAPES), which partially financed my research (Finance Code 001), and Fundação de Amparo à Pesquisa do Estado do Rio de Janeiro (FAPERJ), the Rio de Janeiro state funding agency, for providing invaluable resources and funding. Also, great appreciation is extended to Lisa Bayer, Thomas Roche, and Katherine La Mantia for their guidance and to the anonymous reviewers from University of Georgia Press, whose careful reading and excellent suggestions have greatly improved the book.

I am indebted to friends, old and new, for whose love, joy, support, and advice I will be forever thankful: Leticia Badini, Renata Benveniste, Claudia Berlinski, José Raphael Berredo, Isabel Cantinho, Leticia Carvalho, Paulo Chamon, Ana Carolina Delgado, Marta Fernandez, Jessica Landes, Lia Lopes, Silvia Messer, Natalia Rayol, Rafael Sento Sé, Maira Siman Gomes, Manuela Trindade Viana, and Roberto Yamato. You rock! Also, I am very appreciative of my dear friends Leticia Carvalho, Victória Santos, and Victor Lage for their continued support, helpful reading, and fundamental inputs on early drafts of this manuscript. I can't thank you enough.

Much love and gratitude is extended to my family. My mom, Eliane, whose support in the form of many hugs and words of encouragement was fundamental for the fulfillment of this work. Her sensitivity to others, her curiosity, and her unstinting effort to discover and go after what really makes her happy have always been an inspiration for me. And, of course, I would never have started learning about and from child-soldiers if she had not given me Beah's book in the first place. For that, I will be forever thankful. My dad, Daniel, my greatest example of generosity, discipline, and determination. His words of wisdom and incentive are always in my mind, and they are so powerful. Thank you, Dad, for making me believe that it is always possible to move on and to do better—"Twendai"! I am also very fortunate to have my sisters as my best friends. Sheina, who taught me through her work and words to care about and respect differences, and Bruna, for always being there for me and for making me laugh over my endless anxieties and fears. Knowing that we will always be together—regardless of the geographical distance—is like a safe haven for me. I love you all so much.

Finally, for everything and more, I cannot thank my boys enough for their love and support. To Yaniv, whose love, support, and patience sustained me throughout the writing of this book, and whose critical eye and comments helped me be sure that I was on the right track. Also, thank you for telling me to stop writing (just for a moment) and for helping me rest in your arms when all I needed was to take a deep breath. It is no exaggeration to say that without you there would be no book. To Theo, who has invited me to embark on the most intense and wonderful adventure of my life. Your curious way of looking at the world and your puzzling questions fascinate and teach me every day. Being your mom has brought me hope, light, and happiness. *Eu amo muito vocês hoje e sempre.*

LIST OF ABBREVIATIONS

CAAC	Children and Armed Conflict
CAPES	Coordenação de Aperfeiçoamento de Pessoal de Nível Superior–Brasil
DDR	Disarmament, Demobilization and Reintegration
DRC	Democratic Republic of Congo
FAPERJ	Fundação de Amparo à Pesquisa do Estado do Rio de Janeiro
IASC	Inter-Agency Standard Committee
ICC	International Criminal Court
ICISS	International Commission on Intervention and State Sovereignty
ICRC	International Committee of the Red Cross
ILO	International Labour Organization
IR	International Relations
LRA	Lord's Resistance Army
MONUSCO	United Nations Organization Stabilization Mission in the Democratic Republic of the Congo
MRM	Monitoring and Reporting Mechanism
NGO	nongovernmental organization
OAU	Organization of African Unity
Renamo	Mozambican National Resistance
SDGs	Sustainable Development Goals
SCSL	Special Court for Sierra Leone
SRSG	Special Representative of the Secretary-General
SPLA	Sudan People's Liberation Army
UNCRC	UN Convention on the Rights of the Child
UNDP	United Nations Development Programme
UNICEF	United Nations Children's Fund
UNITA	National Union for the Total Independence of Angola
UN OSRSG for CAAC	United Nations Office of the Special Representative of the Secretary-General for Children and Armed Conflict

THE CHILD AND THE WORLD

Childhood, Its Deviations, and the Governance of the Future

A bright sunny day, a colorful garden, and a child with crayons. The mother by his side keeping him safe and cozy. This scenario does not prompt any kind of concern and needs no further clarification: it is just a happy, playful, innocent moment in an ordinary childhood. However, what happens if instead of coloring the paper, these crayons are ammunition for a weapon the child is carrying? What if the gun is not a toy, but a real AK-47 that is probably taller than the boy?[1] What about the protective, caring mother? She is not there. This situation would not just be disturbing—it would actually be quite unthinkable if it were not for the innumerable stories about children engaged in armed conflicts that are published in the media and international organizations' reports.

Child-soldiers are not imaginary figures, however unthinkable they may be within a particular, albeit generalized, conception of childhood; they are actually a constant in almost every armed conflict around the world. While the participation of children in wars may cast into question the idea of childhood as a "once-upon-a-time story with happy and predictable ending,"[2] it also elicits fear, uncertainty, revulsion, horror, and sorrow by turning the (natural) idea of a protected and innocent childhood on its head. As appalling and destabilizing as the accounts about child-soldiers may be, reflecting on them and exploring what they articulate and (re)produce in terms of the establishment and maintenance of order in international politics is also illuminating. Here, the aim is both to problematize the boundaries that articulate child-soldiers as essentially deviant and pathological in relation to the "normal" child, and to show how these specific limits are instrumental in (re)producing and promoting a particular version of the international political order. The focus, then, is not on investigating the silenced experiences of child-soldiers but on the threat they present by departing from the protected territory of childhood, disquieting everyday international life.

I seek in this book to theorize childhood as a key element in the consolidation of states and the International (or, the Modern International), understood as a regime of power whose emergence in the modern world was able at the same time (1) to articulate sovereign nation-states as the main members of the international system; (2) to produce the model of adult national citizens as subjects of national sovereign states recognized and authorized by other states to act on behalf of them; and (3) to elaborate and deploy a set of norms and practices regulating the relationship among nation-states and individuals inside, if one wants, the international society. I do so by challenging and problematizing assumptions that tend to (re)produce and locate children in a specific universalizing narrative predicated on ideas of innocence, vulnerability, irrationality, and need for protection. Childhood is understood here as a social construct related to the processes by which international politics is ordered. I examine the construction of the limits of a "normal" childhood, which is (re)produced as if it were universal, regardless of locality or context, and how these boundaries forge a (putatively universal) model for the development of mature citizens. Despite the existence of multiple childhoods, a body of international law devoted exclusively to children has been developed since 1924 that prescribes a detailed model of childhood and the child, which I have termed the world-child. In this model, the child has several set features, such as immaturity, vulnerability, and reduced capability until the age of eighteen, and there are certain sets of needs and requirements for it to develop healthily, safely, and happily toward adulthood.

Within this formulation, child-soldiers are invariably framed as an international problem to which only certain subjects, narratives, theories, and responses are admitted. The problem is not addressed in a political vacuum but as a fault line running through the norm of the world-child. At the same time that the child-soldier is an *endangered* child, a victim of war and adult abuse, he or she is also *dangerous*. Rather than offering the promise of a good future, he or she has the potential to put national and international progress in jeopardy by failing to take the steps prescribed in the model of child development. This particular understanding of and response to the child-soldier phenomenon is shaped in a very specific way, suggesting that child-soldiers are an *international emergency*, an exception to normal social life and international order. As such, the child-soldier phenomenon connects the *urgency* of the crisis in virtue of the threat posed by the dangerous armed child with a profound sense of *moral obligation* on the part of international organizations, governments, and (adult) citizens of the world to "save" the endangered child caught up in war. Furthermore, not only must children be saved, but so, too, must the endangered world, whose progressive future is put in jeopardy. At the end of the day, when the report by the NGO Save the Children refers to child-soldiers as "stolen futures," it is worth questioning whose and what futures are actually stolen when childhood is stripped of innocence.[3]

The discourse of the child-soldier as an international emergency (re)produces the notion of risk, which elicits strong demands for immediate international intervention. Since the publication of the report *Promotion and Protection of the Rights of Children: Impact of Armed Conflict on Children* by Graça Machel in 1996, a myriad of interventions have populated the international security and child rights agendas.[4] In the name of "the best interests of the child," these interventions (re)frame child-soldiers as exceptions to the norm and (re)produce them as disruptions of proper normative international life. International order is thus secured while deviant children are relegated to a "space" of silence and illegitimacy, which is often situated beyond—or behind—the boundaries of the (single) world.

Herein lies the central puzzle of this book: the encounter between the compelling and charismatic figure of the child who embodies the potential for a better future and the pathological child-soldier operates here as "site of knowledge."[5] By analyzing this encounter, it is possible to engage in a reflection about order, power, and international governance, which pervade—and limit—understandings of childhood and international politics. In the chapters that follow, I carefully analyze and problematize four important discursive movements that have happened simultaneously: (1) the articulation of an allegedly universal model of the child as immature, irrational, and vulnerable, and in which the child must develop properly in order to become a modern adult citizen; (2) the articulation of childhood as a transitional stage and thus a "site" for investment in the future; (3) the (re)production of the child-soldier not only as a deviation in relation to the norm of the child but also as a pathology in need of immediate solution; and (4) the articulation of a progressive future for international relations predicated on notions of order, stability, and security, to be maintained and (re)produced by modern citizens—namely, the "normal" child projected into the future. Through these discourses, the apparatus of governance for children invests in the construction of a progressive international order that rests on the transformation of the world-child into the world-citizen. Accordingly, international interventions devoted to "rescuing" child-soldiers are not only about recognizing their rights and need for protection but also about their governance and control on account of the threat they pose now or in the future to the stability of the international order.

This approach to the analysis of the mechanisms of child protection and, more specifically, international interventions in child-soldiers does not in any way purport to minimize or question the sentiments and charitable efforts of individuals, international organizations, and governments for helping children. The point, rather, is that this story tells much more about the mechanisms designed to order a particular version of the world that claims to be universal than about children themselves and their childhoods. Critiquing the universalizing model of childhood and the practices of protection based on this particular model, as I aim to do here, is a challenging and uncomfortable exercise. The tension, and perhaps even the contradiction, as Daniel Thomas Cook brilliantly puts it, emerges precisely from identifying multiple, malleable, differentiated childhoods, which in some way contest or relativize at least one perspective on childhood—that of the essentialist, sacralized view held by many, including myself: "All views are not logically possible together."[6] The analysis I propose in this book does not discuss the moral intentions of humanitarian workers, international organizations, or even diplomats, nor does it argue that United Nations protection programs are unworthy or irrelevant. The point, I would contend, is that they are simply not enough. The limits of these programs lie wherever there are children engaged in situations of conflict who do not fit into the single category available for the child-soldier that sees them only as victims. Within this setting, it is fundamental to insist on Cook's questions: "Is innocence perhaps the greatest threat to efforts to allow children to have and name their own childhoods? And whose feet did I just step on with that statement?"[7] Many children who soldier straddle the roles of victims, good citizens-to-be, and children excluded in the name of whatever threat they may pose to the future of the world. While international interventions invite the world to "bring back" former child-soldiers through "rescue" mechanisms, it is surely worth wondering: If these mechanisms are designed to "save" just one specific idea of the child, might they not end up effectively excluding countless other children?

In order to engage with and question the politics of child protection and its relationship with the governance of the future of the world, I think *with* and *through* discourses about the child, child-soldiers, and childhood. In so doing, a whole host of researchable questions come to light, which, in this book, I have limited to just two, which have to do with (destabilizing) order: How do the constructs of the "normal" child and the "deviant" child-soldier contribute toward the promotion and articulation of the boundaries of a particular version of the world? And how do these discourses operate as a "space" for the articulation of a history of linear progress?

THEORETICAL BEARINGS FOR EXPLORING
AN (IN)SECURE WORLD

Only recently, since the UN Convention on the Rights of the Child (UNCRC) was signed in 1989 and subsequently ratified by almost every country in the world, have children come to occupy a more central place in discussions in the field of international politics. Especially in the 1990s, when terms such as "human security," "New Wars," and "Responsibility to Protect" came to the forefront, a particular emphasis on the issue of children affected by armed conflict, and especially their vulnerability, emerged within the international political agenda.[8] However, even today, the child remains a silent force in the discourses of the academic field of international relations. Very few scholars have critically addressed children's role or the implications of conceptualizing it in the specific areas of global politics, the international political economy, or security studies.[9] Here, it is worth highlighting recent scholarly contributions informed by different critical approaches to international relations theory that have disrupted certain received assumptions about childhood, which tend to construct and locate children and youth in security and humanitarian discourses in very particular and circumscribed ways, associating them with vulnerability, irrationality, and dependency.[10]

However, as Alison M. S. Watson adds, "the study of children could be characterised as still being on the fringes of the discipline."[11] Curiously, while international relations research regarding children is still very limited in terms of scope, images of children are on display everywhere across the international community and in humanitarian appeals, following a somewhat conventional format.[12] In them, children invariably appear as objects of protection and are very much marginalized as agents within the international system. Liisa Malkki has studied these images and classified them into five interrelated registers: (1) children as sufferers; (2) children as embodiments of basic human goodness; (3) children as seers of truth; (4) children as ambassadors of peace; and (5) children as embodiments of the future.[13]

In contrast to other fields of knowledge, such as sociology, anthropology, and childhood studies, which have sought to challenge the "universal and natural" vision of children and childhood by recognizing them not so much as naturally occurring, but as historical, cultural, and political constructs, the accounts of children in international relations, especially those articulated within the humanitarian field, are still framed by the above-mentioned images. These images simultaneously depend on and (re)produce the notion of the vulnerable and innocent child who is primarily an object of protection.[14] In this sense, although there is a growing literature in the field of international security about children's participation both in wars and in peacebuilding processes, the notion of children (together with women) as the most vulnerable *civilians* still frames these debates, posing their presence within this research agenda as recipients of humanitarian protection and depoliticized victims of armed conflicts. Likewise, the peacebuilding literature has tended to ignore children's agency in the process of postconflict reconstruction.[15] Although several scholars have started addressing this gap, such as Helen Berents in her work on the experiences of children and young people in Colombia who play an important role in the negotiation of daily life and contribute to the ongoing process of building peace in their community, research still pays little attention to how girls, in particular, experience conflict, how they participate in peacebuilding processes, and how their contribution is influenced—and constrained—by gender norms.[16] Even the vast literature on child-soldiers, which has arisen together with the idea of human security and increasing interest in the so-called new wars, still draws on reductionist accounts of victimhood, which have already been roundly challenged by anthropologists and which disregard other power relations in ways that deny children and youths their potential (and capacity) as political subjects.[17]

In a different approach, but one that equally overlooks children's agency, the widening international security agenda has also made children visible, but in the specific form of challenges or risks to state interests. For example, former child-soldiers who have not been successfully reintegrated into civilian life in a postconflict setting may pose a threat to the long-term viability of peace settlements and state building.[18] In this regard, the introduction of children onto the security agenda is not undertaken for the protection of children at risk but to protect the state and the world from dangerous children. This hampers the process of further unpacking the implications of recognizing children's rights, participation, and protection in conflict and postconflict settings.[19] As J. Marshall Beier points out, simply adding children as victims or potential threats to the international political agenda is not enough. Furthermore, "attempting to 'find' them is beset by the danger of doing no more than that or, worse, making them what they must be in light of commitments and assumptions that precede them."[20] In the end, concludes Helen Brocklehurst,[21] the relationship between the field of international relations and children is tense rather than healthy in virtue of children's nonrecognition and misappropriation.

The way scholars of international relations address children and childhood coincides with the bounded conception of the "normal" child and "normal" childhood (re)produced by and within the field of international politics. Specifically, in security studies, Beier adds that "in their incompleteness they are precisely what Security Studies needs them to be, flowing together with and sustaining dominant understandings of sovereignty, authority, order, protection, and much more."[22] This challenges me to explore the signification of the discourses about the child, childhood, and its deviations, such as child-soldiers, to the (re)production of this particular version of the world, whose limits are carefully articulated by and through these very same ideas of sovereignty, authority, and protection. In this regard, this book aims to elaborate on the account of the child as a conceptual construct that operates as the principle of hope on which the modern promise of a progressive future depends and also a universalizing (but not universal) standard of purity as related to an "original" state of innocence.

At the very most, the discussion I propose here converges on the status and politics of boundaries or exceptions and "on their authorization by subjects who are always susceptible to inclusion or exclusion by the borders they are persuaded to authorize."[23] Although these boundaries may appear or be articulated as clean lines that organize modern political life by dictating that we belong here, you belong there, and they belong elsewhere, throughout the book we see that they are actually anything but straightforward, as they (re)produce inclusions and exclusions that authorize the hierarchies of status, class, kinds of childhoods, and social order not only in domestic life inside nation-states but also in the modern International.[24] To speak about universalism, humanity, the world, and the child is to silence the politics of (re)drawing the connections and distinctions between singularity and plurality, identity and difference, universality and specificity as ordering mechanisms. In this regard, it is important first to identify what I am talking about when I refer to the modern International (or, just International) and the world. Here, I use and emphasize both terms as synonyms in a way to *destabilize* precisely this claim of sameness and universality that occurs when "the International" and "the world" are used interchangeably for describing the supposedly broad context within which modern political life has been possible.

What becomes clear in the book is that the world—or the International—actually challenges the growing assumption that the world is becoming more cosmopolitan. In R. B. J. Walker's words, "the modern world of sovereign politics is a world of constitutive exceptions, and the most important exception [. . .] is the one between the modern and its others/negations that has enabled the construction of a modern politics of sovereign states and subjectivities."[25] In this book, I use the terms "modern International," "International," and "world" as synonyms, not because I agree with the assumption of a shift, especially since the end of the Cold War, from the local or particular to something more planetary, universal, and inclusive, but as a critical reminder of the multiplying boundaries that (re)produce and authorize a particular version of the world, which is not the only one or even the best one.

In another piece, R. B. J. Walker establishes certain "rules" of this "modern International" that must be accepted by all states as a precondition for any specific claim to state sovereignty.[26] One of these rules refers specifically to the distinction between the modern and its others, and it says "no 'barbarians' or non-moderns."[27] Essentially, it operates as a "rule of admission to modern politics": "modern political life must involve a decision about who gets to be treated as a properly human being and who is not fit to participate in the modern international order, not fit to be recognized as a legitimate member of the international community."[28] This rule works in the context of stories. For example, there are available narratives about "the expansion of international society," the "teleology of modernization understood as a process of development," and the "standard of civilization in international law," which set the models and standards that mark out the pathways those who are outside have to follow to be admitted and brought into the world. Within this formulation, international child protection programs could be read as another story or pathway for the transformation of the world-child into the world-citizen. In this context, this rule works as a claim that the entire world could be brought into the International. Especially since the end of the Cold War, discourses about the International have framed it as a more compressed space, a space that is gradually progressing from a state of fragmentation and territorialization toward a "single" space that shares a homogeneous temporality, paving the way for conversations to be pursued and actions to be taken on behalf of one human community, one humanity.[29] However, Walker highlights that it is precisely in this guise that the problem of the *outside* of the International emerges, "against which all teleologies can be articulated as a leap across the divide from pre-modern to modern, from a state of nature to a state of civil society and civilization."[30] Although some claim that the International encompasses everything that is within the modern world, there remains a question about what, and who, has been left outside this process of "internationalization as internalization."[31] In this sense, the idea of humanity can be understood as a process through which a particular version of the world and its subjectivities can be brought into the modern International while simultaneously excluding other worlds.

In this book, the highly complex discussions involving children in general and child-soldiers in particular serve as a window through which we can glimpse some of these borders produced by the International. They are not a mere illustrative example but, rather, a generative site, a locus where those actors authorized to speak in the name of an international society deploy different mechanisms of power to forge and normalize forms of life deemed acceptable. In order to deal with "the problem" of child-soldiers, these actors rewrite the borders of the international system and promote an internationalization of childhood and its possible deviations. Here, the construction of modern individuals is a task taken on by the International, while the need for particularistic mediations, such as nation-states or families, is subsumed to a discourse of absolute universality, working in the name of a better humanity. Children are, in fact, all the same.

One of the United Nations Children's Fund (UNICEF) strategies for dealing with children living in emergency situations is to deliver a "School-in-a-Box."[32] The first element that stands out in this kit is an erasable blackboard, promising that all past (deviant) experiences can simply disappear, to be overwritten by a new (normal) life. The ingredients of a new/normal childhood can also be found in the box: a notebook, a teddy bear, puzzles, story books, and a wooden clock. These objects show that future is just a few developmental steps away. The crayons the children get from the box can be used as a new kind of ammunition: not for loading into a gun, but for inscribing their names as enshrined bearers of a better future. Essentially, this UNICEF solution is not about a *school* in a box, but a *child* in a box that is meant to be "culturally neutral" and can be exported to anywhere in the world.

Figure 1. School-in-a-Box exhibited at the United Nations building, New York, May 2012. Photo by the author.

Furthermore, the idea of sameness contained in the box embodies a guarantee of a better future not only for children but for all humanity. The path of development has to be followed by everyone, coloring the world with the crayons of the modern International. Jens Bartelson highlights that the modern International encompasses a very particular conception of time, which is a succession of events that is always linear, always progressive.[33] This belief in progress enables an interpretation of history as a journey toward a better future: a stable, peaceful world. In this future, humans will be able to *transcend* the borders of the modern International, leave behind its insides and outsides, and inhabit a domesticated, globalized space belonging to a perfected humanity. This idea is operationalized by projects like the School-in-a-Box and also by mechanisms for protecting a universal model of the child (the world-child) and for the treatment and recovery of child-soldiers. As Chris Jenks puts it: "The developing individual is to be watched, monitored, timetabled, regimented and exposed. The private becomes more and more available to the public. Bodies and minds claim an allegiance to the social through dependency, guilt and visibility."[34]

However, if these prevailing discourses about the child and its childhood are only "an unstable victory won at the expense of other possible nows,"[35] the world-child is only one possibility, and the child-soldier is deviant only in relation to this model. This opens up room for questions such as "what is a child?," "what is childhood?," and "what is the signification of child and childhood in the production and reproduction of a particular version of the international political order?" Following these questions, this book draws on the dialogue between childhood studies and critical approaches to international relations theory in order to challenge the boundaries that normalize children and (re)produce pathological others, such as child-soldiers. In this regard, it is possible to think about the relationship between international relations and children beyond the framework of victimization, which glosses over many of the internal variations and complexities of children's experiences, and to explore a more powerful understanding of the role of the child in the articulation of a particular version of the world. Furthermore, as the child is rendered meaningful by its relationship to the category of the adult, problematizing the authorized "truths" about children and childhood means not only challenging the idea that child-soldiers are, by definition, an exception to the norm but also seeing the "conception of adulthood as uncertain and messy, although this is rarely noted,"[36] and the adult, or world-citizen, as a capable "stranger."

ANALYTICAL STRATEGIES

In this book, the construct of childhood as a happy, soothing time of life is challenged by submitting the main discourses about children and childhood to a critical interpretative analysis. As Michel Foucault points out, "[a] critique is not a matter of saying that things are not right as they are. It is a matter of pointing out on what kinds of assumptions, what kind of familiar, unchallenged, unconsidered modes of thought the practices that we accept rest [. . .]. Practicing criticism is a matter of making such facile gestures difficult."[37] Failing to do so means leaving certain understandings about children's morality, children's potential, how children should be raised, and what environment fosters children's development unchallenged, not to mention the "'subterranean' circulations of power by dint of which we casually reinscribe them."[38]

The form of criticism to be used here is discourse analysis. According to Lene Hansen, discourse analysis takes texts that are simultaneously *unique*—each makes its own particular constructions of identity, weaving a series of differentiations and juxtapositions—and *united*—they all operate within a shared textual space and make explicit or implicit reference to previous texts, establishing their own reading and mediating the meaning and status of others.[39] "The meaning of a text is thus never fully given by the text itself but is always a product of other readings and interpretations."[40] Intertextuality is a key concept for discourse analysis, as "it highlights that texts are situated within and against other texts, that they draw on them in constructing their identities and policies, that they appropriate as well as revise the past, and that they build authority by reading and citing that of others."[41] Through an intertextual approach, texts are always understood in relation to others, as part of a broader discursive network that unveils the linkages between texts and the ways in which they construct authority and a kind of stability in dealing with particular subjects. Furthermore, intertextual approaches can take account of different forms of authority and the construction, interconnection, and mobilization of discourses that enable the exercise of power.[42]

In the context of this research, discourse analysis enables the construction of an intertextual network in which it is possible to identify key categories through which the International operationalizes the discourses about childhood that produce both the norm (the model of the world-child) and its many deviations (e.g., child-soldiers). The many possible deviations from the model of "normal" childhood include children who get married, children who commit crimes, and children who work. Child-soldiers are just one other possible deviation, which in this book is the main focus of attention due to its potential to operate as a generative site. In other words, the construct and its supposed deviation (i.e., "normal" child and "abnormal" child-soldier) actually inform each other. The discourses analyzed here constitute ensembles of heterogeneous statements made in distinct contexts with their own regularities and systems of coercion,[43] which play a role in producing, enabling, and limiting empowered/disempowered subject-positions. In line with Foucault, these discourses thus participate in the production and reproduction of certain "truths" or certain "norms" that inform the way a child is supposed to be and behave and the way we are supposed to behave in relation to them.

Specifically, I investigate how these discourses inform the way the international system acts toward children and how it normalizes the boundaries that distinguish children from adults and normal children from pathological others. In doing so, I do not want to relativize the subject but rather to provide an account of the "constitution of knowledges, discourses, domains of objects [. . .] without having to make reference to a subject which is either transcendental in relation to the field of events or runs in its empty sameness throughout the course of history."[44] My critical effort is not an attempt to transcend the world we live in or the present state of things; on the contrary, my goal is to explore this world and the political processes through which it is produced and reproduced. As Vivienne Jabri remarks, "any critical investigation must start with reflection on its own terms, the language within which a project is framed."[45] Likewise, children operate as a fundamental political issue, as objects of knowledge, as reflected practices, which can be situated within the realm of practices of power.

The intertextual network constructed in this book is constituted of four main bodies of research material. This material is based on the reading of a large number of texts from a wide variety of sources (international official documents, NGO reports, academic literature, media, photos, and videos), which include key texts that are often quoted and function as nodes within the intertextual network of debate regarding children and armed conflict, and a large body of general material, which provides the basis for exploring the processes by which the discourses about the world-child and the deviant child-soldier are (re)produced.

First, I draw on official documents devoted exclusively to children—specific human rights treaties or the so-called children's rights milestones—through which the model of the world-child has been constituted and authorized as a completely distinct type of human who is entitled to special rights. The children's rights milestones include the Geneva Declaration of the Rights of the Child, adopted by the League of Nations in 1924, and the documents produced by or in consultation with the United Nations, in particular UNICEF, such as the Declaration of the Rights of the Child (1959); the International Year of the Child (1979); the 1989 Convention on the Rights of the Child (UNCRC); the World Declaration on the Survival, Protection and Development of Children and the Plan of Action for its implementation in the 1990s, adopted at the World Summit for Children in 1990; Convention No. 182 concerning the Prohibition and Immediate Action for the Elimination of the Worst Forms of Child Labour, adopted by the International Labour Organization (ILO) in 1999; the resolution titled A World Fit for Children, adopted by the UN General Assembly at a Special

Session on Children in 2002; and the five-year follow-up to this UN General Assembly Special Session on Children, which ended with the Declaration of the Commemorative High-level Plenary Meeting devoted to the Follow-up to the Outcome of the Special Session on Children, which acknowledges the progress made and the challenges that remain, and reaffirms a commitment to the World Fit for Children compact, the UNCRC, and its Optional Protocols.[46] Also, I analyze two other international standards on human rights that are not devoted exclusively to children but that constitute the group of norms concerning the protection of children and their rights: the Universal Declaration of Human Rights, adopted by the United Nations in 1948, and Convention No. 138 on the Minimum Age for Admission to Employment, adopted by the ILO in 1973.[47] In the 1990s, the concept of protecting children emerged as a core obligation,[48] and this international focus on childhood has been associated with the (re) production of a particular version of the world since the end of the Cold War. Within this scenario, children's participation in wars emerges as an absolute impossibility.

The second set of research material is an ensemble of international legal standards and instruments that aim to distinguish, via a rights-based approach, what is permitted and what is forbidden regarding children's participation in armed conflicts. These documents include the 1977 Additional Protocols to the Geneva Conventions, the 1989 UNCRC, the 1998 Rome Statute, the 1990 African Charter on the Rights and Welfare of the Child, the 1999 International Labour Organization Worst Forms of Child Labor Convention, the 2000 Optional Protocol to the Convention on the Rights of the Child on the Involvement of Children in Armed Conflict, the 1997 Cape Town Principles, and the Paris Principles.[49] Also under analysis here are the twelve UN Security Council thematic resolutions on children and armed conflict, which articulate the military recruitment of children as something that must be outlawed internationally.

Still focusing specifically on child-soldiers, the third group follows Myriam S. Denov's work and explores the way the world's media and policy discourses construct child-soldiers in largely contrasting ways—either as victims or as monsters.[50] My aim is not to describe children's daily challenges and war experiences, but to show how documents such as media reports and studies produced by international organizations stabilize the boundaries between particular versions of the normal child and the pathological child-soldier. These documents try to "give voice" to children by including their narratives about life in those reports, parts of which are reproduced in this book. However, the purpose of their inclusion is to show that these narratives do not so much help us problematize the understandings of the social world as reaffirm the status of children as passive objects, as vulnerable, incompetent beings. In fact, as Ah-Jung Lee points out, such voices are usually followed by accounts of the "horror" of child-soldiering.[51] At the end of the day, the "voices of children" serve as evidence of a picking and choosing of words that reinforces and reproduces the way the world is seen. Also, within this particular construction of the child-soldier, little mention is made of the lived realities of children's participation in wars outside the African continent—contexts and cases that are possibly more numerous, such as in Myanmar or Colombia. Although the characterization of child-soldiers is most often taken out of context, the adjectives used to describe their experiences in armed conflicts, such as "abhorrent" and "barbaric," especially concern the contemporary wars in Africa. Focusing mainly on the African context, these narratives produce the child-soldier as an essentially "African" problem, a problem from a place where violence is an inextricable part of nature, which will be forever dependent on outside intervention, especially from the north.[52] Taken together with the second group of material, these documents (re)produce a general discourse of child-soldiering as an international emergency that is in urgent need of solution.

Finally, the fourth group of research materials comprises fifteen interviews that I conducted in person in New York in 2012, 2013, and 2017 with UN, UNICEF, and NGO representatives and diplomats. My main question to them was how the institutions in which they worked addressed the "problem" of children engaged in armed conflict. The answers given to my questions permeate this whole book and have helped me organize the very fragmented and diverse networks of actors that work on behalf of children daily. As their institutional role was more important to me than their personal opinions, the names of the interviewees are omitted. From these interviews, the idea was to critically reconstruct the operational mechanisms of response to situations of child-soldiering and the way they work as internationally articulated power techniques to frame borders and declare exceptions.

In short, the intertextual network pieced together here reveals how complex and unrelated elements have come to form a familiar account of the child and childhood. I address not just the orderly production and reproduction of the conceptual limits of children, childhood, and the International, but how this order is inherently contingent. In line with Foucault, this discourse analysis adopts the "principle of reversal," which means regarding the discourses as *events*, rather than creation, and thereby trying to identify and grasp the forms of exclusion, the limitations, and the appropriations of discourse to certain categories of subject.[53] In Foucault's own words, "discourse analysis understood like this does not reveal universality of a meaning, but brings to light the action of imposed scarcity, with a fundamental power of affirmation. Scarcity and affirmation; ultimately, scarcity *of* affirmation, and not the continuous generosity of meaning, and not the monarchy of the signifier."[54] In this sense, this form of discourse analysis yields the possibility of thinking about child-soldiers not necessarily as beings waiting to be disciplined, rescued, and brought back within the borders of the world. They are, in fact, inhabitants of a space between boundaries.

PLAN OF THE BOOK

Much of this book reflects on and challenges the limits of the main categories that constitute this research. These categories are reproduced as authorized and universal truths, and the limits of "official actions"—or international interventions—that articulate a single world constituted of absolute differences and exceptions in need of definitive solutions or treatment procedures. Rather than thinking about child-soldiers as essentially a problem of "children without childhood," the following chapters draw on the dialogue between childhood studies and critical approaches to international relations to examine the complexities, silences, and power relations that permeate and are articulated by supposedly ordinary concepts—child, child-soldier, childhood—and how they are instrumentalized in the establishment and maintenance of order in international politics.

Chapter 1, "'Children without Childhood': Child-Soldiers as a Social Problem," outlines the "phenomenon of child-soldiers" and reviews the main ideas or explanations concerning the participation of children in contemporary armed conflicts. In order to explore these contemporary constructions of the child-soldier as an essentially deviant and pathological child—and as such a threat to world stability—this chapter addresses two main perspectives that allow me first to (re)produce the limits that frame the prevailing discourse about children engaged in war and then to problematize these very same boundaries that articulate child-soldiers as deviant in relation to the "normal" child. That is, on the one hand, I analyze the discourse about the child and childhood that defines and (re)produces the child who *cannot* soldier: the innocent, vulnerable being who must be properly prepared to become a rational, productive, educated adult or citizen. On the other, I explore arguments and debates from childhood studies that open room for questioning the kind of social beings children are taken to be, thereby producing a different order of dialogue, reflection, and response from what might be contained in normative, simplistic, good/bad, right/wrong structures of thought that articulate the prevailing discourse about the child-soldier phenomenon.

Then, by aiming to explore the signification of the child-soldier phenomenon—including international responses to the "problem"—in ordering a particular version of the world, I take two entry points: I analyze the discourse about what I have termed the "world-child," which speaks of a general, abstract child as if all children shared an essential set of immutable characteristics, needs, and course of development toward adulthood, and I explore the (re)production of the child-soldier as a pathological deviation in relation to this model of childhood, and as such an international emergency. More specifically, informed by the perspective of childhood studies, chapter 2, "Hope for the Future: The World-Child as a World-Becoming-Citizen," investigates how the children's rights milestones have authorized and normalized both what a child is supposed to be and its journey toward becoming a full modern adult citizen, forging the model of the "world-child." By analyzing these international documents through two interrelated key themes—protection and development—I identify a circularity between the boundaries that set the limits of what a "normal" childhood is supposed to be and their co-option in defining and maintaining a particular version of the world predicated on notions of order, security, and progress.

Chapter 3, "An International Emergency: The World-Child Meets the Child-Soldier," examines how the construction of this model of the world-child produces (and depends on the production of) pathological others, in particular, child-soldiers. In order to explore the boundaries that articulate child-soldiers as an international emergency, which challenges the stability of the international political order and its prospects for progress, this chapter draws on two main discourses: (1) the discourse of the law, that is, international practices that articulate children's participation in war as something that is wrong and must be banned under international law; and (2) what I call the "discourse of the norm," which is analyzed through the three contrasting images of the child-soldier as dangerous and disorderly, the hapless victim, and the redeemed hero, as identified by Denov in her analysis of the discourse articulated by the world's media and policymakers about children caught up in cycles of war and violence.[55] Through and by these discourses, child-soldiers are not only seen as deviant in relation to "normal" children, but also as pathological. This sheds light on how powerful and consensual international interventions in child-soldiers are.

Chapter 4, "(Re)Drawing Boundaries and Restoring International Order: The United Nations Intervenes to Protect Child-Soldiers," is dedicated to carefully exploring these interventions, such as the United Nations Security Council Resolutions on the issue of children and armed conflict, the UN campaign "Children, Not Soldiers," and the United Nations Release and Reintegration Program specifically for former child-soldiers. The force of these interventions resides in the simple but potent message they carry. The fundamental and ultimate justification is to save children's lives and alleviate their suffering. Nevertheless, in the (re)construction of the model of the world-child and framing of the child-soldier as an international emergency, what stands out, especially in my interviews with UN representatives and diplomats, is how these international interventions operate as fundamental mechanisms for ordering the world and protecting the prospects of a progressive future. That is, in the name of securing a particular version of the international political order articulated through the model of the world-child, these interventions (re)declare what constitutes an exception to the norm and relegate child-soldiers to a spatiotemporal *locus* of illegitimacy and silence that often exists outside—or behind—the boundaries of the modern International.

Finally, the conclusion, "Neither 'Beyond' nor 'Behind': Child-Soldiers as Children between Boundaries," is given over to some conclusions (in the form of more questions). Instead of thinking about child-soldiers in terms of "children without childhood," this chapter discusses the idea of what I have termed "children between boundaries": children who do not escape from, but challenge, the limits of "normal" childhood. The idea is to politicize these borders and thus bring forth the enormous complexity of what has come to be treated under the simplified and essentialized ideas of a particular child, a particular adult citizen, and a particular world.

CHAPTER ONE

"Children without Childhood"

Child-Soldiers as a Social Problem

In February 2004, BBC News published a story about the need to disarm and rehabilitate child-soldiers in Liberia as what would be a critical step toward establishing peace in the country.[1] The photograph posted next to the text was of a boy pointing a weapon toward the viewer: he was alone or abandoned, without family or state support, and he was not wearing a military uniform but old clothes and flip-flops. Also, he was carrying a pinky fluffy backpack in the shape of a teddy bear whose contents were unknown to us, the viewers: might it be food, clothes, toys, or bullets to reload the weapon? The single caption, placed underneath the image, read: "The prolonged civil war has damaged a whole generation." This boy-soldier, defined by the weapon he carried, represented a whole—and heterogeneous—generation of children, known as child-soldiers. According to the journalist, "entering the world of Liberia's child soldiers is a disturbing experience. *Normal moral values are put to one side.*"[2] At the end of the story, the readers are none the wiser about that particular boy in the picture: who he was, how he became a soldier, what experiences he had while engaged in war, or if he was still alive. He was *just* a "child-soldier" or, in other words, a "child without childhood," for when being a soldier begins, the child drops out of childhood, understood as a carefree, secure, and happy phase of human existence.[3]

According to the BBC story, the Liberian boy-soldier does not so much stop being a child, although his childhood has been harmed or disrupted by the war experience, as lose his childhood—something rather more abstract and, arguably, more precious. Scottish actor and UNICEF ambassador Ewan Mc-Gregor nicely illustrated this conception of childhood when, in 2012, he called on many to help UNICEF give child-soldiers "another chance at childhood."[4] With the help of international organizations, the child can be rescued from the child-soldier. In other words, child-soldiers can return to their right place, a mythic "walled garden" that all children ideally inhabit.[5] Paralleling this narrative, expressions such as "children without childhood," "children robbed of their childhood," and "children out of place" permeate discussions of the figure of the child-soldier by international organizations, often with humanitarian missions, nongovernmental organizations (NGOs), and the mainstream media.[6] They all stress a single message: children are at serious risk. Expressions such as "without childhood," "robbed of childhood," and "children out of place" emphasize the child-soldiers' vulnerability, understood only as victimization and invariably a site of inaction. Having experienced episodes of violence and loss, these children have become conceptualized as antithetical to "normal" human development.[7] But these statements also have another destabilizing side: if it is the very notion of childhood that identifies children, how it is possible to remove the concept of childhood while the child still exists?[8] If this is so, who are child-soldiers?

These ways of addressing child-soldiers have consequences beyond simple diplomatic or public rhetoric. Rather, this particular prevailing discourse of the essentially innocent and inherently vulnerable child in many ways produces child-soldiers as a new social international problem—a problem that then mobilizes resources, international organizations, and other discourses around the child's "salvation." The child-soldier becomes a social problem in at least two interrelated ways. First, children who soldier have problems that point toward state failure and can only be addressed by dedicated international action and resources. Second, child-soldiers are themselves seen as a social problem—or a threat—by departing from the protected territory of childhood, disrupting, disquieting, and disturbing the everyday social life.

Together, such accounts stand on and lay claim to a binary relationship between adulthood and childhood, which operates as a symbol and pillar of the modern social order. Hence, when children do not behave "like children" (i.e., when they are engaged in armed conflict), the stability of a larger social order is threatened by the foreclosure on the child's future, which itself stands for the thoroughly modern promise of a progressive future. Such accounts characterize the child-soldier not only as threatened by war and adult abuse but also as a threat to the stability of the social order.

This chapter explores the reproduction of the idea of the child-soldier as an *unprecedented* social problem in three parts. First, it examines contemporary constructions of the innocent and vulnerable child who must not soldier as a universalized model and the universalized conception of childhood, understood as a primary and initial stage of human life, marked by purity and innocence. It then turns to the analysis of the constructions of the child-soldier as a new social problem. These articulations are shaped by a common belief that children are particularly vulnerable, irrational, and innocent, that contemporary wars are especially brutal and "uncivilized," and that weapons are smaller and lighter than they used to be. Although these assumptions are questionable, they profoundly frame the discourse about child-soldiers. Finally, in order to explore what is being produced, authorized, and silenced through and by these discourses about childhood, the child, and the child-soldier, the last part of the chapter presents the main arguments and debates of childhood studies, which question both the place of childhood in social relations and the kind of social beings that children have been assumed to be.[9] At the end of the chapter, readers may be thinking about child-soldiers not in terms of "children without childhood" but as children whose life experiences are not perfectly synchronized with a particular version of the "normal" child's childhood.

THE AGE OF INNOCENCE: PRODUCING THE "NORMAL" CHILD AND CHILDHOOD

In the late eighteenth century, Sir Joshua Reynolds painted *The Age of Innocence*, in which a child is located in the center of the picture surrounded by nature. Anne Higonnet guides the reader through the painting, highlighting how the viewer appreciates the innocent and vulnerable girl, who wears a flimsy white dress on her well-fed little body, whose body parts on display are exactly the ones least closely associated with adult sexuality.[10] Around two hundred years later, the photographer Anne Geddes started her child photography business. One of her photos that became globally famous was *Cheesecake*, in which the child is also located in the center of the picture surrounded by nature. The baby in the photograph is naked, but its nudity is diffused by the roses that surround him or her and, especially, by its cuteness, represented in its "gummy smile and eyes squeezed shut[. . . .] We get to see the baby's body and not to see it."[11] As Higonnet argues, in both figures, the viewer is encouraged to take visual delight, eliciting strong "ahh" responses from the viewer, but, very importantly, not in the same way he or she would enjoy looking at an adult.[12] Despite the time difference between those two images, both of them highlight almost the same ingredients of the childhood formula: innocence, nature, fragility, fun, sexlessness, and cuteness. Deprived of these aspects, the "idea of childhood" is not recognized, or is recognized either as wounded or deviant.[13]

In this first part of the chapter, I explore this particular idea of childhood, understood as a distinct social category that cannot be conceptualized except in relation to the notion of adulthood. According to this concept, children are insulated in a designated place, the private sphere—family settings and school being prime spaces for children—and relegated to a specific temporal process, which determines a developmental journey toward becoming a complete adult; that is, a full modern citizen. Although this discourse prescribes a particular kind of childhood experience, this same message is clearly posed in the United Nations Convention on the Rights of the Child, which exports to the world this specific conception of childhood as a universal and uniform experience.[14]

The above-mentioned discourse about childhood has been mainly articulated, since the late nineteenth century, by child developmental psychology. As analyzed later in the chapter, developmental psychology establishes a stage model of child development, which posits a universal, chronological progression from a primal child to an autonomous, principled, subjectively reflective adult.[15] By focusing on and, most importantly, investing in the child's transition to adulthood and increasing participation in society, this particular discourse ignores basic and ontological questions, such as "How is the child possible as such?"[16] In itself, the dualistic view of children as innocent, incompetent, malleable, and in need of protection from adults, who are assumed to be rational and autonomous, is not problematized but is understood as a natural fact of human existence. Consequently, a great many internal variations and complexities are silenced.

Children are frequently asked, "What do you want to be when you grow up?" The question focuses on their future as human beings, since for now—specifically from year zero to eighteen years old—children must be worry free, playing with toys, going to school, and being loved and protected by their families. Within this discourse about childhood, children and adults seem to be fundamentally different types of humans: while "modern children are supposed to be segregated from the harsh realities of the adult world and to inhabit a safe, protected world of play, fantasy and innocence," adults are assumed to be mature and rational beings who must work in order to provide for children.[17] Despite the well-documented diversity of social experiences children go through in different parts of the world—from girls getting married in Bangladesh to children working on the streets in Vietnam or fighting in wars in the Democratic Republic of Congo—in this universalized kind of childhood, as Jo Boyden asserts, there is no place for labor in the factory or mine.[18]

This idea of childhood reflects the modern conception of childhood as a distinct social category that cannot be conceptualized except in relation to the notion of adulthood. As claimed by anthropologists and by the precursors of childhood studies Jennifer L. Hockey and Allison James, four main considerations gave form to this modern conception of childhood: (1) the child is set apart spatially and temporally as different, with childhood being a time of "joy and peace, of playing, learning and growing"; (2) the child is naturally distinct and associated with nature; (3) the child is inherently innocent; and therefore (4) the child is dependent and vulnerable, so he or she needs to mature, broaden his or her perspectives, and gain new experiences in order to become a productive adult.[19] As Jenks indicates, "In sum, these are themes which centre, first, on questions of the child's morality [2 and 3] and, second, on its capability [1 and 4]."[20] In other words, a kind of imaginary of childhood is set up based on a configuration of narratives, images, and ideas and is reproduced as innate to childhood itself.

According to the first aspect highlighted by Hockey and James,[21] childhood appears as a transitional stage represented by expectations as to the child's future as an adult. Commonplace expressions such as "children are the future of society," "children are apprentice citizens," and "children are our most precious resource" are illustrative, as they tend to deprive children of existence as human beings in favor of the notion of them as "human becomings."[22] Once constituted as "a becoming," the child is essentialized as a tabula rasa, dependent and incomplete, while childhood is understood as the phase of life that lays down the foundations and shapes the individual in order to prepare him or her for the future, when he or she will participate in the adult world. The age criterion is thus significant for defining and constituting the child, as it marks these "processes of temporality."[23] Children are known not only by their name, gender, race, religion, class, and other social categories, but also—and perhaps more importantly—they are marked off and organized according to their age.

As Allison James argues, "*beings of a lesser age*, it would seem, what children are!"[24] Chronological age is naturalized arbitrarily under the terms of the UNCRC, which establishes that eighteen years of age is the temporal point at which age no longer matters, as it marks the transition from the child to the adult.[25] This gradual segregation of children from adult society, as noted by Michael Wyness, reflects "modern sensibilities on the child as both the embodiment of innocence and purity and an investment in the future."[26]

Within this discourse of childhood, the adult world is assumed to be not only rational, complete, and firmly established but also, and perhaps more significantly, desirable. As Jenks points out: "It [the adult world] is a benevolent and coherent totality which extends a welcome to the child, invites him to cast off the qualities that ensure his differences, and encourages his acquiescence to the preponderance of the induction procedures that will guarantee his corporate identity."[27]

Articulated as different (or non-adult) beings through mechanisms of protection and practices of care, children are sent on a journey toward a knowable future: their participation in the adult world as full citizens. In this sense, children are forced into a position of waiting; included in social power relations as potential citizens of future society, they are waiting to become adults, to mature, to become competent, to acquire rights, to become useful.[28] Interestingly, children's *inclusion* in the social political realm derives precisely from their *exclusion* at the present time.

Furthermore, through this dichotomy between beings and becomings, the adult, with its connotations of stability and completeness, functions as a kind of standard model of human being that the child should become in the future. This binary relationship that articulates the child as "the citizen to be" and the adult as the "full citizen" operates in terms of a gradation of maturity. Instead of a contradiction, the dichotomy is reproduced within a teleological framework: the relationship between the child and the adult is marked by this progressive linearity, in which the final destination is adulthood. As a standard model, the adult thus stands ready to be used to measure and evaluate children's incompleteness and process of development.

The relationship between adults and children is thus marked by the simultaneous presence of two different interrelated (and mutually constitutive) temporalities. While adulthood is premised on the notions of a temporal stability through which "the adult" is produced as a mature, developed, contradiction-free citizen who has already completed his or her social journey, the temporality of childhood is predicated on an in-process notion. The child is in the process of grow*ing*, learn*ing*, and matur*ing* in order to become a rational adult. Within these terms, the childhood/adulthood dichotomy is bound up in a gradualistic dualism between time of development and time of accomplishment, which resonates in other related dualisms, such as vulnerable versus competent and dependent versus autonomous. In this sense, adults should provide for children economically and morally by working and earning income. For their part, until the "beings of lesser age" turn eighteen, they have no moral or economic obligations, and their points of view, desires, and opinions are often ignored because their age has been taken as a sign that they are still immature, irrational, and are not yet worth listening to.

Thus, the modern discourse about childhood, based on ideas of development and progress, articulates not only the experience of children in society but also the projections and aspirations of adults. Through this dichotomization between human beings and human becomings, the child has come to symbolize the promise of a good future, which is understood in a progressive vein. Both children and childhood are (re)produced as assets to be invested in for the future of modern society, and as such they must be safeguarded.

This formulation reveals an ambivalent meaning of the child: at the same time that the child is (re)produced as a symbol of the promise of a progressive future, he or she also serves to display to adult society its own state of once untutored and undeveloped difference. Either way, children's high profile in modern society cannot be denied. As Erica Burman points out, "childhood becomes a site of multiple emotional as well as political investments: a repository of hope yet a site of instrumentalisation for the future, but with an equal and opposite nostalgia for the past."[29] In turn, the idea of children as the epitome of goodness and knowledge linked to the risks associated to the child's undeveloped or still uncivilized stage makes them subject to different forms of regulation and training based on modern ideas of their development, protection, conditioning, and innocence.[30]

Because of this process of regulation and training of the child, children are not only set apart temporally but also insulated spatially. A key element of the modern discourse about childhood has been the segregation of children into the private sphere: children's homes are seen as "safe havens," the appropriate place for them to be raised, facilitating their physical and social protection from the outside world. At the same time that the private sphere is (re)produced as a safe place for children, there is an increasing perception of risk and vulnerability associated with children's participation in public life. As a result, protection—understood as actions designed to prevent children from being physically harmed—involves not only delimiting children's places but also regulating their participation in public life: where they go, with whom, for how long, for what purpose.

In this sense, the places for children are very restricted. In addition to their homes, there are two other corners of the institutionalized triangle that circumscribe children's daily lives and shape their social experiences: recreational institutions (designated by adults as the proper places for them to play) and schools (for them to study).[31] Children must occupy these particular spaces, or else they are considered conspicuous for their inappropriate or precocious invasion of adult places. From this perspective, phrases such as "child labor," "child marriage," "child prostitution," "street child," and "child-soldiers" evoke a profound sense of incompatibility and victimization, since they refer to children's engagement in the wrong places, places other than the ones considered natural for children.

The production of children as human becomings and the physical and social placement of children in designated spaces are mutually confirming. Jiri Kovarik, for example, conceptualizes the articulation of childhood experience in terms of "stages and scripts" in which space and time are closely interwoven.[32] At the same time that children are insulated and distanced in terms of space, their gradual emergence into a wider and distinct adult world is understood as a process that may happen by accident (e.g., the humanitarian depiction of children's engagement in wars), by degrees (e.g., the discourse of child development psychology), as an award, or as part of a gradualist rite of passage.[33] Based on Kovarik's reflection, Jenks concludes: "These stages and scripts, being primarily the family, the school and the peer group, generate not just the 'where' and 'when,' but also the 'what' and 'how,' questions that relate to children's environments."[34]

The placing of children in designated spaces and their relegation to a particular developmental journey toward adulthood shed light on the aspects Hockey and James highlight as having given form to this modern conception of childhood.[35] That is, the delimitations on both "where" the child should be (at home or at school, protected from the dangers of public life) and "when" (the degrees or stages the child must follow in order to become a rational adult) are premised on and, at the same time, articulate the figure of the "natural child," who is seen as inherently vulnerable and exuding innocence. In this regard, even when children participate in public social life, stepping away from the "places for children," this tends to be interpreted through the notions of dependence and vulnerability.

Based on the formulation of the (adequate) spaces and times for children, the borders of this particular idea of the child are also articulated through the notion of "natural growth," which associates children's biological immaturity and the physical signs of anatomical change that accompany childhood to social development. The conflation of the realms of the natural and the social is perpetually reinforced, universalizing childhood as a uniform experience.[36] Children's achievements, such as learning how to walk or how to speak, are understood as symbolic markers of this gradual social development process. Also, children's interests or desires—both biological and social—are understood and articulated as needs. These needs, such as asking for food or care, are seen as intrinsic to children themselves, something they possess, something endowed to them by nature and detectable in their behavior.[37] In this regard, "children's needs" are understood as unquestionable facts rather than socially constructed, culturally specific and, thus, up for political discussion. Moreover, the particular idea of the child being naturally dependent and vulnerable associated with the discourse of "children's needs" (re)produces the asymmetry of power between the child as the one to be serviced, protected, and provided for, and the adult as the dominant provider. Instead of this kind of dualism being regarded as only one way of seeing the complex and multifaceted social relationship between children and adults, it is articulated as a natural fact, authorized by biological factors.

Based on these ingredients, Allison James and Alan Prout argue that the modern conception of childhood can be understood as a self-sustaining model, which is related to three predominant themes: rationality, naturalness, and universality. "Rationality is the universal mark of adulthood with childhood representing the period of apprenticeship for its development [. . .] the naturalness of children both governs and is governed by their universality. It is essentially an evolutionary model: the child developing into an adult represents a progression from simplicity to complexity of thought, from irrational to rational behavior."[38]

In short, this prevailing modern discourse about childhood (re)produces children as innately innocent, dependent, and vulnerable beings (or becomings) in both physical and social terms, which makes any link between children and violence particularly problematic. Hence, the ambivalence that inhabits the discourse of modern childhood authorizes children to be controlled, segregated, and placed spatially and temporally in a distinct social group that is utterly disempowered, but doing so is "in their best interests."[39] In other words, by securing the proper places and times for children, the child, understood as the epitome of innocence, goodness, and the promise of a progressive future, must be protected and invested in, while, at the same time, the child understood as undeveloped, not yet civilized, even savage—a potential source of disruption—must be contained and disciplined.

From this analysis, three main elements appear fundamental for this particular articulation of childhood and the child: (1) a foundational belief that the child's inherent vulnerability is related to an original state of purity and innocence; (2) the trope of the child as a full citizen in potential; and (3) the child developmental model that relegates children to a specific temporal process that structures their journey toward the rational world of the adult. As Mills notes, this discourse institutes a slip from the description of the child to the prescription of his or her life based on a set of methods and rules of play from the field of child developmental psychology.[40] In Foucauldian terms, child developmental psychology works as "discursive policing" or a principle of control over the production of discourse about the child and childhood by fixing the limits of what can be said about children.[41]

This ambivalent meaning of the child is in close dialogue with child developmental psychology, as children themselves can acquire the abnormal or pathologized status of risk if they fail to fit the normalized process of development. As is explored here, it is precisely the normalization of the process of child development and maturation articulated by child developmental psychology that makes abnormality possible. Thus, unlike the notion of development as a natural progression, in this work, development is understood as if "[it] is always *of* something, *to* somewhere, as evaluated *by* someone."[42]

The idea of development is a powerful key concept within the modern discourse about childhood. In this discourse, social and individual development practices are associated with other terms, such as growth, change, and progress. When framing the child's development toward adulthood, there is a strong sense that these changes in the physical and, perhaps more importantly, the psychological and social realms follow an ordered rule-governed plan leading toward a more advanced, complex, or sophisticated level of organization.[43] Although this notion of development appears as if it were an inevitable, natural, universal progression, it also includes the permanent possibility of rupture or discontinuity, which is itself envisaged in terms of deviation, pathology, or inferiority. The possibility of the rupture of the developmental process authorizes external interventions, so that its linearity can be restored. This message is reproduced, for example, by the common use of an arrow as the metaphor of time transition or, in Kofsky Scholnick's words: "a push towards change, not as a force that simultaneously transforms and is transformed."[44]

However, it was not until the late nineteenth and early twentieth centuries that this notion of development, grounded in the idea that children's attributes should be linked along the dimension of time in a single sequence, became so pervasive within the discourse of childhood. At this time, as Hugh Cunningham affirms, it was believed that science from the particular perspective of evolution could help explain the mysteries of children's minds, measure the maturation of children, teach mothers how to rear their children, and provide guidance for children whose development deviated from the standard norms.[45]

Some of the priorities of child development derive from this: first, to describe the major developmental milestones (biological and social changes) that the child goes through, which mark their progression toward adulthood; secondly, to explain what drives the processes of growth and change underlying child development; and third, to identify the causes and environmental factors involved in shaping deviations from the norm of growth and development (that is, the presumed linear movement toward the production of a modern [adult] citizen).[46] In this regard, child developmental psychology also aims to identify what role deviations from normality may play as causal factors in maladjustment, delinquency, or other social risks.

Child developmental psychology was made possible by the work of the clinic and the nursery school. Such institutions were fundamental in that they allowed for the observation of numbers of children under controlled, experimental conditions. They simultaneously standardized and normalized through the collation of comparable information on a large number of subjects and analyzed it in such a way as to construct norms. A developmental norm, as argued by Nikolas Rose, "was a standard based upon the average abilities or performances of children of a certain age on a particular task or specified activity."[47] In the psychology of childhood, growth and temporality were principles of organization that described and produced individual children in terms of their location on this axis of time in relation to what was supposed to be "normal" for their age. At the end of the day, this developmental norm not only presented what was normal for children of a certain age but also made it possible to rank and order, include and exclude, in comparison to the norm.

Arnold Gesell, in the work he carried out at the Yale Clinic of Child Development, founded in 1911 for the assessment and treatment of children having problems at school, was one of the first to draw up the norms and milestones that underlie developmental stages checks. It also promoted the first maturational view of development as a process of natural unfolding, whereby development is equated with growth.[48] In the Yale clinic, there was a huge, glass-enclosed dome that established a shell within which a researcher could present a stimulus to a baby and observe its reactions, as recorded by an "objective observer"—a newly available movie camera on the left of the room. Believing that he could remove the "biases" of contextual, personal factors, Gesell did repeated tests of many children and assembled a massive data bank of young children's behavior at various ages and stages of development. This information was tabulated, and variations across ages were compared to establish chronological and group norms.[49]

In other words, these children were transformed into a visible, observable, and analyzable *object* within child developmental practices that made a claim to truth about the natural stages of early development of the child.[50] Even today, Gesell's findings—or, as he called them, his "normative findings"—remain the organizing principle for the milestones on which the American Academy of Pediatrics bases its advice.[51]

Through these experiments, Gesell (and numerous researchers since then) sought to identify "universal, rule-governed patterns of behavior, thinking and reasoning, and especially how far these follow a predictable, stage-like sequence."[52] Although individual differences in developmental processes were recognized, the emphasis was on what children had in common. The main goal of these studies was to identify "normal" patterns of development, articulating any deviation from the standard model in terms of developmental delay or precocity. As Burman argues, the focus of child developmental psychology has been not on particular social experiences of children but on a totalizing, coherent, and abstract child as exemplar, as the norm.[53] Martin Woodhead comments further that "the use of the singular noun 'child' in textbooks on 'Child Development' has been a highly informative 'calling card' for the paradigm!"[54]

In terms of the second priority of child developmental psychology, which aims at explaining the processes underlying the development journey, Jean Piaget's work may be considered the source of the idea that development was the product of the maturing child's activity in constructing an internal representation of their environment.[55] That is, beginning in early childhood years, children interpret, organize, and use information from the environment to construct their own conceptions ("mental structures") of their social and physical worlds.[56] Children's intellectual development, according to Piaget, does not only mean accumulating knowledge and skills but, more importantly, the progression of their intellectual capacity along a series of qualitatively distinct stages. Based on Piaget's empirical studies, a child's process of development begins from sensory-motor intelligence immediately succeeding birth and proceeds through preconceptual thought, intuitive thought, and concrete operations up to the level of formal operations, which for most people occur in early adolescence. As a universal recipe for "childishness," Piaget establishes the stages of a chronologically and hierarchically arranged process that starts from low-status, infantile, "figurative" thought to high-status, adult, "operative" intelligence.[57]

Within Piaget's approach, children are depicted as social actors—and not just objects of the adult world—in the construction and interpretation of their own worlds. However, the focus is still on individual development and the appropriation of the world by one single child isolated in his or her own terms, silencing both the role played by children's relationships with other children and adults and the variety of social and cultural circumstances that also shape children's lives.[58] Piaget's theory also produces a homogeneous notion of the childhood experience, which is depicted as a progressive graduation through stages to ever greater competence and maturity, with the end point being adulthood, a phase articulated as stable and rational. This framework, then, takes the dominant view that children are, first and foremost, sites of investment for the future. Children's position of waiting is continuously (re)produced, and any deviation from their normalized journey toward transition to the adult world is articulated as pathology.

Hence, within the child development discourse, understood as a scientific model, normative descriptions of the modern child slip into naturalized prescriptions. When normative and scientific discourses combine, it is possible to locate within the child both more knowledge about the (good) future and, by virtue of the child as a human becoming in process of maturation, the route to knowledge.

Overall, what emerges from the analysis of child developmental psychology is how it sets the limits for the discourse about both the (abstract) child as the norm and childhood. It articulates the identity of the child, which takes the form of a permanent reactuation of the rules regarding what a child is, where it must be placed, and how it must develop. Based on these reflections on the particular discourses about the child and childhood, the next section focuses on the possibility of rupture by considering the specific case of child-soldiers—that is, children who deviate from the normalized course of development. By having experienced episodes of violence and loss, child-soldiers transit between the notion of the child as victim, who must be protected and rescued from the war setting (an adult's place par excellence), and the notion of the child as a monster who has not followed the natural stages in becoming a "normal" adult. In both cases, the child-soldier is articulated as a social problem that has gained increasing attention from international society since the end of the Cold War.

CHILD-SOLDIERS: A *NEW* SOCIAL PROBLEM?

A child-soldier, age sixteen, gave the following testimony: "I was attending primary school. The rebels came and attacked us. They killed my mother and father in front of my eyes. I was 10 years old. They took me with them . . . they trained us to fight. The first time I killed someone, I got so sick, I thought I was going to die. But I got better. . . . My fighting name was Blood Never Dry."[59]

In a similar vein, Human Rights Watch describes the plight of children engaged in war in Myanmar:

Once they are deployed to battalions throughout the country, child soldiers in the Burma army continue to be brutalized by their commanders and they are also forced to be brutal to civilians[. . . .] Their commanders beat them for little or no reason, steal their pay and their rations and then send them out to the villages to steal their own food and round up villagers for forced labor. Fearful of the beatings and punishments they will face if they fail their assignments, they round up women, children and the elderly to fill the specified numbers for forced labor, or kick and push civilians who are carrying army supplies to make sure they reach the camp on time. When participating in combat for the first time, most young boys say they were afraid; they cried or closed their eyes and fired their guns into the air. They are ordered to commit human rights abuses which they know are wrong[. . . .] A mental health professional who reviewed transcripts of interviews with one of the boys indicated that his responses were consistent with the symptoms of post-traumatic stress disorder.[60]

At first blush, what comes to mind through these narratives and other reports about child-soldiers published by international humanitarian organizations, NGOs, and the world's media is a relationship between extremes: the extreme violence of the child-soldiering "phenomenon," the extreme brutality of contemporary wars, and the extreme fragility of the states where this phenomenon takes place. In such discourse, there is no room for ambiguities. The complexity of wartime is lost. Child-soldiers' experiences are occluded, and they are essentialized as deviant children, supporting the argument of how certain children are capable of committing violent acts that other, normal children are not.

Pictured as a *new* phenomenon, child-soldiers are then articulated as a growing feature of war. Despite the recognition that some children have been present in armies in the past,[61] these are considered the exceptions to what the rule used to be—that is, that warfare was the domain of adults. Since the end of World War II, the participation of children in armed conflict not only as victims but also as perpetrators of violence has been increasingly present in the debates in the field of international politics.[62] Considered by some authors to be one of the main symbols of the so-called new wars,[63] child-soldiers have attracted enormous media attention and have also become a priority in the humanitarian field: narratives about boys (mostly) carrying weapons such as AK-47s emerge on front pages of newspapers, are incorporated into academic debates, and have become popular themes in the movie industry and in fictional literature. Although the constructions and imageries vary, the discourse about the child-soldier articulates a clear message: there is a serious *crisis* of childhood. That is, instead of innocent and happy children, child-soldiers are associated with a clearly defined "adult role," one that exhibits all the features of the social world that differentiates adults from children.[64]

From the 1977 Additional Protocol to the Geneva Conventions, which is the first systematic legal attempt to directly address the issue of child-soldiers, to the Paris Principles and Guidelines on Children Associated with Armed Forces and Armed Groups,[65] it is possible to identify a great expansion of what is meant by the social category that refers to children engaged in warfare. Under the first international documents, the regulation (or prohibition) of children's participation in war and their protection were contingent on their role as combatants, varying, for example, with the nature of the conflict or the age of the child involved. However, in the latest international document, the Paris Principles, which serves as the basis for UNICEF's programs, the broad definition of child-soldier given in the Cape Town Principles is provided, and the concept of child-soldier is formally abandoned in favor of the concept of a "child associated with an armed force or armed group," which refers to "any person *below 18 years of age* who is or who has been recruited or used by any armed force or group in *any capacity*, including but not limited to children, boys and girls used as fighters, cooks, porters, messengers, spies or for sexual purposes. It does not only refer to a child who is taking or has taken a direct part in hostilities."[66]

According to UNICEF and other international humanitarian organizations, the change of labels was justified because the term "child-soldier" obfuscated the range of roles that children undertake when they participate in war and are recruited by military groups. By seeking to protect children involved in warfare, both the Cape Town Principles and the Paris Principles expanded the concept of "soldier" far beyond what most people would intuitively recognize.[67] In particular, the Paris Principles reflect the changing discourse around the child-soldier, which articulates it as a social problem: from a specific concern with child combatants to an attempt to build an absolute barrier between childhood and military life. At the same time that this broader concept makes possible the international protection of an increasing number of children, it unites under one single category children who are assumed to share essentially the same characteristics or practices. By doing that, the various roles played by children when in war and the different meanings these experiences may have in the local context are left unacknowledged or unexplored.[68] In order to analyze these silences and to work through stereotypical referents and associations, I consider this broad definition under the term "child-soldier" as a critical reminder of what it stands for.

Furthermore, in most accounts of child-soldiers by international organizations (mainly, humanitarian ones), NGOs, and the mainstream media, the concept is not hyphenated. But here, the addition of the hyphen—connecting unconnectable categories—operates as a way of problematizing the utmost barrier between being a "child" and being a "soldier": the idea that childhood and war are mutually exclusive. Even when these children are categorized as soldiers, they are hardly compared to legitimate servicepeople who lawfully kill on behalf of the state. That is, child-soldiers are articulated as neither authentic soldiers, because they are not yet adults, nor as "normal" children, since their experiences do not coincide with the behavior prescribed for the normalized child. As dually deviant, child-soldiers therefore exceed both the limits of what it means to be a child and what it means to be an (adult) soldier. The hyphen, then, simultaneously challenges and (re)produces three fundamental categories of modern society: war as an exclusive domain of adults; the (adult) soldier as the legitimate combatant in charge of defending his or her nation-state; and the "normal" child as an innocent being who should be protected and excluded from war.

According to David Rosen, this discourse about the child-soldier refers to a recent account of this category of children involved in warfare.[69] Although child-soldiers have always been present on the battlefields, they have been articulated in many different ways, such as war heroes or natural companions of adults during war in medieval times, when, as Philippe Ariès reminds us, there was generally an indifference to age.[70] Thus, Rosen argues that the discourse about the child-soldier *reverses* traditional images of the child-soldier and suggests that "rather than mythologiz[ing] the past and render[ing] invisible the thousands of child soldiers who fought in wars of national liberation, we should ask why there was no international child-soldier crisis at that time."[71] Following Rosen's suggestion, I turn the focus toward the analysis of the main assumptions that frame the discourse about the child-soldier, in which its identity as deviant and pathological in relation to the child-norm is (re)produced without being problematized.

In 1996, Graça Machel, an expert appointed by the secretary-general of the UN and a former minister of education of Mozambique, presented a report to the United Nations General Assembly titled *Promotion and Protection of the Rights of Children: Impact of Armed Conflict on Children.*[72] In it, she suggested that more than three hundred thousand under-eighteens were fighting at that time in thirty-one conflicts around the world. This study prompted much international attention, advocacy, and programming on the "phenomenon" of child-soldiers and also led to the creation of Child Soldiers International (formerly Coalition to Stop the Use of Child Soldiers), made up of prominent humanitarian and human rights organizations. The report included a number of concrete recommendations for the protection of children in armed conflict and was, according to Machel, an urgent call for ending the exploitation of children as soldiers.

The report was based on interviews with child-soldiers, NGO representatives, members of different communities impacted by war, and government representatives. Machel narrated in detail how children were recruited into armed groups and armed forces and discussed their different experiences while involved in war not only as victims but also as perpetrators of violence. Moreover, Machel emphasized that states must recognize the recruitment and use of child-soldiers in order to be able to include special provisions for demobilization and reintegration of children in peace agreements and related documents. In sum, Machel's message was very clear: children must not take part in warfare. "The international community must denounce this attack on children for what it is—*intolerable* and *unacceptable*[. . . .] *The needs of all children are the same:*

nutritious food, adequate health care, a decent education, shelter and a secure and loving family. *Children are both our reason to struggle to eliminate the worst aspects of warfare, and our best hope for succeeding at it.*[73]

As one of the main documents responsible for taking the issue of child-soldiers to international consideration, Machel's report sets forth the main ideas about the child-soldier. There are three discursive pillars that articulate the child-soldier as a new social problem: (1) children are presumably vulnerable and innocent; (2) the new wars are particularly brutal and "uncivilized"; and (3) weapons are smaller and lighter than they used to be. Although these assumptions are questionable, they have been (re)produced and articulated by and through international organizations, NGOs, and the mainstream media since the publication of the report in 1996.

Considering the above-mentioned statement, what becomes clear is the (re)production of the notion of the "natural child," who is presumably vulnerable and innocent and whose needs, both biological (e.g., "nutritious food") and social (e.g., "a secure and loving family"), are coalesced and universalized. In this sense, it is interesting to note that although Machel emphasizes that most of the underaged engaged in war are adolescents, the term she uses to refer to them is "child" or "children," based on the fact they are all under eighteen.[74] Similarly, most of the international reports by international agencies and NGOs do not differentiate children from adolescents. The use of the term "child," rather than "children and adolescents," which would mark different stages of temporality and maturation, homogenizes and (re)produces the idea that this is a group of people who are particularly vulnerable and as yet irrational. As Rosen puts it, "As a result, the child soldier who volunteers is conflated with the child soldier who is kidnapped; the teenager is conflated with the vulnerable toddler."[75]

From this perspective, child-soldiers do not have real agency in their military participation.[76] Even where most recruitment is reportedly voluntary, the NGO Watchlist on Children and Armed Conflict (hereinafter Watchlist) report titled *Where Are They . . . ? The Situation of Children and Armed Conflict in Mali* (2013) downplays the voluntary aspect of children's enlistment by emphasizing that armed groups took advantage of poverty, idleness, or lack of adult care by targeting "vulnerable children, including children on the street and children out of work."[77] It says that armed groups incentivized recruitment by offering children or their families

money, reportedly wide-ranging monthly sums of 40,000 to 400,000 CFA francs (approximately US$ 80–800); goods, such as televisions or bikes; free education at a time when most schools were closed; or simply the promise of payment and three meals a day[. . . .] As one source put it: *"When you have nothing and are given something, you take it."* To attract children, Ansar Dine and MUJAO threw candy from vehicles or distributed gifts to children. Young children ran small errands in exchange for money and shared meals with the armed groups. In these ways armed groups began associations with at-risk children that they then recruited.[78]

Specifically, on military recruitment, Rosen notes that children are articulated in these narratives as emotional decision makers: they only believe, feel, or sense; they do not know, understand, judge, or decide as adult soldiers do.[79] For instance, in Machel's report, children volunteer to be soldiers because "they *believe* that this is the only way to guarantee regular meals, clothing, and medical attention" or because "they may *feel safer* [. . .] if they have guns in their hands" or "*feel obliged* to become soldiers for their own protection."[80] Following on the same idea, in the review on the progress made in relation to children's protection in armed conflicts since the publication of her report in 1996, Machel argues that it is misleading, in a war setting, to consider a child's decision to join the military as "voluntary."[81] As in Machel's first report on the impact of war on children and the Watchlist report, the term "voluntary" is usually placed within quotation marks in international organizations' reports, indicating that it should not be taken literally when addressing child enlistment.[82]

This discourse resonates with UNICEF's position in relation to the participation of children in warfare. According to a UNICEF senior adviser at the Child Protection in Emergencies unit, the voluntariness of children's choices to join the armed groups cannot be accepted:

> Is it really voluntary when you have no food at home, there is no money to go to school or you've just watched your whole village get attacked by this rebel group and family members have been killed and raped? I mean it is not really voluntariness under those circumstances. There are pressures and there are circumstances. What I find is often the children who have joined armed groups through that rather than being abducted is that they regret their decision, because they didn't know what they were getting into.[83]

Also, in the Save the Children report *Child Soldiers: Care & Protection of Children in Emergencies: A Field Guide*, this argument is clearly posed: "Although children may come forward to join an armed group without conscription or press-ganging, this type of recruitment is rarely *truly* voluntary. Children may have no other option for survival in a conflict where they have lost family members or access to other forms of protection. Finally, *children do not yet have the cognitive developmental skills to fully assess risks and choices* that they may make under these conditions."[84]

However, rather than silencing children's agency, Brocklehurst argues that child-soldiers may be understood as active participants with varying degrees of self-awareness.[85] When children decide to engage in war, they may be motivated, as these reports emphasize, by threats such as starvation, isolation, or domestic violence, to name but a few. Still, instead of silencing these hard and complex decision-making processes, Brocklehurst points out that these children may choose to join the armed groups to live—so as not to kill or be killed.[86]

Nevertheless, not only is the focus of humanitarian discourse on abductions of children, masking the fact that voluntary enlistment often outnumbers forced recruitment in certain locations,[87] but these narratives frequently describe the forced recruitment of children as being linked to specific acts of terror, such as compelling the new recruits to kill family members or co-villagers. The Human Rights Watch 1997 report on child soldiering in northern Uganda, in turn, underlines the brutality of the kidnappings of children through the testimonies of child-soldiers: "We were all tied up and attached to one another in a row. After we were tied up, they started to beat us randomly; they beat us up with sticks."[88] Moreover, reports of the use of drugs, such as "brown-brown," reiterate the vulnerability of child-soldiers: "Children are easily controlled and very brave when given drugs. Has no second thoughts and can always perform."[89]

Also, the presumed immaturity or irrationality of the child can also be equated with naïveté about the consequences of actions or can be understood as malleability. Children are depicted as being programmed to function like robots or brainwashed to commit terrible abuses that they can neither appreciate nor control.[90] Even when child-soldiers are given some agency, Alcinda Honwana describes it as "tactical" or "agency of the weak" rather than strategic agency, which requires a basis of power, mastery of the larger picture, and some comprehension of the long-term consequences of actions in the form of political gain.[91] But, according to Honwana, "the majority of child soldiers seem to have entirely lacked such a perspective."[92] In the UNICEF report *Will You Listen? Young Voices from the Conflict Zone*, this idea is reaffirmed through this child's testimony: "Many of us, especially the boys, are forced to join various armed forces. They then put us in the front of the battlefields or force us to spy on the opposition. They brainwash us into believing that we are fighting to defend our rights and our communities."[93]

However, this idea of child-soldiers as "killing machines" is a mistaken interpretation, because in situations of harsh discipline where dissenters may risk summary torture and execution, it becomes *rational* to exhibit obedience and not question orders for survival's sake.[94] A clear example comes from Neil Boothby's interviews with former child-soldiers in Mozambique, in which they reported that those children who resisted were often killed and those who obeyed became junior leaders or received other rewards such as extra food or more comfortable housing.[95]

Even so, Machel, among others, insists on the assumption that child-soldiers are more "malleable" than adult soldiers and reiterates that some military commanders have even noted the desirability of child-soldiers because "they are more obedient, do not question orders and are easier to manipulate than adult soldiers."[96] An illustrative example of this discourse about the child-soldier is the description made by a reporter from Radio Netherlands Worldwide:

> Children make very effective combatants. They *don't ask a lot of questions.* They follow instructions, and they often don't understand and *aren't able to evaluate the risks of going to war.* Victims and witnesses often said they feared the children more than adults because the *child combatants had not developed an understanding of the value of life.* They would do anything. *They knew no fear.* Especially when they were pumped on drugs. They saw it as *fun* to go into battle.[97]

In face of this discourse, a common conclusion is posed by Machel in her report: "Children [child-soldiers] are dropping out of childhood."[98] This notion is indeed evident in many of the common titles found in works about child-soldiers: *Innocents Lost: When Child Soldiers Go to War* or *No Childhood at All: Child Soldiers in Burma.*[99] Again, although there are situations in which children do indeed suffer in armed conflict and are brutally exploited, the risk of this particular discourse is that it silences the possibility of analyzing and comprehending the experiences of military recruitment through a different grammar than the one of victimization of children, which considerably undermines their status as political beings.

The second assumption that frames and (re)produces the discourse of the child-soldier as a new phenomenon is the idea that it is closely related to the development of a "new," far more brutal type of conflict, the new war, which has prevailed since the Cold War, or, as Gates and Reich put it, "in the age of fractured states."[100] According to Mary Kaldor, the new wars, although localized, draw on a globalized social and economic arena and need to be understood in this context of intensified global interconnectedness.[101]

Simply put, these new wars can be contrasted with earlier wars in terms of a blurring of distinctions, which are characteristic of the (re)production and institutionalization of both the modern nation-state and modern war. Different from the wars of the eighteenth century, which were articulated as an activity based on clear ideas about the appropriate role and limits of force of diplomatic relations, the new wars have rendered those fundamental boundaries unrecognizable. Kaldor, then, lists the distinctions that have been challenged, such as the one between private and public; the one between what took place within a clearly defined territory of the state and what took place outside it; the separation of economic activity from public state activities; and the separation between combatants and civilians, which, according to Kalevi J. Holsti, becomes unclear through, for example, the lack of distinctive uniforms, which symbolize this institutionalization and serve as a visual marker of armed forces.[102] This distinction is particularly important in defining the child-soldier, who in many situations does not wear a military uniform, as the picture of the Liberian boy in the BBC story exemplifies. The absence of the military uniform together with the presumed vulnerability and innocence of the child (re)produces the imagery of the child-soldier not only as a victim of war but also as not competent enough to be an authentic soldier with a full uniform. Finally, above all these distinctions, the separation between war and peace is vague, and when peace does appear, it seldom holds for long. One of the characteristics of these new wars is their duration. Within such formulation, Peter Singer, for example, justifies the participation of child-soldiers in terms of fulfilling the continuous demand for combatants to maintain the conflict: "With their ready availability and easy transformation into combatants, children now represent a low-cost way to mobilize and generate force when the combatants do not generally care about public opinion. This creates the doctrine of child soldiers, a new way of enacting violence that prescribes the methods and circumstances of children's employment in battle."[103]

Paralleling Kaldor's construction of the new wars, Machel, in her report on the impact of wars on children, defines warfare in postcolonial states, where the majority of child-soldiers are found, in terms of the "abandonment of all standards" and a "sense of dislocation and chaos."[104] Moreover, Machel describes the "callousness of modern warfare" as resulting from the breakdown of traditional societies brought about by globalization and social revolutions. The report cites such phenomena as the vestiges of colonialism, internal dissent, structural monetary adjustments, uneven development, the collapse of government, the personalization of power, and the erosion of essential services as factors contributing to a breakdown in the rules of warfare. This breakdown has led to the loss of distinctions between combatants and civilians, especially high levels of violence and brutality, and the use of any and all tactics, including systematic rape, scorched-earth policies, ethnic cleansing, and genocide. As emphasized in the report, the abandonment of standards has brought about human rights violations against women and children, including the recruitment of children into armed forces and groups.[105]

In face of this assumption about a new type of warfare, many scholars have questioned whether these qualitative changes that have occurred in the nature of violent conflict would justify thinking of "contemporary" or "modern" conflicts as a departure from "earlier" forms of conflict.[106] Edward Newman, for example, questions the extent to which contemporary forms of organized violence qualitatively reflect new patterns in terms of actors, objectives, spatial context, human impact, and the political economy and social structure of conflict in the twentieth century.[107] However, irrespective of this debate about whether the factors that characterize the new wars have been present throughout the last century, it is worth exploring what is articulated and (re)produced in terms of the understanding of the child-soldier when children engaged in armed conflict are conceived as one of the main symbols of these new wars, which are clearly associated with the failure of statehood.

First, the temporal aspect reflected in constructs such as new wars provides an indication of the transformation of the contingent event into the new norm.[108] From this formulation, the child-soldier appears as a symptom that became a normalized mark of these supposedly new "barbarous and uncivilized" wars. Moreover, in highlighting the limitless character of these contemporary wars, which dismantle the traditional conceptions of state boundaries and their associated rules, the discourse about the new wars renders the state permeable, beyond control by government or its institutions. Child-soldiers, as a social problem (or as one of the prime examples of incivility), emerge from this context of "fragmentation of the certainties of modern life," fusing two very contradictory and powerful ideas, namely the "innocence" of childhood and the "evil" of this kind of warfare. From this outset, child-soldiers are, thus, aberrant and abhorrent.[109]

Within such a formulation of armed conflict as the "abandonment of all standards" or "chaos," the potential reversal of such fragmentation can either emerge from the victory of one faction over all others, so that a renewed monopoly over the means of violence is established, or through forms of external intervention that aim to control emergencies and put in place governmental practices aimed at the reestablishment of the social order, the protection of civilian populations, and the assurance of respect for human rights.[110] Specifically, for the child-soldiers, the only solution is to be saved by international society, since their own families, societies, and states are disqualified for this role, occupying the realm of the uncivilized, and must be either rehabilitated or punished and reconstructed through international interventions.

Finally, the third assumption is that technological improvements in small arms enable child-soldiers to be effective participants in warfare. According to this discourse, the simplification of their use is as important as their light weight. As Michael Wessells notes, in previous ages, young children lacked the size and strength to wield effectively the weapons of their days, such as swords, spears, shields, and heavy muskets.[111] In her 1996 report, Machel also associates the participation of children as soldiers in armed conflicts with the "proliferation of inexpensive light weapons."[112] According to the UN expert, if previously the more dangerous weapons were either heavy or complex, in contemporary contexts the weapons are "so light that children can use them and so simple that they can be stripped and reassembled by a *child of 10*."[113] The age criterion here is important, since it isolates the child and articulates him or her based on a particular chronological stage marked by his or her fragility, irrationality, and immaturity. From this single piece of information, it is assumed that although a child is not yet fully developed or as strong as an adult, he or she can still use a gun.

In addition, through the black market, official and unofficial military organizations can acquire weapons very cheaply and easily. Thus, at the same time that the easy access to deadly weapons is assumed to transform any local conflict into a bloody slaughter, the cost of turning children into soldiers is significantly lower. A report by the Small Arms Survey states this idea clearly: "Light weapons are becoming more lethal, more portable, less expensive, and more durable, increasing the prospect of their proliferation, especially to non-state armed groups."[114] For example, Machel comments that in Uganda "an AK-47 automatic machine gun can be purchased for the cost of a chicken and, in northern Kenya, it can be bought for the price of a goat."[115]

However, by drawing on historical examples of participation of children in war, Rosen argues that it is not possible to establish a direct link between the spread of small arms and the recruitment of children by armed groups and armed forces.[116] The most popular weapon for child-soldiers, the Russian AK-47, has been available since 1949; it was the key weapon of national liberation groups, rebels, and insurgents long before the child-soldier phenomenon, which gained strength after the end of the Cold War. In addition, there is the weight itself. Rosen highlights that at 4.3 kilos, so the AK-47 is similar in weight to or even heavier than many of the rifles used in the American Civil War, in which the number of child combatants was significantly higher.[117] For instance, the U.S. rifle musket of 1861, which went into mass production during the American Civil War, was a simple and durable weapon that weighed 4 kilos.[118] Moreover, weapons such as machetes and knives were still prominent in armed conflicts in countries such as Sierra Leone and Rwanda.

Therefore, small arms can be used to kill populations during wars, but their role in fostering child-soldiering is at best indirect. Again, what becomes clear from the assumptions about both new wars and "new" weapons is that they articulate and translate the participation of children in war as a new and emerging event characteristic of these barbaric armed conflicts, calling for immediate intervention on the part of external actors. Furthermore, these assumptions (re)produce and emphasize the first claim discussed here, that child-soldiers are particularly vulnerable and are exploited by adults in "barbarous" contexts of armed conflict.

In short, the discourse about the child-soldier as a new social problem is articulated by the presumed link between children's putative vulnerability and innocence, the technological advance of the arms industry, and supposed changes in the nature of most contemporary armed conflicts. As Lorraine Macmillan notes, the child-soldier has been constructed as a "bounded category, to which only certain subjects, narratives and theories are admitted."[119] In this sense, a single discourse about the child-soldier, regardless of the varied experiences of children who soldier, has become the focus of international sympathy, fear, charity, pity, and intervention.

According to this discourse about the new phenomenon of child-soldiering, the approach to otherness, the child-soldier, is ambivalent. When child-soldiers' "childishness" is not recognized, the identification of these children as "vulnerable and innocent" and a hostility or fear toward them as "not really like our children" coalesce. Child-soldiers are not only subject to social problems but are also a *threat* to humanity. As Machel emphasizes in the beginning of her 1996 report, "Children are both our reason to struggle to eliminate the worst aspects of warfare, and our best hope for succeeding at it."[120] International programs for rescuing former child-soldiers and aiming to give them another chance at childhood are, thus, justified and authorized. The "normal" child—together with the promise of a progressive future—is (re)produced as the norm, while the child-soldier is located in a network of power relations through which these children are classified and fabricated as deviant and pathological.

In order to explore what is being produced, authorized, and silenced through and by this particular discourse about childhood, the child, and the child-soldier, the next and final section presents the main childhood studies arguments and debates. By seeking to problematize the modern dichotomy between child and adult in terms of human becoming and human being, childhood studies makes room for analyzing and discussing the anomaly—that is, childhoods—in which the hallmark of innocence is not necessarily present,[121] and uncontrolled children challenge the idea of the child as a vulnerable, immature, passive object in an adult world.

THINKING DIFFERENTLY: CHILDHOOD STUDIES AND THE STUDY OF CHILDREN

Children's experiences of war, migration, famine, and poverty confront the so-called modern world with different accounts of childhood. In *Vietnam's Children in a Changing World*, Rachel Burr depicts the experiences of street children and challenges the modern premise that all forms of child labor are bad.[122] According to Burr, one problem is that those who oppose what children do really don't know their or their families' circumstances: "work means different things to different children, and children's experiences vary considerably."[123] Other examples of ethnographical works about children are by Kristen E. Cheney, who focuses on "different" childhoods, including the experiences of child-soldiers in northern Uganda, and by Olga Nieuwenhuys about child labor in India.[124] As claimed by Nieuwenhuys, the fact that these children step out of what is considered the "morally correct" way of being a child should not mean that they have no childhood or are robbed of it.[125] In the absence of a valid criterion across cultures of what a happy and normal childhood is, the decision about where to draw the line between "right" and "wrong" childhoods is always a political one.

It is in this vein that the paradigm of childhood studies, as proposed by James and Prout, seeks to challenge the "universal and natural" vision of childhood by articulating childhood as a social construct that varies depending on social, economic, and political contexts.[126] Thus, James and Prout suggest six principles for guiding the new field of childhood studies: (1) childhood is a social construct, meaning that it is a cultural and structural element of all societies; (2) like other variables such as gender, class, and race, childhood should be included as a variable in all social analyses; (3) children should be studied in their own right; (4) children are social, active, creative agents who are simultaneously able to construct their own social lives and contribute to the (re)production of societies in general; (5) ethnography is a useful methodology for the study of childhood; and (6) proclaiming a new paradigm also means engaging in the process of (re)constructing childhood in society.[127]

The debates within childhood studies have been significantly influenced by the work of the historian Phillipe Ariès, specifically his book *Centuries of Childhood* (1962), on the history of the modern family and childhood.[128] By seeking to understand the particularities of modern society in comparison with the past, Ariès locates the genesis of the modern conception of childhood, which derives from the dichotomization between children and adults, in the eighteenth century. In medieval society, he argues, although children were plentiful (and visible), they did not constitute a conceptual category; that is, there was no awareness of the particular nature of childhood, that particular feature that distinguishes the child from the adult. For example, children and adults used to wear the same type of clothing, and games that now are considered inappropriate for children (such as gambling) used to be part of the day-to-day lives of every child. Put another way, the only difference between these two phases of life—childhood and adulthood—in medieval society was their physical size. Children were essentially mini-adults. As soon as they could live without the constant solicitude of their mother, nanny, or cradle rocker, children were understood as belonging to adult society.[129]

In order to examine the particularities of modern childhood and modern children, in "The Idea of Childhood," part 1 of *Centuries of Childhood*, Ariès investigates changes in the concepts of age, the portrayal of childhood in pictures, children's clothes, the history of games and pastimes, and the development of the idea that children are inherently innocent. In short, he concludes that in the eighteenth century, there were two concepts of childhood: the first was to be found within the family circle in the company of little children. Children, by virtue of their sweetness, simplicity, and drollery, became a source of amusement and relaxation for adults, a feeling that Ariès calls "coddling."[130] This coddling consisted of a celebration of children's incompetence and clumsiness: "The less capable in the management of their bodies and the less subtle their handling of social relationships, the greater the love and attention given to them."[131] The second concept of childhood was rooted outside the family in moralists, who emphasized how children were fragile creatures of God and needed to be protected and disciplined in rational manners.[132] In the eighteenth century, these two elements were present within the family sphere in addition to a new one: concern about hygiene and physical health.

In the next two parts of the book, "The Scholastic Life" and "The Family," Ariès explores the two institutional developments he considers as crucial for the (re)production of this idea of childhood. First, the introduction of a modern system of schooling, in which the need to isolate, protect, and discipline children was apparent in the way classrooms were designed and became containers for the assessment and regulation of children's social and moral development. The importance of the school system is in close dialogue with the argument made by reformers who held that as part of the "moralization of society," children should have an education. The school system replaced the ways children had previously learned and been educated (from their direct participation in "adult society"). Commenting on Ariès's work, Cunningham notes: "Children came to be subjected to a 'sort of quarantine' before they were allowed to join adult society. Parents were taught that they had a duty to ensure their children were sent to school."[133]

The second change, which made the first one possible, was the privatizing of family life, which increasingly revolved around children, distancing them from the rest of the community. In modern society there was a new feeling within the family: parents were interested in and oversaw their children's education. In other words, children were insulated in a private world in which adults were obsessed by the physical, moral, and sexual problems of childhood. Children came out of the anonymity they had experienced in medieval society and gained such an important role in the modern family that losing them caused enormous pain.

Based on Ariès's analysis, the construction of childhood is a continual process that is never fixed or constant. Within this approach, the modern discourse about childhood may be understood as only one way of conceptualizing children's and families' experiences. As noted by Ariès, the modern discourse about childhood is linked specifically to major social changes in the late seventeenth century that opened room for—and articulated—a particular idea of childhood. Although this specific idea of childhood was socially constructed, it has since been (re)produced as a natural, universal fact, entitling all children throughout the world to certain common ingredients and rights of childhood. In this sense, Ariès's work is a significant breakthrough in developmental psychology thinking—and enlightening for the scholars of childhood studies—as it depicts the possibility of a variety of childhoods, which are lost and found at various junctures of history depending on different locations and cultures and not only based on biological factors.[134] As Brocklehurst argues in her book *Who's Afraid of Children?*, perceptions of childhood and adulthood may vary with the political (adult) priorities of society.[135] Engaging with this idea, this book focuses specifically on how a specific notion of childhood articulates (and is articulated by) a particular process of ordering the modern International.

By challenging the understanding of childhood in a fixed and bounded way, the borders of its discourse might be problematized so its internal variations and complexities can be explored. For example, it is possible to question the notion by which childhood appears as a transitional stage and to focus on the importance of studying children in their own right, independent of the perspectives and concerns of adults.[136] Through this approach, children may be analyzed as human *beings*, and possible discontinuities between "places for children"—as designated by adults—and "children's places"—as negotiated or constructed by children and adults—can be brought to the fore.

In this sense, it is important to highlight how, in the arena of childhood studies, distinctions have been drawn between three key concepts: childhood, children, and the child. Differently from the use of the concepts of adult and adults, the child as a singular term is often used uncritically and comes to represent an entire category of people: children. Indeed, as James highlights, the idea that the adult could be used as a concept to represent adults in general contradicts the very notion of the individual as a fundamental constituent of adulthood in modern societies.[137] In this regard, the possibility of uniting children under a singular umbrella phrase, the child, not only dismisses the individuality of children but also reduces their significance as social actors. According to James, this unquestioning generalization reflects the conceptualization of children in terms of their developmental stage: the only aspect that matters about children's lives is what they will be when they grow up.[138]

In order to step away from these generalizations, Daniel Thomas Cook suggests that we can think of childhood as a social institution that preauthorizes biographies by establishing a particular (or appropriate) configuration of relations that give social shape and cultural meaning to children's initial membership in human society.[139] In the same vein, Elizabeth Chin argues that childhood creates a territory whose boundaries, like all human constructions, are subject to change and to history.[140] Following this idea, the term "children," according to James, is a classificatory label given to the group of people who, regardless of their multiple social and biological constructions, are grouped together for inhabiting the social category of childhood.[141] Cook's argument does not minimize children's agency but leads to examining children's ability to negotiate descriptions of and prescriptions for how to be a child from different sources:

from the family sphere and the school environment to the international arena.[142] In this regard, the child-adult relationship, despite its power imbalance, should not be comprehended as a relationship of dependence versus independence, but in terms of *interdependencies*, in which children negotiate the constraints of the bounded world and reaffirm their relative autonomy within the constraints that limit their choices.[143] In other words, the adult's power over children is not absolute and is subject to resistance when children make and create their own meaningful worlds, even in armed conflict zones.

Finally, the term "child" should be used to refer to an individual social actor. In this sense, James suggests a different use of the concept "child" from the one within the developmental psychology discourse, where the term "child" in the singular form is articulated as a generalized one. That difference is clearly posed by James when she emphasizes that although our day-to-day encounters with the individual child are necessarily informed by understandings of the analytical and universalized concepts of childhood and children, they should not be dependent on them.[144]

These reconceptualizations of childhood and of the child open room to explore the extent to which children are potentially competent social actors and "active in the construction of their own lives, the lives of those around them and of the societies in which they live," complicating the normalized idea of childhood and of the child as the generalized form.[145] The idea of children as social agents turns out to be very important for this study, since it enables us to challenge what Nick Lee calls the "vulnerability complex," in which children and, more specifically in this study, child-soldiers, are continuously placed.[146] According to Lee, children's innocence is equated with being inherently vulnerable, which authorizes and legitimates children's political exclusion and adults' right to talk on behalf of them. At the same time, children's exclusion is linked to their lack of voice, taken here as a sign of their incompetence rooted in their biological and psychological immaturity rather than the outcome of any political process. By problematizing the idea of children as incomplete adults, the arguments and questions raised by childhood studies have contributed significantly to the debate on children's agency and participation. Although their participation has become an ever more popular policy demand, and international moves toward their political inclusion have multiplied, challenges still remain, such as tokenism, limited impact on decision making, and lack of sustainability, especially within child protection.[147] This central tension between children's participation and child protection, which is further explored in the next chapter, (re)produces and at the same time is articulated by the particular way of understanding the child, where children's capacity to participate in identifying their own concerns and solutions is limited by the normalized and universalized ideas of the child's innocence, vulnerability, and irrationality.

In order to move the focus away from adult definitions and adult actions to children's own words and experiences, childhood studies claims to study children in their own right, which often means stepping away from the modernist duality of childhood and adulthood, envisaged to bring about more stability and coherence, since it also limits the space available for ambiguity and complexity. While engaging with the debates put forward in childhood studies, this book does not purport to overcome these dichotomies or to replace one essentialist argument (that children are incompetent) with another (that they are competent), but to explore and problematize the concepts and categories and, more importantly, how they articulate specific kinds of subjectivities, life experiences, and objects. Along similar lines, in their recently published book, Spyros Spyrou, Rachel Rosen, and Daniel Thomas Cook invite scholars to *reimagine* childhood studies and to engage in further dialogue about the nature and boundaries of the agentive, competent, knowing child who makes meaning with regard to her or his own lifeworld.[148] As they argue in its introduction, "the thrust of approach and conception continues to favor singular—if socially, culturally, and historically embedded—subjects who display, or must be allowed to display, creativity and active engagement in the world in the here-and-now."[149]

That is, instead of investing in a zero-sum game of replacing the vulnerable and dependent child with one who is a competent social actor, this new effort in the field of childhood studies argues for the need to turn attention to the relational and interdependent aspects of children's lives, such as other persons, objects, technologies, epistemes, and politics that characterize them. Seeking an alternative pathway, Sarada Balagopalan argues in her chapter in *Reimagining Childhood Studies*: "An analytical exploration of these relational complexities contains the potential to propel the study of children and childhoods as central to, and not as a by-product of, current efforts to re-imagine the contemporary political terrain."[150]

Thus, besides questioning what a child is and what childhood is, as was first proposed by the scholars who defined the new childhood studies paradigm, it is also worth questioning what the significance of childhood is and what is produced and reproduced in the social order through the discourse of modern childhood.[151] In this sense, both "childhood" and the "child-norm" operate here as "analytic prisms" through which it is possible to explore the power relations that permeate and constitute the modern child, the modern subject, and, specifically in this book, the modern International.[152]

If the chapter started by defining what childhood and the child are in a very coherent and clear-cut way, in this final section, informed by childhood studies, it seeks to destabilize the boundaries that normalize these discourses in order to shed light on and problematize their limits, silences, and power relations. As the boundaries between child and adult, "normal" child and "deviant" child, are problematized, it is possible to analyze the discourse of the child-soldier without necessarily reproducing these children as deviant—or pathological—in relation to the view of the universalized and natural child. In this sense, instead of (re)producing these discourses as facts, room is opened for exploring challenges (such as the child-soldier) to the articulated coherence of the modern social order, thereby contributing, I contend, to an expanded view of the risks and social possibilities these challenges imply.

Finally, by drawing on the three pictures described in this chapter, I identify the key notions of the "natural child" and the "deviant child." The painting by Sir Joshua Reynolds and the photograph by Anne Geddes (re)produce the ingredients of the modern childhood formula, such as innocence, cuteness, happiness, asexuality, as well as the formula's presumed universality. The child-soldier from Liberia carrying the fluffy pink teddy bear backpack while he points his weapon toward the viewer brings forth the idea of a child whose childhood has been ruptured, lost, or stolen. From this understanding, the idea of the child-soldier as deviation and pathology is articulated precisely within and by the modern discourse that produces the "normal" child.

The child-soldier thus emerges as a fissure in the norm of the child. Through the ambivalent meaning of the child, the child-soldier is the child *at risk*, a victim of war and adult abuse, but he or she is also a *risky*, dangerous, savage child who constitutes the unpredictability in the present time for not following the steps prescribed in the model of child development. Within this discourse, the child-soldier must be treated so that the child and his or her childhood can be saved. Thus, in addition to the temporalities of the adult (a "temporary stability") and of the child (predicated on the notion of being "in process" of formation), the temporality of the child-soldier is premised on the notion of a *temporary emergency*. And this is what makes the international response an imperative, in an urgent bid to rescue child-soldiers so that they may have another chance at a (normal) childhood.

CHAPTER TWO

Hope for the Future

The World-Child as a World-Becoming-Citizen

We the Children is the title of the 2001 report by former secretary-general of the United Nations Kofi Annan that sought both to analyze the achievements related to the well-being of children a decade after the World Summit for Children and to renew the international commitment to create a "world fit for children."[1] Although the report's title may suggest it was written *by* children, no room in its 102 pages is set aside for children's own words—only a variety of photographs of children through which the UN celebrates the diversity of childhood. Regardless of the absence of children's own claims within the report, it analyzes their needs, such as those related to health, education, and safety. In view of this fact, it is worth questioning who these children—or, "our children"—are and what a "world fit for children" means.[2] Moreover, for the purpose of this book, it is fundamental to investigate how deviant children—such as child-soldiers—are articulated in and by the discourse about "our children," which claims to be universal.

Taking into consideration the modern conceptions of childhood and the child discussed in chapter 1, the focus here is on exploring how these particular discourses are articulated by and through the (re)production of what I call the world-child and what Annan calls "our children."[3] The discourse about the world-child speaks of an abstract and generalized child as if all children, irrespective of age, gender, culture, social class, race, and other particularities, shared an essential set of immutable characteristics and needs. In this sense, the *world* feature of the child is fundamental, as it lays claim to this universalistic aspiration through which childhood is (re)produced as a natural, homogenous experience that is ideally lived by "our children." Also, the child is not connected to any form of world, but to a particular version of the world—or, the International—that is authorized by the normalized ideas of childhood and the child, which are themselves articulated by this very same notion of the world and its mechanisms for ordering the relationships between people and states. Unlike the hyphen in the term *child-soldier*, the hyphen in *world-child* does not (re)produce any barrier between childhood and world. Rather, it stands for a circularity between the boundaries that articulate the limits of what a "normal" childhood is supposed to be (based on a supposedly universal model for the development of mature citizens) and that are instrumental in defining and maintaining a particular version of the world predicated on notions of order, security, and progress.

Considering the debates and questionings of childhood studies, this chapter investigates how the ambivalent meaning of the child-norm has been articulated and addressed in the discourse about the world-child. In this sense, the focus is on international practices devoted exclusively to children—the child-specific human rights treaties, or the so-called children's rights milestones—through which the world-child has been constituted and is continuously reproduced not only as fundamentally different from the adult but also as a completely distinct type of human who is entitled to special rights. By analyzing these practices through two interrelated key themes—protection and development—it is possible to identify how they articulate not so much different ways of codifying children's behavior as ways of normalizing what a child is and the journey it takes to become a full (adult) citizen who is competent and educated enough to participate in the particular version of the world described above.

The notion of discipline as a method of control for forming *docile* individuals is thus a central idea in this analysis.[4] The protection and development practices articulated through the children's rights milestones are understood here as disciplinary operations that (re)produce the docile child—a child who is still dependent and must be prepared to become an adult—and the docile adult, who is presumed to be capable, mature, rational, and free of contradictions; that is, the modern "world-citizen" par excellence. In particular, this chapter explores how, by guaranteeing the manufacture of docile children, these disciplinary operations address the ambivalent meaning of the child and, as a consequence, control the child's potential to become a source of threat to the international order or this particular version of the world.

The children's rights milestones include the Geneva Declaration of the Rights of the Child, adopted by the League of Nations in 1924, and the documents produced by or in consultation with the United Nations, in particular UNICEF, such as the Declaration of the Rights of the Child (1959); the International Year of the Child (1979); the 1989 Convention on the Rights of the Child (UNCRC); the World Declaration on the Survival, Protection and Development of Children (hereinafter World Declaration) and the plan of action for its implementation in the 1990s, adopted at the World Summit for Children in 1990; Convention No. 182 concerning the Prohibition and Immediate Action for the Elimination of the Worst Forms of Child Labour, adopted by the International Labour Organization (ILO) in 1999; the resolution A World Fit for Children adopted by the UN General Assembly at a Special Session on Children in 2002; and, finally, the five-year follow-up to this UN General Assembly Special Session on Children, which ended with the "Declaration of the Commemorative High-level Plenary Meeting devoted to the Follow-up to the Outcome of the Special Session on Children," which acknowledges progress made and the challenges that remain, and reaffirms a commitment to the World Fit for Children compact, the UN-CRC, and its Optional Protocols.[5] Also under analysis here are two international standards on human rights that are not devoted exclusively to children, but that comprise the group of norms concerning the protection of children and their rights: the Universal Declaration of Human Rights, adopted by the United Nations in 1948, and Convention No. 138 on the Minimum Age for Admission to Employment, adopted by the ILO in 1973.[6]

In addition to the analysis of these international practices, some of the interviews I conducted with UNICEF and UN representatives and diplomats also compose this intertextual web. Although these international practices constitute very heterogeneous statements formulated in different contexts and with their own forms of regularity and systems of constraint, it is possible, on the basis of these narratives, to identify a new regularity, which is formed by including or excluding, justifying or brushing aside, this or that statement regarding the world-child. In other words, I explore how these practices have been recomposed in the epistemologically coherent and institutionally recognized figure of the world-child.

Irrespective of the change of a few words, the message articulated through such discourses is clear: there is no nobler action than promoting children's well-being and development toward a brighter future. As Vanessa Pupavac emphasizes, the cause of children is regarded as capable of transcending national, political, and social divisions and enlisting people globally to counter social problems and militate against disorder and conflict.[7] For its part, the Plan of Action for Implementing the World Declaration justifies this global sensitivity toward children by affirming: "There is no cause which merits a higher priority than the protection and development of children, on whom the survival, stability and advancement of all nations—and, indeed, of human civilization—depends."[8]

With their "promise of a good future," children have been submitted to incisive new forms of disciplinary normalization, which Foucault tells us consist first of all in positing an optimal model—here, the world-child—that is constructed in terms of a certain outcome and is used to evaluate precisely what complies with the norm and what does not; that is, the abnormal.[9] Within these terms, it is possible to grasp how the position of children in international relations changes from one in which children were legally indistinguishable from adults to one in which the child is articulated as a separate, distinct, protected being—or "becoming."

THE GOVERNED WORLD-CHILD

In 1946, in support of the United Nations Relief and Rehabilitation Administration, the UN, together with the United States War Department, produced a short black-and-white documentary called *Seeds of Destiny* about the situation faced by displaced and refugee children in the wake of the Second World War.[10] The very first frame is a citation from the Gospel of Matthew: "A good tree cannot bring forth evil fruit, neither can a corrupt tree bring forth good fruit" (7:18). The movie goes on to feature images of children with missing limbs, dressed in rags, stealing, begging, and smoking. Then it proclaims that it is critical that postwar children avoid the "ruin, doubt, defeatism, and despair that will breed more Fascism, Hitlers, Tojos, and Mussolinis"; instead, "we" must invest in the development of "Einsteins, Toscaninis, Manuel Quezons, Madame Curies, and Sun Yet Sens."[11]

In the movie, there is a clear concern about a future that may be at risk, when children—or seeds—growing in bad (abnormal) conditions face a perilous destiny. In other words, a corrupt tree brings forth bad fruit. This feeling of apprehension resonates within the ambivalent meaning of the child, which was analyzed in the previous chapter. If, on the one hand, the child is (re)produced as the epitome of goodness and the symbol of the promise of a progressive future, on the other, it also stands for that which is still undeveloped and may become a potential source of disruption. In this sense, it is important to ask the same question as Burman asks in relation to ChildAid cards with their message about hope for the future: "whose future is being addressed since, for most children in need, the real danger is that there will be no tomorrow."[12] Burman argues that it seems as if it is our hopes as modern adults, not those of children in need, that are at stake. I would add that it is the imagined (and promised) future of the world-child that is the focus of international attention and aid practices. Children's common—or normal—experiences and demands are silenced, or articulated as deviation, through the protection and development practices that advocate a normalized child, a world-child, who must follow the "right" steps in order to become a "good," "educated," "productive" (adult) citizen.

In this sense, following Jacqueline Bhabha's questioning,[13] it is fundamental to ask: What sort of human is the world-child? The limits of this category are carefully (re)produced through discourses that denote a single, progressive, direct line of reasoning oriented toward a stable end point. Through these discourses, both the object of knowledge (the child) and the subjects of knowledge (international, aid, and diplomatic organizations, to mention a few) are constituted on behalf of the *world*. By (re)producing certain standards for childhood, the children's rights milestones simultaneously articulate and authorize such international subjects to define childhood and the child. This definition entails attributing distinctive rights and duties to both children and adults, determining the objects and agents of protection, setting the scope and time limits for protection and development programs, identifying violations of such protections, and establishing punishments in cases of violation.

Based on the analysis of the children's rights milestones together with the above-mentioned publications and interviews, I identify and work with three overlapping and interrelated discourses that articulate the borders of the bounded category of the world-child. The first of these includes statements about what could be called a "natural child," in which "objective" conceptions of children's social and biological needs are established and promoted. Associated to the very idea of children's universal needs, the second discourse (re)produces the world-child as being inherently innocent and vulnerable and, as such, the object of *international protection*. The third discourse articulates childhood as deserving of investment in the future by expressing concerns about children's *development* toward becoming productive members—or citizens—of society. At the end of the day, these discourses express and reproduce conceptual links between three elements—international order, development/protection, and the natural child—and thereby articulate and authorize the world-child as the norm.

Long before the first Universal Declaration of Human Rights in 1948, the special international status of children as distinct bearers of such rights was formally articulated in 1924, when the League of Nations adopted the World Child Welfare Charter, written by an early progressive child advocate, Eglantyne Jebb, as the Geneva Declaration of the Rights of the Child, commonly known as the "Declaration of Geneva." At that time, most philanthropists insisted that childhood was *neutral*—free of religious conflict—making it possible for all to come together.[14] In five short sentences, the document called for the national and international provision of children's needs, heralding a series of international documents that contributed to the vision of the twentieth century as the "century of the child."[15] The main idea was to map out a territory called "childhood," understood as a garden of delight, within which children would be cared for and would acquire the habit of happiness.[16]

The provisions of the Declaration of Geneva were premised on the understanding that "mankind owes to the Child the best that it has to give." Specifically, the second provision says: "The child that is hungry must be fed; the child that is sick must be nursed; the child that is backward must be helped; the delinquent child must be reclaimed; and the orphan and the waif must be sheltered and succored."[17] Biological needs, such as those associated with hunger and illness, psychological issues, such as those related to being "backward" in relation to some kind of normality, and moral aspects, such as treating the "delinquent," are conflated together and must all be addressed by "men and women of all nations." In John Wall's words, this overall provision-based approach pointed toward chiefly developmental grounds: "Society owes children the necessary means for growing up to become healthy and productive members of the world."[18]

From this second provision, it is possible to identify the three dichotomies that Harry Hendrick sees as informing child-related policymaking in the twentieth century: an emphasis on either the bodies or the minds of children; the child as victim or threat; and the child as normal or abnormal.[19] Or, in other words, these oppositions articulate the aspects that have given rise to the natural child as a different sort of human, who is assumed to be innocent, vulnerable, immature, and still lacking reason, and whose needs can be universalized and understood as natural facts rather than socially and culturally constructed. Furthermore, within this approach, the model of the natural child as the norm not only contains a judgment about which children's needs are desirable but also prescribes the goal to be achieved, against which the idea of "backwardness" and "delinquency" can be judged or determined. Thus, all children are entitled to a childhood that provides *protection* in the form of health, nutrition, and a family setting, and *preparation* in the form of education and child development practices so that abnormalities can be monitored and their potential for becoming a threat can be kept under fierce control.

Accordingly, even though the title of the treaty suggests that the child is conceived as having individual rights, its language evokes certain impositions on adults in their behavior toward children. In this vein, the Declaration of Geneva can be better thought of as a "symbolic enterprise," whose merit lay in introducing the term "rights of the child" into the international arena.[20] If we just focus on the use of the term "child" and look at the titles of the three twentieth-century international children's rights agreements—the Geneva Declaration of the Rights of the Child (1924), the Declaration of the Rights of the Child (1959), and the Convention on the Rights of the Child (1989)—it is worth questioning which rights holder is covered by these treaties: "children," understood as a diverse group of people who inhabit the social institution of childhood, the "child" as an individual, as in James's argument,[21] or the world-child norm? Specifically, in the UNCRC, Anna Holzscheiter reports that most drafters pleaded in favor of "the child" in order to place the child as an individual instead of submerging him or her in the vast totality of children.[22] However, the other declarations and resolutions that are not focused particularly on children's rights, but on state leaders' responsibilities toward them, use the term "children" in their titles. This difference can be seen as an international articulation of "children" as innocent, vulnerable, dependent becomings, with an associated emphasis on victimization, instead of "the child" in the singular form as a political subject.

However, in my analysis of these three international treaties devoted exclusively to the rights of the child, what emerges is not the "child" as a subject of rights but an abstract being, a generalized form, an optimal model: the world-child, who, as established in the preamble to the UNCRC, should grow up "in a family environment, in an atmosphere of happiness, love and understanding" for his or her "full and harmonious development."[23] Principle 6 of the Declaration of the Rights of the Child adds that he or she "shall, wherever possible, grow up in the care and under the responsibility of his parents, and, in any case, in an atmosphere of affection and of moral and material security."[24] And the UNCRC's preamble goes a little further by saying that this atmosphere for maturing is fundamental so the child can be "fully prepared to live an individual life in society."[25] In this regard, the possibility of living an individual life comes with the process of developing and being prepared to be a social and political subject, which culminates in the temporal transition to adulthood when the child turns eighteen, a universal age criterion established by the UNCRC in 1989.

As the convention affirms: "a child means every human being below the age of eighteen years unless under law applicable to the child, majority is attained earlier."[26] According to a program officer of the UN Office of the Special Representative of the Secretary-General for Children and Armed Conflict (hereinafter the UN Office of the SRSG for CAAC), the UNCRC, despite its internal ambiguities, articulates a specific identity for children: "it created a *standard*, which is important. It created a norm that says that ideally a child is a person that is under eighteen."[27] Furthermore, as Afua Twum-Danso Imoh argues, this treaty was an attempt to promote a particular experience of childhood for children globally and to set a universal approach for protecting all children around the world.[28] The UNCRC is the most ratified international legal agreement ever: the only country to have signed it but not ratified it is the United States.

This gold standard for children is not only based on the age criterion but more fundamentally on the idea of there being objective, universal needs for people from birth to age eighteen. Through this particular grammar that articulates and (re)produces the notion of the natural child, the complexities of childhood (like those of adulthood) are left to one side, so that "children's needs and wishes [. . .] are not difficult to understand."[29] Both international treaties devoted exclusively to the child—the Declaration of the Rights of the Child and the UNCRC—justify Annan's words in their preambles when they state that "the child, *by reason of his physical and mental immaturity*, needs special safeguards and care, including appropriate legal protection, before as well as after birth" (emphasis added). In this sense, a child needs to be protected on account of his or her status as a natural child. The use of the expression "by reason of" acknowledges and affirms the difference of this group of people, whose special right to be cared for and protected against harm is granted insofar (and possibly only insofar) as he or she is naturally a child.[30] Following on from this idea, Principle 4 of the Declaration of the Rights of the Child (1959) emphasizes: "The child shall have the right to adequate nutrition, housing, recreation and medical services."[31] Interdiscursive links between the idea of the naturally innocent, vulnerable child who should be entitled to a happy and fun-filled childhood and the need to formulate a set of norms to assure children's special requirements (re)produce universalized, but not necessarily universal, understandings of childhood and the child. If granted these special rights, the child "may have a happy childhood."[32] A whole catalog of international norms for children offers protection for the future of both the child and the world against any possible subversive or destructive traits.

In its second paragraph, the Plan of Action for Implementing the World Declaration acknowledges the diversity of children's demands around the world, stating that the "needs and problems of children vary from country to country, and indeed from community to community."[33] Nevertheless, it concludes that "parents, elders and leaders at all levels throughout the world have certain *common aspirations* for the well-being of their children."[34] These common aspirations articulate and are authorized by the particular conception of the child established in the second paragraph of the 1990 World Declaration, which reads: "The children of the world are *innocent, vulnerable and dependent.* They are also curious, active and full of hope. Their time should be one of joy and peace, of *playing, learning and growing.* Their future should be shaped in harmony and co-operation. *Their lives should mature,* as they broaden their perspectives and gain new experiences."[35]

The semantic field of innocence, with its emphasis on the child's vulnerability, immaturity, dependence, and playfulness, is also matched by the gerund constructions of the verbs "playing," "learning," and "growing," which mark a temporality predicated on an "in process" notion, the temporality of the natural child and of childhood as a transitory phase to adulthood. Eleven years after the adoption of the World Declaration by the state leaders at the United Nations, the world fit *for* children—but not necessarily constructed *by* children—is still prescribed as one that emphasizes and (re)produces the very same idea of the child-norm, or the world-child. In this particular version of the world, "all girls and boys can enjoy childhood—a time of play and learning, in which they are loved, respected and cherished, their rights are promoted and protected, without discrimination of any kind, in which their safety and well-being are paramount and in which they can develop in health, peace and dignity."[36]

Every document analyzed here articulates in some way or other some supposedly universal conditions and guiding principles for shaping a healthy and happy childhood based on a specific idea of who children are. Most of these conditions are associated with biological or physical needs within a decontextualized discourse. The social, economic, historical, and cultural settings in which children grow up, which can be very diverse, are left unexplored.[37] This is clear from the language of the declaration reporting on progress made five years after the adoption of A World Fit for Children: "Fewer children under five are dying each year. More children are in school than ever before. More educational opportunities are being equally extended to girls and boys. More medicines are available for children, including those infected by HIV/AIDS. More laws, policies and plans are in place to protect children from violence, abuse and exploitation. Our present and future actions should build upon those important gains."[38]

In this vein, one of the most groundbreaking innovations of the Declaration of the Rights of the Child, the principle of the "best interests of the child," can be read as the principle that makes the child an object of intervention on the part of states and the International.[39] As Pupavac argues, "'the best interests of the child,' rather than the child's views, [. . .] are 'to be of primary consideration.'"[40] This principle is mentioned twice in the 1959 Declaration; it is subsequently reproduced in Article 3 of the UNCRC, in the 2002 resolution A World Fit for Children, in which it is mentioned eight times, and in its follow-up declaration (paragraph 3), from 2007.

An exploration of these international practices points toward the full range of ideas connected to the modern conception of the child, the natural child, which operates as the norm, and which in turn justifies the rights of the child and (re)produces them as strong demands. That is, based on the conception of children as a different sort of humans, as dependent, immature, irrational human *becomings*, children of the world naturally need to be cared for, protected, and developed. The "children's needs" formulation is a very powerful one in the sense that it articulates a specific conception of the child as passive, to be serviced, protected, and provided for, rather than to be engaged with as an active participant.[41] In other words, the discourse that (re)produces the natural child is simultaneously associated with and authorizes the discourse of the child as an object of international protection. In order to investigate this second discourse in particular, the focus of attention now turns to the complex relationship between children's right to participate and their right to be protected. Specifically, through the children's rights milestones, I analyze in the next section how the idea of the natural child, rights to protection/participation, and mechanisms of ordering the modern International are intertwined in the making of a "politics of protection" within the context of the (re)production of the world-child.[42]

PROTECTING THE WORLD-CHILD:
NATURALLY INNOCENT, NATURALLY SPECIAL

Since the early twentieth century, anxieties concerning the (re)production of the universalized child have occasioned a panoply of practices aimed at codifying and regulating children's right to special protection. In this maze of treaties and reports, the world-child—as an idea and a target—has become inextricably connected to the aspirations of international subjects, such as the UN and, more specifically, UNICEF. In the period following World War II, international practices—in particular, UNICEF advocacy—concentrated on the physical well-being and protection of children as encapsulated by the Declaration of the Rights of the Child, which complements the rights established in the Declaration of Geneva with an emphasis on the explicit right to protection in order to guard children against violence and harm.[43] Within the context of establishing and guaranteeing children's rights "against every form of exploitation," *physical* protection is at the core of UN practices devoted to children in normative documents and programs, such as the ones undertaken by UNICEF in the fields of health and nutrition, which remain the cornerstone of the organization's work today. For example, paragraph five of the plan of action for implementing the World Declaration by the year 2000 stated the major goals for the survival, protection, and development of children included reducing severe and moderate malnutrition among under-fives to half of 1990 levels and assuring universal access to safe drinking water and sanitary means of excreta disposal.[44]

Meanwhile, in its second principle, the 1959 Declaration of the Rights of the Child states that "the child shall enjoy special protection, and shall be given opportunities and facilities, by law and by other means, to enable him to develop physically, mentally, morally, spiritually and socially in a healthy and normal manner and in conditions of freedom and dignity."[45] Later, in Principle 9, it affirms that "the child shall be protected against all forms of neglect, cruelty and exploitation."[46] In a similar vein, Article 3 of ILO Convention No. 138 (1973) establishes eighteen years as the minimum age for admission to any type of employment or work that could jeopardize the health, safety, or morals of young persons.[47] This same message of the unique value of children, putting emphasis on their protection and rejecting the notion of their engaging in paid employment, is reiterated in the ILO's Worst Forms of Child Labour Convention, which requires immediate and comprehensive action for the effective elimination of the worst forms of child labor.[48] In 1979, the UN General Assembly introduced—and justified—the International Year of the Child by stating it was "*deeply concerned* that, in spite of all efforts, far too many children, especially in developing countries, are undernourished, are without access to adequate health services, are missing the basic educational preparation for their future and are deprived of the elementary amenities of life."[49] Finally, Article 19 of the UNCRC, which serves as guidance for UNICEF child protection practices, reads: "States Parties shall take all appropriate legislative, administrative, social and educational measures to protect the child from all forms of physical or mental violence, injury or abuse, neglect or negligent treatment, maltreatment or exploitation, including sexual abuse, while in the care of parent(s), legal guardian(s) or any other person who has the care of the child."[50]

In these fragments, I highlight the frequent use of the term "special" to qualify child protection and the focus on children's physical well-being in child protection practices. The drive behind the establishment of children's rights is therefore framed in terms of children's special status as a vulnerable population group who are in need of advocacy on their behalf.[51] Furthermore, the idea of the natural child, (re)produced by the focus on children's physical well-being within child protection practices, associated with a discourse that articulates the world-child as an object of international protection, frames a hierarchical relationship between the child—naturally special and naturally innocent and in need of protection and services—and adults, as the dominant providers, as if it were the only possibility. As Annan affirms in *We the Children*, "'we as *adults*' have an irrefutable duty to *create* a world fit for children, that is the kind of world that children deserve."[52] This raises a crucial question: Who is this "we" that has the capacity to speak authoritatively about solutions for the entire mass of children?

In this sense, in the current context of children's rights, only adults, with their duties of childrearing, may be articulated as the potential problem, never the child itself. Within this context, practices designed to preserve and mold children have gained centrality in the international political agenda, and while the lives of their families and communities have been exempted from detailed prescriptions of conduct, they remain exposed to moralizing and normalizing interventions from outside.[53] As Pupavac argues, "international organizations assume that external actors are required to intervene to define social norms and ensure their institutionalization," thereby protecting the world and the child.[54]

The world-child's protected (and regulated) life has its spaces circumscribed to an institutionalized triangle, whose vertices are home, school, and recreational centers.[55] Public spaces, for example, are usually (re)produced as *risky* places for children because they present some kind of danger or threat to the child at the present time or to the adult the child will become. In the documentary *Seeds of Destiny*, which draws attention to children whose childhood has been disrupted in virtue of their experiences of war and the consequences of the Second World War, none of the children are portrayed living in homes or with families; instead, they appear in public spaces or in institutional care. Moreover, as Tarah Brookfield highlights, the film contrasts these experiences with images of "normal" places, such as quiet middle-class suburban homes and schoolyards in America.[56] Following the same idea, the UNICEF report *The Progress of Nations* affirms that the places of "lost children" have already been cataloged: "They are in the tents and barracks of Africa. In the brothels of Asia, the slums of Europe and North America, the sweatshops of Latin America."[57] In contrast to these (public) places, the private, domestic, family sphere is reaffirmed and reinstituted as the correct and safe place for children. However, when being at home is not an option, when the "tents and barracks" of camps for the displaced in Afghanistan, Chad, and Liberia are the only possibility, the UN establishes that the world must provide "safe places for children," where they can "play or learn" in safety.[58] These areas are sometimes labeled "child-friendly spaces" or "safe play areas."[59] Both UN documents—one stating places that are not for children and the other aiming to create places for children in settings not designed for them—take us back to the importance of a "special" space for growing children, with the family playing a central role.[60]

As first established in the Universal Declaration of Human Rights, the family unit is a fundamental group of society and the *natural environment* for the growth and well-being of all its members, especially children.[61] In Article 25.2, the mother is highlighted as a figure who, together with children, is entitled to special care and assistance. Within this approach, the Declaration of the Rights of the Child states: "he [the child] shall, wherever possible, grow up in the care and under the responsibility of his parents, and, in any case, in an atmosphere of affection and of moral and material security."[62] The preamble of the UNCRC reproduces the idea of the family environment as a safe and loving place—fundamental aspects for the development of a still dependent, vulnerable, and innocent being.

The World Declaration also calls attention to the high number of mothers who die each year from causes related to childbirth, stating, in the fourteenth goal, that "safe motherhood must be promoted in all possible ways. Emphasis must be placed on responsible planning of family size and on child spacing. The family, as a fundamental group and natural environment for the growth and well-being of children, should be given all necessary protection and assistance."[63] Its plan of action, then, associates "the full and harmonious development of their [the children's] personality" to maturing "in a family environment, in an atmosphere of happiness, love and understanding."[64] Mirroring this same message, the resolution A World Fit for Children affirms that "the primary responsibility for the protection, upbringing and development of children rests with the family," for which reason the family should be strengthened and entitled to receive comprehensive protection and support.[65]

This particular understanding of the family as a happy, loving environment where the world-child should grow and develop articulates not only the conception of a particular child but an entire social system that makes this child possible. When these international practices refer to the relevance of the family environment for the world-child's normal development, they are not simply articulating the child as a particular being (or becoming); they are also implying that they should have certain kinds of family relations and structures. In other words, these discourses that articulate the world-child also presume a world-family structure, a patriarchal nuclear family, as the prevailing reference point for child-rearing and development. The mother, it is assumed, will have primary responsibility for guaranteeing that her children develop appropriately, while the state must perform a policing role, intervening whenever the family does not act appropriately. Should the state fail, then the international community must step in as both provider and protector so the child does not lose its childhood and the world does not miss out on its chance for a progressive future.

To use Didier Bigo's classification, the world-child's protection, identified through the children's rights milestones, may be associated with the idea of *tutore*, which means "to look after." In Bigo's words, protection as *tutore* is "*to help in the present and for the future. It reinforces the monitoring and the surveillance of the protected but in the name of love. It is a caring voice which substitutes the will of the protected for the will of the protector.*"[66] Here, we could substitute "in the name of love" for "in the best interests of the child," calling attention to the world-child as an object of external intervention. In this case, protection as *tutore* is thus associated with caregiving, monitoring, and disciplining children in accordance with the model of the world-child. In this setting, the protector (the subject of knowledge)—which could be an international organization, an aid agency, or diplomatic corps—is articulated as having the capacity to know children's needs better than children themselves or their communities.

From this understanding, the discourse that articulates a child as an object of protection enacts a relationship of dependency between the protected and the protector, in which the political agency of the protected child is annulled or "extracted."[67] However, Michael Freeman, one of the most eloquent children's rights authors, argues that this conception of the child as a protected being whose political agency is silenced was formally challenged for the first time by the UNCRC in 1989, when it added an entirely new category of children's rights: their rights to *participation*.[68] Although the word "participation" is not actually mentioned in the convention, there are six rights in the UNCRC that address this topic: the right to be heard (Article 12); the right to freedom of expression (Article 13); the right to freedom of thought, conscience, and religion (Article 14); the right to freedom of association and assembly (Article 15); the right to privacy (Article 16); and the right to access to appropriate information and mass media (Article 17).[69] Along with the adoption of the UNCRC, another important event defined UNICEF's activities in the 1990s: the World Summit for Children, held in 1990, where 159 countries undertook to follow a plan of action to ensure "children's survival, protection and development" and to grant children a participatory role, indicating a global commitment to the child entitled to full rights as an individual.[70] In the words of the World Declaration, adopted at the summit, "among the partnerships we seek, we turn especially to children themselves. We appeal to them to participate in this effort."[71]

In 2009, the UN Committee on the Rights of the Child referred to participation directly in its General Comment on Article 12: "This term has evolved and is now widely used to describe ongoing processes, which include information-sharing and dialogue between children and adults based on mutual respect, and in which children can learn how their views and those of adults are taken into account and shape the outcome of such processes."[72] E. Kay Tisdall concludes that this definition of participation "emphasises relationships and respect, with reciprocal information-sharing and dialogue. Children and young people should receive feedback, to learn how their views have been considered, and the definition presumes that children and young people's views should be taken into account and shape outcomes."[73] The convention is the result of child policies and debates in the international political arena that have, since the second half of the twentieth century, as Freeman argues, departed from a language of "salvation" and shifted from protecting children to protecting their rights.[74]

Taking these shifts into consideration, Bhabha argues that the main achievement of the UNCRC in relation to previous children's rights agreements is that it establishes a framework for thinking about children as rights-bearing subjects and agents, as well as objects of adults' protective attention.[75] Article 12.1 of the UNCRC is probably the best example of the coexistence of the vulnerable and the competent child in international human rights law: "1. States Parties shall assure to the child who is capable of forming his or her own views the right to express those views freely in all matters affecting the child, the views of the child being given *due* weight *in accordance with the age and maturity of the child.*"[76] A decade later, the resolution A World Fit for Children (re)produced this message: "Listen to children and ensure their participation. Children and adolescents are resourceful citizens capable of helping to build a better future for all. We must respect their right to express themselves and to participate in all matters affecting them, *in accordance with their age and maturity.*"[77] The addition of the term "adolescents" and the idea of their being "resourceful citizens" are worth noting. The 2007 declaration on the five-year follow-up to A World Fit for Children reinforces the importance of children's participation: "As we welcome the voices and the views of children, including adolescents, heard at the commemorative plenary meeting, we strive to strengthen their participation in the decisions that affect them, *in accordance with their age and maturity.*"[78]

At the same time that the above-mentioned documents open room for children's participation, they still emphasize that it should vary according to their age and maturity, which takes us back to the modern conception of childhood that establishes children's development as a progressive gradation through stages, marked by years, to ever greater competence and maturity. Based on scientific criteria, cognitive development, emotional development, and physiological development are all understood to proceed along this general progression articulated in rather binary terms, such as child versus (or "heading toward") adult or object versus (or "heading toward") subject. The rather ambiguous conception of children's right to participation set forth in the UNCRC is clearly articulated by Lothar Krappmann, a member of the UN Committee on the Rights of the Child, when he emphasizes that although many children cannot make decisions for themselves, they have to be heard. Then, articulating the parallel between children's development and their stage of maturity, he argues that "their evolving capacities have to be considered to the extent that in some areas children's own responsibilities are guaranteed."[79]

Specifically, Article 12.1 clearly articulates the ambiguity of children's right to participate by attaching two conditions to it, as David Archard notes. First, this right is assured only to a child "who is capable of forming his or her own views."[80] Because children are constantly referenced to their future potential and possibilities, not all children can exercise this right; their present actions are downplayed, and their capacity is that of an irrational and vulnerable child, which is one of the central ingredients for distinguishing the child from adults. In this sense, it is worth questioning who, under Article 12, is authorized to determine whether a child is mature or capable enough for their view to be heard and heeded.[81]

Chin argues that of all the criteria used to evaluate children's capacities and process of "evolution," their chronological age is the most arbitrary: "chronological age is naturalized rather than natural—and is also the only measure that does not assess capabilities."[82] Therefore, age can be used to reflect a child's development, but its role as a fundamental criterion to evaluate children's capability to participate is, at best, indirect. However, the second condition identified by Archard is that the *weight* of children's views should be proportionate to their age and maturity.[83] The use of the term "due weight" is crucial: it is simply assumed that the older a child is, the more developed, mature, and capable he or she will be to participate in social life. In such an approach, Archard tells us, age "may be taken as a reliable index of maturity."[84]

While the world-child starts out being essentially excluded (or included by exclusion) from the very architecture of modern human rights because children are presumed not to be capable of using their free will and reason to legislate over their desires, on the other hand, they are assumed to follow a particular journey of "stages and scripts." By following the required developmental steps, the child gradually accumulates special "participation" rights until they turn eighteen and reach their transition to adulthood, the phase of life presumably marked by autonomy and full citizenship. This can be seen in the schema created by UNICEF, which is depicted in the form of a child figure nestled within concentric circles of relationships, which represent spaces for children's participation that extend from family to society.[85] Above the figure, the UNICEF report explains: "As children grow and develop, their opportunities for participation expand from private to public spaces, from local to global influence."[86]

Based on this, the domains of children's participation are clearly associated with (and premised on) both the spatial depiction of relationships—what the "natural" places for children are—and the developmental stages a child should follow in order to become a fully competent adult.[87]

However, as Jason Hart argues, events such as armed conflict and mass displacement, the HIV/AIDS pandemic, environmental degradation, and rural-urban migration have all challenged this bounded "site" for children's participation by creating responsibilities for children that inevitably involve them in a range of settings that extend far beyond the home, school, and immediate neighborhood.[88] Or, on the contrary, such as in the situations Kristen E. Cheney analyzes in Uganda, the trope of the "ideal child"—or, in this case, the world-child—may embody contradictions that prevent children from becoming fully functional in local praxis.[89] This fact, Cheney argues, "challenges the common motto, 'Develop the child; develop the nation.'"[90]

Ultimately, the convention is just one more example of how the idea of the natural child, with its emphasis on children's needs in terms of care and control, compromises the potential to view children as participants and political agents.[91] Focusing specifically on child protection, Tisdall argues that "the focus moves to adult definitions and adult actions, prevention and protection, rather than children and young people's participation in identifying their own concerns and solutions."[92] Despite the criticism voiced by children's rights movements against the "tutelage status" of child protection practices, such narratives also reproduce the hierarchical relationship of dependencies—not *interdependencies*—between children as objects of protection and adults as the dominant providers.[93] When it comes to children's agency, the conversation should not only be about the possibility of attributing agency to children but also about examining what agency means, and what children as autonomous agents do. As David Oswell argues, rather than a property of an entity, agency is always relational: "[it] is always in-between and interstitial," where "the capacity to do and to make a difference is necessarily dispersed across an arrangement."[94] Furthermore, by considering the different spaces of children's experience and experimentation, we can investigate how children's agency impacts on modern understandings of adulthood and citizenship and, consequently, on the modern articulation and promotion of a particular version of the social and international order today and tomorrow.

From this analysis, one fundamental question must be raised: How can these tensions between child protection and child participation be negotiated successfully to the benefit of children and young people, their families, and societies at large?[95] More specifically, the challenge is, as Bhabha puts it, to figure out how to honor children's rights of agency and participation without abandoning international obligations to their protection.[96] The "phenomenon" of child-soldiers is a good case for analysis, since it enables the spaces for children's autonomy and agency to be investigated in a situation where their protection is considered to be most needed. Twum-Danso Imoh is of the view that no matter how hard children's experiences may be to swallow, there is a need to problematize such black versus white, good versus bad dichotomies.[97] By so doing, spaces may be opened up for children who live their lives in shades of gray and who are not necessarily interested in being held up as sacred or assumed to be innocent.[98]

The challenge, however, is that the limits of children's participation start with the ambivalent approach to the child. That is, the international obligation to protect children is authorized by this particular articulation of the natural child as an inherently irrational, innocent adult or human in the making. Protection mechanisms are designed to assure a process of development informed by both the universalized idea of childhood and a very clear telos to children's development. It is as if correcting—or preventing—potential deviations in the transformation of the world-child into the world-citizen will prevent ruptures that might jeopardize the promise of a progressive future ahead of "us." If, for some children, the end of this childhood trajectory will be a transition to adulthood and the chance to engage in society as full citizens, for many children with a troubled past, such as child-soldiers, protection practices produce multiple boundaries that punish, exclude, shape, enable, and delimit their political possibilities.[99]

To draw on Bigo's discussion, we could argue that protecting the world-child may be linked to the idea of "a route to not being harmed."[100] It still involves help, the duty to provide assistance, aid, support, and care. However, it may also be associated with management, monitoring, surveillance, and the (re)production of a specific profile of a world-child destined to develop and become a "normal" adult capable of making voluntary choices in full cognizance of dangers and protecting themselves against their violent impulses. Of global appeal, the special status of the world-child, holding out the promise of a progressive future, puts him or her in the unique position of being singularly vulnerable and still undeveloped and thus the target of special attention.[101] Accordingly, it is not just the protection of the child that is at issue but, more importantly, whether he or she will come to constitute the kind of adult who is capable of building a better world.

In this sense, the protector as a tutor, acting on the behalf of humanity, organizes the life of the world-child and directs him or her toward freedom (that is, the transition from childhood to adulthood). Protecting, or monitoring, Bigo tells us, is not only about delimiting spaces where the protected must be placed, but about time.[102] These child protection practices are, thus, about monitoring children's experiences in the present while preparing them for their future and, by doing so, investing in the world's progress. This particular way of articulating protection as *tutore* is even clearer in the discourse about the natural child as being universally neutral, expressed in international politics as a "zone of peace" and a site of investment in the future. The remarks by UN Secretary-General

António Guterres at a special event to mark 2017 World Children's Day build on this idea of the world-child: "Whenever I meet children—including and especially those living in the poorest, most desperate situations, suffering terrible hardships—they never fail to inspire me with their *smiles*, their *laughter*, their vision and their hope. *In a world that can so often seem to be a hopeless place, we need children's hope, more than ever.*"[103] If children are (re)produced as a zone of peace, their treatment, Holzscheiter argues, serves as an indicator of "civilization."[104] This message is clearly posed by Kofi Annan in the report *We the Children*: "A society whose children are malnourished, abused, undereducated or exploited cannot truly claim to be progressing or to be developed, however impressive its economic growth or per-capita income levels might be."[105]

These preoccupations with children's development toward becoming useful members of society permeate all the international practices under analysis here, articulating the third discourse that (re)produces the borders of the bounded category of the world-child. The discourse on childhood as a site for investment in the future is explored in the last section by focusing essentially on two issues: (1) how the notion of childhood as a transitional stage is articulated through and by the (re)production of the idea of school education as a fundamental element of the world-child's preparation for the future; and (2) the articulation of the promise of a progressive future for international relations predicated on notions of order and stability which are maintained and (re)produced by world-citizens—that is, the future profile of the world-child.

THE "STAGES AND SCRIPTS" OF THE WORLD-CHILD: PREPARING FOR A BETTER FUTURE

In 2002, the United Nations outlined its vision of a world fit for children, in which its notion of the "child fit for the world" was (re)produced through the themes of protection and development (or preparation):

> A world fit for children is one in which all children get the best possible start in life and have access to a quality basic education, including primary education that is compulsory and available free to all, and in which all children, including adolescents, have ample opportunity to develop their individual capacities in a safe and supportive environment. We will promote the physical, psychological, spiritual, social, emotional, cognitive and cultural development of children as a matter of national and global priority.[106]

This joint commitment reflected the same goal already established a decade earlier at the World Summit for Children, where state parties undertook to give every child a better future. What first calls attention here is how the focus of international practices is devoted to children's future—instead of investing equally in a better present—despite the fact that for some children, the major concern is that there will be no tomorrow. This raises an important question: Whose future is at stake when there is an urgent appeal to pursue the "best interests of the child"? Moreover, by investing in progress for children, no room is left for reflecting on the future or the present as encapsulating social relations that can always be (re)produced not only *for*, but also *by* children.

If we analyze the children's rights milestones through this suggested question, it is interesting to note how the health, welfare, and "normal" development of the child has been linked in thought and practice to the fate and responsibilities of the nation-state and the world. This idea is clearly (re)produced in the International Year of the Child resolution: "Recognizing the fundamental importance in all countries, developing and industrialized, of programmes benefiting children *not only for the well-being of the children but also as part of broader efforts to accelerate economic and social progress*."[107] In the same vein, the World Declaration affirms that giving high priority to children's survival, protection, and development will ensure the *well-being* of all societies.[108] The message is even more explicit in its plan of action, which relates children's development to the progress of humanity: "Progress for children should be a key goal of overall national development. It should also form an integral part of the broader international development strategy for the Fourth United Nations Development Decade. As today's children are the *citizens of tomorrow's world*, their survival, protection and development is the *prerequisite* for the *future development of humanity*."[109] That is, (re)produced as a site for investment in building a brighter international future, the world-child—or, the "citizen of tomorrow's world"—must be protected and developed appropriately. Investing in children's health, nutrition, and education is, the plan of action tells us, the "foundation for national development"[110] and, I would add, for keeping alive the modern promise of a progressive future for international relations.

Within this formulation, children are not just an abstract symbol used to promote peace and a progressive future or, as ChildAid cards say, "hope for the future"; the bodies and minds of both "endangered" and "healthy" children are the targets for the investment, authorization, and (re)production of the promise of a better future. Hence, progress for the world-child and the progress of the International coincide or, rather, are co-reproduced. That is, two important discursive movements happen simultaneously: (1) the articulation of the world-child as an immature, irrational, vulnerable becoming whose time is predicated on the notion of a particular desirable developmental journey toward adulthood; and (2) the establishment of the idea that international development promotes the reconciliation of a linear *progress* (seen as an inevitability) with *order* and *security*, which are maintained and (re)produced by world-citizens.

Effectively, when the child is developed, the promise of a progressive future for the international order is protected. Or, by disciplining the child, risks of international instability and insecurity may be kept at bay. In UNICEF's words, the "progress of nations" should be judged not by their military or economic strength, but by "the protection that is afforded to the growing minds and bodies of their children."[111] Kofi Annan reiterates the same message in his report: "it is children whose individual development and social contribution shape the world's future—and it is through children that entrenched cycles of poverty, exclusion, intolerance and discrimination can be ended."[112] This parallel drawn between the aspirations of the international regarding the promise of a progressive future, political concerns in relation to children's development, and social anxieties about the need to guarantee order and security is worth investigating further.

In the fragments cited above, the connection between children's development and national and international security and progress may also be read through a familiar political narrative whereby it is not only "morally right" to protect and care for children, especially those in poor circumstances, but not doing so could lead to wars and political instability. This correlation between development and international security resonates in the words of a diplomat who, when she gave the interview, was a member of the UK's Permanent Mission to the United Nations and the Security Council Working Group on Children and Armed Conflict. Talking about the UN's efforts to convince armed groups to demobilize child-soldiers, who were, she said, at a "very delicate developmental stage," she argued: "It's a struggle for UN people, and they have to tell the people leading [the armed groups] that it's not in their own interest to have a gun in children's hands. Because once the conflict is over and hopefully everything is fine in the end they [child-soldiers] will be the people leading the country, then you want them to have something other than knowledge of how to use the guns."[113]

Exploring similar views about the incorporation of war into the development discourse, Mark Duffield argues, "Insofar as development is able, for example, to reduce poverty, improve well-being or generate hope, it is also felt to have a concomitant potential to promote local and international security."[114] Within this context, developing and transforming the still uncivilized child into a known safe other—the modern citizen—is an important mechanism for promoting social stability and safeguarding the promise of a modern progressive future. As Duffield puts it, by fostering the development of "the other"—in this case, guaranteeing a particular process of child growth—we improve "our" security.[115] Or, according to the concluding paragraph of the five-year follow-up to the UN General Assembly Special Session on Children, A World Fit for Children, the best interest of all *humanity* (not necessarily "the best interests of the child") is served by ensuring the well-being of all children in all societies, with a collective sense of "urgency."[116]

The discourse of the world-child that relates child development to international progress makes some spaces normalized as places for children and others inappropriate for children, such as working in a factory or down a mine or taking part in wars, as described by the Worst Forms of Child Labour Convention.[117] If, in terms of child protection, the family sphere is the fundamental unit for providing for children's needs, in regard to their preparation for adulthood, school education is articulated as crucial, since "it will [...] promote his [the child's] general culture and enable him, on a basis of equal opportunity, to develop his abilities, his individual judgment, and his sense of moral and social responsibility, and to become a useful member of society."[118] Twenty years later, the UN General Assembly resolution on the International Year of the Child reaffirmed the international commitment to children's education in exactly the same terms as the 1959 Declaration of the Rights of the Child.[119] It went on to add, "the child shall have full opportunity for play and recreation, which should be directed to the same purposes as education."[120] Article 29 of the UNCRC, for its part, refers specifically to children's right to education, saying that it must be directed to "the development of the child's personality, talents and mental and physical abilities to their fullest potential" (item A) and, in this sense, to the child's preparation for a responsible life in a free society (item D).[121] Finally, the World Declaration stated that the state leaders gathered at the World Summit for Children would together provide educational opportunities for all children in order to "prepare children for productive employment and lifelong learning opportunities, i.e. through vocational training; and that enable children to grow to adulthood within a supportive and nurturing cultural and social context."[122]

From these narratives, it seems that the goal of schooling is to prepare for the future, to develop the children's "fullest potential." As Rose argues, education is at the same time imposed and recognized as a personal right for the child and as a social and collective right, since it implies the "duty of each individual to improve and civilize themselves for the benefit of the social health of the community."[123] Moreover, as long as the process of learning is oriented primarily toward the future, preparing the child by imparting knowledge so they can "become a useful member of society," education can be valued not so much for what it may promote in terms of a child's well-being and empowerment in the present—that is, as a child—but for how it contributes to the formation of future (normal) citizens who have the responsibility to participate in the (re)production of a (stable) modern social order. It is interesting to note how specifically Sustainable Development Goal 16, "Peace, Justice and Strong Institutions," makes reversing the high rate of children leaving primary school in conflict-affected countries a key factor for building a more sustainable future.[124] In addition to that, target 16.2 establishes in particular the need to "end abuse, exploitation, trafficking and all forms of violence against and torture of children" so a more just and stable world may be constructed.

In this regard, the universalized compulsory nature of schooling imposes a disciplinary dynamic where children are placed in classrooms organized by rows and broken into tables or groups for specific activities: "None of this speaks of the child's experience as being the experience of a 'neutral' space."[125] Rather, the school locks the child in a process of production by instructing its conduct, supervising and evaluating its learning process ("Has the child attained the expected or required level of expertise?"), and correcting it by rectifying any childhood pathologies. In the name of promoting a better future for children, the school institution operates as a tool for governing "others" through which not only is the child as a norm—the world-child—(re)produced, but so is the (desired) adult the child will become.

As disciplinary techniques (as conceptualized by Foucault),[126] child protection and child development practices authorized by the discourse of the natural child reveal an evolutionary time frame that articulates progress toward a stable point in the child's transition to adulthood and, simultaneously, a progressive future for international relations. The maturing of the world-child is not just one of seriation (a sequence of moments and tasks) but a continuous and cumulative journey from being a "savage" to becoming a "modern citizen." Children's multiplicity is dissolved into individual docile bodies that can, in Foucault's terms, be kept under surveillance, trained, used, transformed, and improved.[127] Finally, the borders of the bounded category of the world-child, articulated and authorized by the three overlapping and interrelated discourses identified in the children's rights milestones, continuously (re)produce a totalizing, coherent, abstract child as exemplary, as a norm, and as a particular version of the world, which cannot be disconnected from one another and which is only possible though a certain syntax of order, responsibility, and progress. Or, as the former UNICEF Executive Director Henry R. Labouisse said in his acceptance speech when the UN agency was awarded the Nobel Peace Prize in 1965: "each time UNICEF contributes [. . .] to giving today's children a chance to grow into useful and happier citizens, it contributes to removing some of the seeds of world tension and future conflicts."[128]

As already discussed here, what is distinctive about the discourse of the world-child is how the ambivalent meaning of the child is addressed. In this sense, the social and international regulation of children's lives is not just about recognizing their rights but is designed for their governance and control on account of the threat to the stability of the modern social order they pose in the present or will pose in the future. Within this discursive formulation, where the risks associated with the ambivalent meaning of the child are always present, potential deviations in relation to the world-child as the norm are not excluded or extinguished. Actually, notions of normality are extrapolated from the international attention directed toward those children who deviate from the normalized course of development. In this sense, following on Rose's discussion of the governance of the child,[129] the world-child operates in four guises: as that which is natural and healthy; as that against which children are judged and found deviant or pathological; as that which is to be produced by (developmental and protection) programs; and as that which provides the rationale for intervention when "reality" and "normality" fail to coincide. Children and worlds are, thus, made visible or articulated only through the articulation of the model of a single world-child, allowing some of them to be modified, normalized, universalized, and included in the group of "our children," while many others are left out.

Lastly, it is worth questioning what happens when the world-child meets the child-soldier. Will this encounter be engaging or effacing? Equitable or hierarchical? Hospitable or hostile? While in this chapter we focus on the (re)production of the world-child as the norm, in the next chapter we focus on "children-at-risk," a cause of concern for families, courts of law, teachers, doctors, nation-states, and the International. In particular, the next chapter explores the "border areas where real-life children engage with global child-hood"—or, "world-childhood"—through the discourse about the child-soldier, who, far from holding out any promise of a good future, may put national and international progress in jeopardy.[130]

CHAPTER THREE

An International Emergency
The World-Child Meets the Child-Soldier

Child. War. To explore the connections between these two terms is to weaken the hyphens that structure and organize the monolithic ideas of the child-soldier and the world-child. Put another way, the participation of children in armed conflicts—not only as combatants but also as spies, porters, cooks, and sex slaves—is invariably a "problem," since it brings to the forefront the supposed untenable linkage between children's vulnerability and need for protection and the extreme violence of contemporary conflicts. This leads Honwana to ask: "How can an innocent child become a soldier?"[1] It is unthinkable not only because it suggests that children are involved in a particular political crisis but also, and more importantly, because the child-soldier is an oxymoron that articulates a more generalized crisis of humanity. Such a powerful logic can be seen at work in the campaign called "Kony 2012," which was launched by the NGO Invisible Children in 2012. In a thirty-minute documentary, Jason Russell, cofounder and chief creative officer of Invisible Children, urges the "people of the world" to join the NGO's cause and help arrest Joseph Kony, the leader of the armed group in northern Uganda called the Lord's Resistance Army, who is accused of recruiting thousands of children and transforming them into soldiers.[2] By the end of the campaign, Kony had not been arrested (it is not even known if he is still alive), but the idea of a moral obligation to save and protect Ugandan children, which lay at the very heart of the campaign, was immediately shared: just three days after the release of the video, more than seventy million people had viewed all or parts of the video, causing the issue to trend on Twitter and in much of the mainstream media.[3]

The video draws on strict binaries: "happy childhood" versus "unhappy childhood"; "victim" versus "protector"; "good guys" versus "bad guys"; "chaotic Uganda" versus "civilized United States." Russell's little boy, Gavin, appears in the video wearing nice clothes and playing. Indeed, "he loves jumping on the trampoline, being a ninja, and dancing" (Russell tells us, the viewers, in voice-over). From these colorful, playful, loving scenes, the video suddenly shifts to images of an almost black-and-white Uganda: poor, unhappy children dressed in rags and full of fear. A young boy and former child-soldier called Jacob talks about his brother, who was killed by the rebels, whom Jacob saw cutting his brother's neck. Jacob says he would rather die than live on this earth. While Gavin smiles, has a loving family, and lives in a safe house, Jacob cries and cannot go back home because he is afraid of being abducted by the armed group again. So he sleeps in a big, cold, crowded hangar alongside other threatened children.

Next an important and telling dialogue ensues between Gavin and Russell, who tries to explain to his son about the armed conflict in Uganda and his work at Invisible Children. Russell asks Gavin to say what he does for a living, to which Gavin replies, "You stop the bad guys from being mean." Then Russell asks, "Who are the bad guys?" Gavin thinks for a bit and then answers innocently: "Star Wars people." Russell then asks him, "Can I tell you the bad guy's name?" and shows him a picture of Joseph Kony. He then shows Gavin a picture of Jacob, who he immediately recognizes, and Russell says, "Joseph Kony, he has an army and what he does is he takes children from their parents and gives them a gun to shoot and he makes them shoot and kill other people." The dialogue then ends with Gavin asking hopefully, "But they're not going to do what he says because they're nice guys, right?" Fade out. Then we hear Russell in voice-over as we are shown the image of a child being abducted while sleeping, saying: "I couldn't explain to Gavin the details of what Joseph Kony really does, because the truth is Kony abducts kids just like Gavin."

Within this formulation, Gavin is presented as an example of a "normal" child according to the norm of the world-child, who lives in a "world fit for children." Jacob and the other (invisible) children from Uganda are all, irrespective of their particularities and complexities, depicted as deviant children who must be saved by the "good guys" who can "stop the bad guys from being mean." The construed features of this characterization revolve around the idea of childhood as a state of vulnerability and victimhood. This explains why Russell says that Ugandan child-soldiers are kids *just like* Gavin—in the sense that they are all under eighteen and have basically the same needs—but that they need (outside) protection, since their childhood has been lost or stolen. Jacob, for example, does not play, does not go to school, and does not have a loving family.

As the signifier of the child in need—or "at risk"—Jacob articulates three dynamic relationships, which have been pointed out by Burman in her work on child-saving activities.[4] First, it underestimates all those people in need, reproducing the hierarchical discourse that "they can't look after themselves." Second, it frames parents, communities, and the nation-state (in this case, Uganda) as "neglectful or irresponsible in failing to meet the needs of their children," while never articulating the child itself as being responsible or the potential problem. And finally, children's suffering and distress are reproduced in the video without making the slightest reference to the social, geographical, and political conditions that gave rise to the armed conflict in Uganda. The problem is decontextualized, naturalized, and depoliticized, "so that we, as spectators and potential rescuers, avoid implication in producing the situation."[5]

In addition to these three relational dynamics, I would include a fourth one that is clearly articulated by the Invisible Children video: the interrelation between the two imageries of child and childhood—Jacob and Gavin. Without the image of the deviant child, Jacob, the normal child, exemplified by Gavin, would be incomplete, and vice versa. In other words, the discourse that (re)produces child-soldiers as deviant in relation to "normal" children plays an important role in articulating them as being simultaneously *at risk* and *posing a risk* to social stability, and in doing so it is neither natural nor neutral. Rather, it works to authorize its converse—the norm of the world-child with its prescribed "happy, innocent, and safe" childhood—and the desire to restore it. In this regard, this particular discourse about the child-soldier can be read as simultaneously supporting and challenging the constitution of the world-child and its future profile as a modern citizen.

As it considers the prevailing discourse about the child-soldier, whose most iconic figure is a poor, vulnerable African boy who carries a gun bigger than he, this chapter investigates how child-soldiers are invariably framed as an international problem in need of solution. While the need for effective child protection policies is beyond doubt, it is important to critically analyze this question and the categories that are constructed by this particular version of the child-soldier subsumed in a vocabulary of crisis and danger. The very use of the word "phenomenon" is critical insofar as it already articulates the presumed immediacy and unusual state of affairs of a child participating in contemporary armed conflicts.[6] As discussed in chapter 1, regardless of many historical examples of children's participation in war, the child-soldier is assumed to be a *new* international problem, an *exception* to the norm of the world-child, owing primarily to the outbreak of *new* wars in the post–Cold War era. As such, it must be *urgently* addressed. Graça Machel states this very clearly in her report, which indicates the inclusion of the issue of child-soldiers on the international agenda as a matter of concern: "It is unconscionable that we so clearly and consistently see children's rights attacked and that we fail to defend them. It is unforgivable that children are assaulted, violated, murdered and yet our conscience is not revolted nor our sense of dignity challenged. This represents a *fundamental crisis of our civilization*[. . . .] Each one of us, each individual, each institution, each country, must initiate and support global action to protect children."[7]

Following the same narrative as *Kony 2012*, Machel also speaks of child-soldiers as victims who have problems that must be addressed by international action and resources. The crisis, seen in this way, is related to modern civilization's inaction in face of the atrocities committed against children. But who is the "we" associated with "our civilization"? Are child-soldiers included in this bounded "we"? Or, to look at it the other way around, do they themselves constitute a potential threat to "our civilization"? In order to explore the many facets of this "fundamental crisis of our civilization," the next two sections analyze how the understanding of and response to the child-soldier phenomenon are shaped in a very specific way—one that suggests they are an international emergency, abnormal, "exceptions to normal social life and global order: sudden, unpredictable, and carried strong moral imperatives for immediate action."[8]

The focus turns to the discourses that articulate and authorize the limits that (re)produce the child-soldier as an international problem, setting boundaries within which only certain subjects, narratives, and theories are admitted.[9] On the one hand, I analyze what I have termed the "discourse of the law," composed of the international legal standards related to the child-soldier problem, which aims to build an insurmountable barrier between child and soldier, making the military recruitment of children *wrong*. On the other hand, I examine what I call the "discourse of the norm," which is analyzed through three contrasting images of the dangerous, disorderly, hapless victims and, more recently, the redeemed heroes, who have been identified by Denov in the world's media and policy discourses about children caught up in the cycle of war and violence.[10] The discourse of the norm creates a space for—or makes visible—child-soldiers as a pathology, excluding their aspects of disorder, dysfunction, and risk from the accepted boundaries of the world-child. In this case, it is not only that children's participation in wars is wrong, but it is absolutely *abnormal*. Therefore, the child-soldier is constructed through a logic of exception: whatever qualities apply to a "normal," ordered childhood are absent in the lives of child-soldiers. For these children in particular, the borders of the triangle that circumscribes the world-child's happy life—family home, school, and recreational centers—have been completely blurred.

While the efforts of civil society and international and national authorities to stop the use of child-soldiers have managed to build and sustain awareness of the issue, they have, at the same time, come to articulate the child-soldier as a "limit-concept" that occupies an ambiguous position at the dividing line between the child and the adult.[11] In doing so, it expresses the limits of a certain logic of intelligibility—in this case, the ordering of social and international life. When (universalized) protection and development practices are violated, all that remains is the natural child as the vulnerable, irrational, immature becoming in need of others' (adults') help and guidance. However, when the natural child has a weapon in his or her hands, a vacuum of modern categories, ideas, and values emerges, and all that remains is no longer a child but a "beast of no nation," whose childhood has been lost together with any semblance of the civilized world-child's world.[12] Neither the world nor the child is recognized in the figure of the child-soldier. As such, the child-soldier is an emergency that evokes fear, uncertainty, revulsion, horror, and sorrow. By itself, the child-soldier phenomenon connects the *urgency* of the crisis triggered by the threat—or danger—posed by the dangerous armed child with a heightened sense of *moral obligation* on the part of international organizations, governments, diplomatic corps, and (adult) citizens of the world to "save" the endangered child with arms caught up in these violent situations. It is as if protecting child-soldiers, as bearers of the world's future, is not only an act of humanity but an act *by* humanity and *for* humanity.[13]

THE DISCOURSE OF THE LAW: BANNING THE USE OF CHILD-SOLDIERS

Known as the "Century of the Child," the twentieth century witnessed a gradual prioritization of child protection and development practices on the international agenda.[14] Despite the international recognition that mankind "owes to the child the best it has to give," children's experiences of war, migration, famine, and poverty cast into doubt whether it is still possible to preserve in any way the territory mapped out as a happy and healthy childhood.[15] What emerges from these experiences is, as Watson says, a crisis in childhood: somehow these children's lives are far from what is presumed to be "child-like" and also far from the progress implicitly promised for the future of mankind through children.[16] A case in point is the participation of children in armed conflict not only as victims but also as perpetrators of violence.

Although children have always been present on the battlefields, their international treatment has changed considerably since the end of the Cold War.[17] On the one hand, the high number of state ratifications of the UN Convention on the Rights of the Child and the World Summit for Children in 1990 has inaugurated a time in which the protection of children has come to occupy a central place in the international human rights and security agendas alike. On the other hand, the accumulation and publicization of atrocities, for example the murders, mutilations, abductions, and rapes committed by groups such as Sierra Leone's West Side Boys, has lent urgency to the expansion of the international movement toward the elimination of the participation of children in any kind of regular or irregular armed group.[18] Within these terms, the "child-soldier phenomenon" has emerged as a humanitarian and political issue. As a program officer of the UN SRSG Office for Children and Armed Conflict (Office for CAAC) comments, "The global culture on child soldiering is changing and so they [armed groups] do use them [children], but they hide it. So it's not a point of pride anymore, or it's not a point of development anymore[. . . .] Nobody thinks it's ridiculous to bring child-soldiers' cases to the Security Council. The discourse is now changing. So now it is a no-brainer."[19]

The essential quality of child-soldiers, according to these discourses, is their vulnerability: they are dependent, exploited, and powerless.[20] The "remediation" of the child-soldier problem comes primarily via a rights-based framework together with UNICEF rehabilitation programs. Through these practices, child-soldiers are (re)produced as having their development process severely disrupted by their role in hostilities and as being victims who have been "acted upon but not acting, at least not of their own volition."[21] This section focuses specifically on the "response" to the child-soldier problem via the rights-based approach—or the discourse of the law—which distinguishes what is permitted and what is forbidden in accordance with a specific code, while the next chapter explores the international rehabilitation programs. Specifically, I analyze here how international legal standards—including the 1977 Additional Protocols to the Geneva Conventions, the 1989 UNCRC, the 1998 Rome Statute, the 1990 African Charter on the Rights and Welfare of the Child, the 1999 International Labor Organization Worst Forms of Child Labor Convention, and the 2000 Optional Protocol to the Convention on the Rights of the Child on the Involvement of Children in Armed Conflict (hereinafter Optional Protocol)—and two international instruments adopted by UNICEF that have a key role in the debates on the definition of the category child-soldier—the 1997 Cape Town Principles and the Paris Principles—articulate children's participation in armed conflicts as wrong and something that must be outlawed internationally.[22]

Protecting children in situations of armed conflict was one of the earliest concerns of international laws on children's rights. The Geneva Convention on the Protections of Civilians, for example, contains seventeen articles specifically on the need to provide general protection to children as civilians.[23] However, the four Geneva Conventions of 1949 are silent on both the recruitment of children into the armed forces and their participation in hostilities. Indeed, the first systematic attempt to directly address the issue of child combatants can be found in the 1977 Additional Protocols to the Geneva Conventions. Under the Additional Protocols, the regulation of children's involvement in war is contingent on both the nature of the conflict—international armed conflict (which is addressed in Additional Protocol I) and non-international conflict (which is addressed in Additional Protocol II)—and the age of the individual involved—younger children (under fifteen) and older children (aged fifteen to eighteen).

In particular, Additional Protocol I imposes the least restrictive requirements on sovereign states: it does not actually prohibit child recruitment but only addresses the youngest category of children by requiring states parties to take all "feasible measures" to prevent children who have not reached fifteen years of age from playing a "direct part in hostilities" (Additional Protocol I, Article 77), which means active combat, but excludes other military activities, such as spying, supply transportation, and cooking. It also requires states to "refrain from recruiting them into their armed forces." Regarding the category of older children, its only requirement is that if and when states recruit children between fifteen and eighteen years old, they should "endeavor to give priority to those who are the oldest" (Additional Protocol I, Article 77). The treaty's language is far less strong than originally proposed in a draft treaty by the International Committee of the Red Cross (ICRC). Initially, the ICRC proposed that state parties "take all *necessary measures* in order that children under fifteen years shall not *take part in hostilities* and, in particular, they shall refrain from recruiting them in their armed forces or accepting their voluntary enrollment."[24] It is worth mentioning that the final treaty does not say anything specific on the definition of "recruitment," so the word could be construed to cover both the compulsory and the voluntary enrollment of children into armed groups.

The protections for children in Additional Protocol II are much stronger. Its restrictions against child recruitment are clear: "children who have not attained the age of fifteen years shall neither be recruited in the armed forces or groups nor allowed to take part in hostilities" (Additional Protocol II, Article 4). In this sense, Additional Protocol II creates a comprehensive ban on the use of any person below the age of fifteen as a soldier in any internal conflict. One of the reasons that may explain this difference in the language of the two protocols was brought to the fore by the Canadian delegation during the drafting of Article 77 of Protocol I. According to Canada, people aged sixteen to eighteen are often better physically equipped for fighting than their fathers are. If international law obliges states to prohibit the recruitment of children and their participation in hostilities, it would mean depriving them of an important pool of effective combatants.[25] Furthermore, limiting the use of child-soldiers by rebel groups and insurgents, as Additional Protocol II does, is an effective way of hampering their access to the advantages the use of child-soldiers would bring.

What emerges from the analysis of this first international agreement is that there are two main pillars supporting and articulating the ban on the involvement of children in armed conflict. First, there is the idea of "militarization," which can be understood in a more restrictive sense, considering only children's direct participation in hostilities, or from a broader perspective, embracing not only combatant children in state and nonstate forces but also noncombatant children's involvement in supporting roles, working as spies, cooks, porters, messengers, and so forth. Secondly, there is the age of the child, which serves as a parameter for defining whether they are capable of playing certain social roles. Specifically, on the age issue, it is important to explore how this is also related to contemporary debates on the possibility of children taking responsibility for their actions versus their presumed ignorance, either because they are too young to commit such violent acts or because they just do what they are told to do by adults. These are some of the aspects that are examined in further detail through the analysis of these international practices that seek to eradicate the problem of child-soldiering.

In regard to the first pillar, the militarization of children, the UNCRC, the African Charter on the Rights and Welfare of the Child, and the Optional Protocol reproduce the 1977 Additional Protocols' exact vocabulary by affirming that children should "not take direct part in hostilities."[26] However, the Optional Protocol actually parallels Additional Protocol II insofar as its strongest restrictions are directed against nonstate armed groups: "armed groups, distinct from the armed forces of a State, should not, *under any circumstances*, recruit or use *in hostilities* persons under the age of *18 years*."[27] In this sense, this particular agreement reproduces two conceptions of the child-soldier: children cannot participate directly in hostilities as combatants on the behalf of state parties, while irregular armed groups are prohibited from using children "in hostilities." This differentiation could also be read as states assuming that indirect participation in international conflicts is safer than indirect participation in the so-called new wars.[28]

In a language somewhat different from the UNCRC, the Rome Statute, which is considered one of the most significant recent legal developments in limiting the use of child-soldiers, adopts a broader idea of militarization by abandoning the use of the term "direct."[29] It defines the use of children to "participate actively in hostilities" as a war crime.[30] However, as highlighted by Radhika Coomaraswamy, former special representative of the secretary-general for CAAC, the scope of this provision's application to real-life situations has yet to be determined by the courts.[31] The first trial involving this legislation heard at the International Criminal Court (ICC), in 2009, was that of the Democratic Republic of Congo (DRC) rebel leader Thomas Lubanga Dyilo, and it was based exclusively on counts of the charge of conscripting or enlisting around three thousand children under the age of fifteen or using them to participate actively in hostilities in the Ituri region of eastern DRC. Found guilty, Lubanga was sentenced on July 10, 2012, to a total of fourteen years in prison.

In the same vein, the International Labour Organization (ILO) Worst Forms of Child Labor Convention includes among the worst forms of child labor the "forced or compulsory recruitment of children for use in armed conflict" (Article 3) and requires all state parties to take "immediate and effective measures to secure the prohibition and elimination of the worst forms of child labour as a matter of urgency" (Article 7).[32] Whatever a child's role in an armed conflict, it is already qualified as one of the "worst forms of child labour" and must be eliminated. Nevertheless, the ILO convention is not as far-reaching, as its focus is only on children's forced involvement in hostilities.

A broader concept of child-soldiers in terms of "militarization" is finally articulated by the two international agreements regarding the interdiction of the involvement of children in armed conflict: the Cape Town Principles and the Paris Principles.[33] As discussed in the first chapter, the fluidity of the concept of the child-soldier was first addressed in 1997 at a symposium organized by UNICEF and the NGO Working Group on the CRC, when the Cape Town Principles and the Best Practices on the Prevention of Recruitment of Children into the Armed Forces and on Demobilization and Social Reintegration of Child Soldiers in Africa were adopted. The Cape Town Principles expanded the concept of "child-soldier" and adopted a more inclusive terminology of "children associated with armed forces or armed groups," which refers to "any person under 18 years of age who is part of any kind of regular or irregular armed force or armed group in *any capacity*."[34] Then, a decade later, UNICEF organized a review of the Cape Town Principles, which resulted in the Paris Principles and Guidelines on Children Associated with Armed Force and Armed Groups. The Paris Principles formally abandoned the concept of child-soldier in favor of the concept of a "child associated with armed group or armed force" to avoid implying that children, when recruited, will directly participate in wars as combatants.[35]

Regarding the second pillar that structures the discourse of law—the issue of age—the definition of the child-soldier contradicts to some extent the internationally accepted definition of the child. The UNCRC is the best example: at the same time as it establishes the eighteenth year of life as the transition point to adulthood, Article 38 repeats the language of Additional Protocol I, making it the only provision of the convention that does not contain the general age limit of eighteen years:

> 2. States Parties shall take all feasible measures to ensure that persons who have not attained the age of fifteen years do not take a direct part in hostilities.
>
> 3. States Parties shall refrain from recruiting any person who has not attained the age of fifteen years into their armed forces. In recruiting among those persons who have attained the age of fifteen years but who have not attained the age of eighteen years, States Parties shall endeavour to give priority to those who are oldest.[36]

Those who advocated banning the use and recruitment of child-soldiers saw this as a major flaw in the treaty and tried to fix it with the supplementary treaty, the Optional Protocol, which states that "*raising the age* of possible recruitment of persons into armed forces and their participation in hostilities will contribute effectively to the implementation of the principle that *the best interests of the child* are to be a primary consideration in all actions concerning children."[37]

However, the Optional Protocol does not eliminate the contradiction surrounding the age of child-soldiers. In Article 4, it states that "armed groups, distinct from the armed forces of a State, should not, *under any circumstances*, recruit or use *in hostilities* persons under the age of *18 years*."[38] As a diplomat who, at the time of the interview in 2013, was a member of the UK's Permanent Mission to the United Nations and of the Security Council Working Group on Children and Armed Conflict, affirmed: "That's where the boundaries come in. We don't give the right to choose to children under eighteen. It's the minimum that we can do to enable them to have access to education, to opportunities, and to face a secure environment."[39] When asked about the military recruitment of British youth fifteen to seventeen years old by the UK forces, her explanation for such flexibility lay in the unquestionable idea of the UK as a responsible nation-state: "they [children] are never exposed to some kind of danger until they're eighteen. So, it's very mature. They never leave the country. Essentially, it's working in the Ministry of Defence. They might have some military training, but they're not going to leave the country or go to a hostile environment."[40] This affirmation, however, finds some divergence in face of evidence about at least 22 British under-age soldiers who were sent to Afghanistan and Iraq between 2003 and 2010.[41] According to the NGO Child Soldiers International, in 2018, the British army enlisted 1,690 children (26 percent of British army recruits), 920 of whom were aged sixteen.[42] Legally, the UK is not doing anything wrong: Article 3 of the Optional Protocol states that children who are fifteen or over may be *voluntarily recruited* into the armed forces of a state, provided that "such recruitment is done with the informed consent of the person's parents or legal guardians."[43] As the UK diplomat affirms, "We have signed the Optional Protocol and Protocol 2, and we think we are not violating any of the agreements because we have a lot of caution."[44] Regardless of its internal inconsistency, the Optional Protocol has become one of the main symbols of what has come to be known as the "straight-18 position," which calls for an international legal standard banning the recruitment into armed forces and the use in combat of anyone under the age of eighteen.

Furthermore, the Optional Protocol clearly advances in setting a distinction between compulsory versus voluntary recruitment. The implications and reasons for this difference resonate with the child rights debate about child protection versus children's right to choose and participate. It is as if the child-soldier stood at a gray dividing line between these two positions: while it could be argued that the restrictions placed by international legal standards on the minimum age for recruitment interfere with the rights of the child to freedom of association and freedom of expression, the violence of war and the presumed chaos of the new wars is seen to work in favor of the (re)production of the child as vulnerable, innocent, and in need of (international) protection. The Optional Protocol therefore enables some children to decide and others not, depending on their age but more importantly on who the recruiter is: the modern nation-state, which claims to monopolize the legitimate use of violence, or the multiplicity of "irrational," "chaotic," and "dangerous" irregular armed groups.

While voluntarily enrolling to join a state's armed forces can be accepted as a rational, acceptable choice even for a child, joining an armed nonstate group is interpreted as invariably against the child's best interests, constituting a form of child exploitation and abuse. Thus any autonomous decision taken by a child can only be read between quotation marks.

In addition to the Optional Protocol, the "straight-18 position" was strengthened by the adoption of two treaties, the ILO's Worst Forms of Child Labour Convention and the African Charter on the Rights and Welfare of the Child, which define children as all persons under the age of eighteen.[45] When it comes to children and armed conflict, the UN and, in particular, UNICEF regard the Cape Town Principles and the Paris Principles as the core documents that reflect a common understanding of the child-soldier and efforts toward eradicating this practice.[46] According to these principles, the idea of "militarization" must be as broad as possible in order to embrace all children who are involved with armed groups, state or otherwise, and the age limit to participate in war must be eighteen. Nevertheless, it is worth noting that international humanitarian law is still guided by the Rome Statute, which defines "conscripting or enlisting children under the age of fifteen years" as a war crime.[47]

While the "straight-18 position" makes progress in the protection of a larger group of children, children whose engagement in war involves a multiplicity of complex experiences are all grouped together under a single legal category imbued with the idea of victimhood that insists on children's separation from politics and the denial of their agency.[48] An illustrative example is the figure on the first page of a training manual developed by the NGO Geneva Call, titled *Protecting Children in Armed Conflict: Key Rules from the Geneva Call's Deed of Commitment*, geared toward armed nonstate actors.[49] The figure consists of a large number 18, with two children (a boy and a girl) standing on the bottom of the number 1, which is marked like a tape-measure. In this image, children's biological immaturity and the idea of "natural growth" are conflated with children's social development and capacity to participate. Put another way, the notion of biological size is related to chronological age, thereby determining when a child's capacity and maturity will be developed enough for them to become a soldier.

However, this story gets even more complicated when age is used as a criterion not only for evaluating children's capacity to choose to participate in war but, paradoxically, for denying the possibility of holding children accountable for their acts. That is, although children are considered capable enough to be soldiers as of age fifteen, the fact that they are still children means they are presumed to be inherently innocent and irrational and thus unable to assume legal responsibilities. The Rome Statute is a case in point. While it allows for the conscription and enlistment of children from the age of fifteen, Article 26 in particular provides for both the trial and the imprisonment by the ICC of people charged with and convicted of recruiting children, provided this person is not under the age of eighteen. As a result, in its aim to prevent children from being tried in court, the statute not only fails to address the legal responsibility of children who commit war crimes but also presents a disturbing gap that may incentivize adult soldiers to use children of fifteen to seventeen years of age to perform heinous crimes and recruit other children.[50] The Special Court for Sierra Leone (SCSL), established in 2002, took a similar position. Although it was the only international court that had jurisdiction to try persons aged above fifteen, the SCSL decided not to prosecute any children, since they were considered unable to bear the "greatest responsibility" of the crimes they were "forced to commit."[51]

By drawing on the four main pillars of the modern conception of childhood, as described by Hockey and James, the dilemma (re)produced both by the Rome Statute and the SCSL can be understood precisely as what arises when questions of children's *morality*—that they are inherently and distinctly innocent—fail to coincide with questions of children's *capability*.[52] Accordingly, child-soldiers end up being articulated as "emotional decision-makers" whose agency is not seen as a strategic one that requires being able to understand the larger picture of the armed conflict or having any comprehension of the long-term consequences of their actions in the form of political gain as adult soldiers do.[53] Coomaraswamy, for example, cites children's vulnerability and early stage of development as a justification for their participation in war. In other words, children are first and foremost *victims*:

> Children are involved in armed conflict at an important moment in their psychological and moral development. They are desired as recruits, because they are more easily intimidated and indoctrinated. In some cases, they are exposed to forced alcohol and drug abuse and pushed into perpetrating atrocities, such as torturing, killing and plundering. Sometimes, children are even forced to inflict harm against their own families and communities, in order to break off ties with the past and become a full grown member of the group. In summary, children most commonly lack the mental maturity and judgment to express their consent to engage in armed violence, and therefore should be shielded from criminal liability.[54]

Over the course of forty years, the participation of children in armed conflicts has been transformed from a practice loosely regulated and focused on children's role as combatants to one that is problematized and subject to greater control. While an international legal consensus about the age and military activities that define the child-soldier has yet to be reached, the notion of a *right* childhood as one that is lived outside war is neither challenged nor problematized but is formalized and universalized by the discourse of the law. As a consequence, children's involvement in war is (re)produced as invariably wrong and as something that must therefore be eradicated. From such a formulation, in which the hyphen that *dis*connects the child from the soldier is not questioned, there is no room left for ambiguities or space for considering children's own motivations or their ability to understand their own circumstances and express their own views regarding their participation in hostilities or the local social constructions of the roles suitable to children according to their gender and age. After all, the view of the child-soldier as abnormal is (re)produced through the same ordering strategies that are meant to protect them. The next section turns to the assumptions and categories that give social coherence to the discourse about child-soldiers as an apparent pathology. Through the analysis of three images (reproduced in writing, orally, or visually) that permeate and articulate the bounded category of the child-soldier as deviation—the victim, the monster, and the redeemed hero—I explore the discourse of the norm.

AGAINST THE NORM: THE CHILD-SOLDIER AS AN INTERNATIONAL EMERGENCY

"The Making, and Unmaking, of a Child Soldier." Although this is the title of an autobiographical article by the now-celebrated former child-soldier Ishmael Beah, a very similar construction could equally be applied to other children who have crossed out of the "space" of the child-soldiering phenomenon and "found" their "lost childhood."[55] First a hapless victim recruited by evil adults, then turned into a dangerous monster in the context of war, the child-soldier can, if saved by the International, be unmade and become a child again, like a redeemed hero, recovering his or her lost—or stolen—childhood. Despite their different attributes, these three images of child-soldiers, as discussed by Myriam S. Denov in her enlightening critical analysis of child-soldiers in the Sierra Leone war, somehow articulate the identity of *deviation*, in which the horrors of the war experience prevail, calling attention to the risks involved when the world-child departs from its "natural" course of development.[56] The messy, ambiguous, and sometimes paradoxical experiences of child-soldiers in wars are muted when these children are articulated in problematic frameworks and static identities constructed through a logic of extremes that speak of their innocent victimhood or their monstrous behavior.[57]

Beah's own story is retold through these images, from the first battle, when all he felt was fear, to his transformation into a ruthless, violent combatant. At the beginning, Beah, who was recruited by the National Army at age thirteen during the Sierra Leone civil war, says: "I have never been so afraid to go anywhere in my life as I was that first day. As we walked into the arms of the forest, tears began to form in my eyes, but I struggled to hide them and gripped my gun for comfort. We exhaled quietly, afraid that our own breathing could cause our deaths."[58] However, after the first week of going out on raids to kill people, combined with the use of drugs, "the idea of death didn't cross my mind, and killing had become as easy as drinking water. After that first killing, my mind had stopped making remorseful records, or so it seemed."[59] The unmaking of the child-soldier, then, starts when Beah is already sixteen years old and is taken by UNICEF representatives to a rehabilitation center, where, as he explains, he "*relearn[s]* boyhood." At the first moment, though, Beah and the other former child-soldiers do not seem to accept being at the center and still behave very aggressively, especially when the ones who were recruited by the rebel group Revolutionary United Front and the ones who fought together with the National Army were put in the same space. As Beah put it, "we thought that we were part of the war until the end." But then, after a several months, things started to change. The phrase that Beah had heard from every staff member and that he had always hated—"None of what happened was your fault. You were just a little boy"—began to make sense, and he started to believe it. From that moment on, Beah was no longer a monster or a hapless victim, but a redeemed hero who had survived war and had "learned how to forgive himself, to regain his humanity, and, finally to heal."[60]

These fragments from Beah's article shed light on three important movements that occur simultaneously in the discourse of the norm, which is (re)produced within the politics and practices of childcare, child watching, and child saving. The first movement is the articulation of the child-soldier as an anomaly and a pathology in comparison with the model of the world-child. The second movement is the (re)production of the world-child as a norm by locating the child-soldier in a network of power relations through which child-soldiers are classified as a deviant and inferior. In this sense, the child-soldier's relationship with the world-child norm can be described as a kind of "inclusive exclusion," in which child-soldiers are included in the discourse of normality only by virtue of their exclusion from the normal conception of the child and ordered spaces of childhood.[61] Finally, the third movement—together with the discourse of the law—frames the child-soldier not only as a child rights violation but also as an international emergency. The idea of the child-soldier phenomenon as an emergency plays an important role in building and controlling the limits of the category of the child-soldier in that it casts these children's life experiences—represented through static images of victim, monster, and redeemed hero—as a problem in need of immediate solutions formulated by specialists. Furthermore, while the concept of emergency excludes the child-soldier from the terrain of order and normality, it also (re)produces certain boundaries that delimit the model of the child and a particular version of the world that children with weapons insist on challenging, overstepping, or sidestepping.

To critically analyze these three movements, I follow Denov's work in exploring the contrasts in how the world's media and policy discourse constructs child-soldiers.[62] The interviews I conducted with diplomats and the UN and UNICEF staff also clearly authorize and (re)produce the discourse of the child-soldier as an emergency. These narratives, combined with the discourse of the law, compose a general discourse of the child-soldier as an international emergency, which is dominated by a problem-solving logic that defines children's participation in armed conflicts as both wrong and abnormal and in urgent need of solution. Not only is this perspective uncritical of the prevailing ordering mechanisms and their power relations; it also limits critical thinking on what constitutes a "normal" form of social and international life.

"Forgotten Fighters" is the title of a report by the NGO Human Rights Watch about child-soldiers in Angola, where, according to the 2001 Global Report by the Coalition to Stop the Use of Child Soldiers, around seven thousand children served with the Angolan Armed Forces and the largest opposition armed group, the National Union for the Total Independence of Angola (UNITA).[63] The title of the report raises at least two questions: Who are these child fighters? Who has forgotten them? According to Human Rights Watch, while some children received arms training and were active in the fighting, many others acted as porters, cooks, and spies. However, regardless of their duties, "the work they performed was hazardous and has had an emotional impact on many of them."[64] Within this formulation, children's experiences in war—the particularities and complexities of which are already overlooked—are once again silenced, or homogenized, under the image of the exploited victim. It is unquestionable that these children, like all the civilians, are victims of the conflict. However, while the report focuses only on children's testimonies about their coercion into military service to commit horrific human rights abuses, the diversity of the children's experiences while engaged in war is disregarded. Put another way, children's relationship with war is far more complex than can be expressed through the simple image of the victim.[65]

The image of the victim revolves primarily around forced recruitment or abduction; children being forced to kill or slaughter, especially a family member; children witnessing extreme acts of violence, especially against other children; children being the object of humiliation, brutal beatings, rape, sexual slavery, slave labor, and hunger; and children unprepared for involvement in combat. Most of the reports by humanitarian organizations end up stating that all these children want is to get back their "lost childhood," of which peace and school are crucial ingredients.[66] Vulnerability in particular is articulated as the equivalent of victimhood, but this is not necessarily what emerges from children's experiences. As Marisa O. Ensor argues, many children in Sudan joined the Sudan People's Liberation Army (SPLA) voluntarily and were adamant about their right and capacity to fight as adult soldiers.[67] However, in humanitarian narratives, the victimization of child-soldiers prevails, with the emphasis being put on brutal recruitment methods and punishments. In two Human Rights Watch reports, this image is (re)produced through children's testimonies:

> Early on when my brothers and I were captured, the LRA [Lord's Resistance Army] explained to us that all five brothers couldn't serve in the LRA because we would not perform well. So they tied up my two younger brothers and invited us to watch. Then they beat them with sticks until two of them died. They told us it would give us strength to fight. My youngest brother was nine years old.[68]

> After the first training I had special training on carrying heavy weapons. We carried them around the playground. One day I had cramps and fever and said I couldn't come. They poured hot water on my body and back as punishment. This left a burn mark.[69]

In these testimonies, the correspondence between childhood, vulnerability, and victimhood is clearly articulated. Paralleling these accounts, Roméo Dallaire, a distinguished human rights activist, depicts the child-soldier as an "end-to-end weapon system" and a "tool"; moreover, children are "vulnerable and easy to catch, just like minnows in a pond," while the adults involved are described as "evil."[70] Child-soldiers are thus articulated first and foremost as victims who are easily convinced to obey the armed groups' leaders and are not capable of evaluating the risks of being a soldier. A report by Amnesty International, for example, explains why in some countries there is a "trend" to deliberately recruit children rather than adults: "both governments and armed groups use children because they are easier to condition into fearless killing and unthinking obedience."[71] In a similar vein, in an interview, a UNICEF adviser at the Child Protection Unit argued that armed groups could mobilize children in wars more easily "to take risks" because "adults have this factor of caution [. . .], the children go and take the risk and sacrifice, and they can easily be used."[72] As a fifteen-year-old boy formerly associated with an armed group in the Democratic Republic of Congo highlights, "We are put on the frontline because children are not scared of fighting."[73]

In this discourse about the child-soldier, children are depicted as hapless victims who are essentially irrational and are thus unable to understand or identify the risks of entering combat. In one sense, it is precisely their "childish" nature that makes them the ideal target of recruiters and the object of adult abuse.[74] Or, in Coomaraswamy's words: "These children are not just getting caught in the crossfire, they are being forced and manipulated to give expression to the hatred of adults."[75] This same idea seems to serve as the basis for structuring the UN's six grave violations against children during armed conflicts (the killing or maiming of children; the recruitment or use of child soldiers; rape and other forms of sexual violence against children; the abduction of children; attacks against schools or hospitals; and the denial of humanitarian access to children), which have been specified in several Security Council resolutions that form the architecture of the UN Security Council's thematic agenda on Children and Armed Conflict. Focusing solely on children's victimhood and vulnerability, these violations have set the research agenda for much of the global program for the defense and protection of children in situations of armed conflict.[76] According to the reports on the six grave violations, Katrina Lee-Koo argues that despite the multiplicity of child-soldiers' experiences in the field, "children are entirely dominated by the ravages of conflict, which are unnaturally brought to bear upon their lives and which they are unable to shape, resist or mitigate."[77] These reports shed light on just one possible and extreme account of being a child-soldier: the hapless victim whose agency in conflict is completely stifled.

Terms such as "used as/for," "forced to," "brainwashed," and "manipulated" appear frequently in these narratives, articulating and authorizing this idea of the child whose agency—or possibility of political participation—is completely silenced. Even though the SRSG report for CAAC that celebrates ten years of the Machel Report affirms that "we should recognize the capacities and agency of children and youth, and avoid characterizing children and youth as vulnerable or as delinquents who pose a threat to security," the text goes on to state that "moreover, adults are responsible for environments of conflict and violence."[78] In such ambiguous formulations, although children are recognized as agents, they are still (re)produced as objects of adult abuse or manifestations of adult hatred. As such, these children are still kept in the role of irrational, dependent, vulnerable minors incapable of taking responsibility for their actions.[79] Coomaraswamy makes this argument even clearer when she affirms, based on Melissa A. Jamison's discussion of her concerns regarding the detention of juveniles, that "even when children behave like 'adults' during war their emotional and psychological vulnerability and the forced nature of their acts should be taken into account."[80] The first thing worth questioning in this statement is what "behaving like adults" means. If the answer is "combating, killing, or even raping," the question should be turned toward the nonproblematization of the adult soldier, who is naturalized as someone who is able and mature enough to be a soldier and voluntarily adopt certain types of corrupt and destructive behavior.

If one follows on from Peter Nyers's critical analysis of the inevitable construction of the refugee as a problem, it is possible to see how this discourse about the child-soldier as an emergency is constructed through a process of differentiation that is structured through a dichotomous logic.[81] When it comes to the image of the victim, the adult soldier is presumed to be autonomous and able to feel hatred and do harm to other people, while the child-soldier is articulated as a vulnerable, immature, innocent child. As Nyers suggests, this oppositional relationship between order—here, the self-governing adult—and crisis—in this case, the exploited child—is not natural or symmetrical but operates as a differentiating power that has the capacity to keep things apart.[82] As such, the child-soldier cannot be considered a legitimate (adult) soldier, a noncivilian sanctioned to take part directly in hostilities,[83] nor is he or she a "normal" child; rather, he or she is a victim of war. A program officer of the Office for CAAC emphasizes this differentiating power by highlighting the way child-soldiers are dressed: "In the Ivory Coast, I also met with children, around fifteen years old, armed as well, with pieces of uniform. It's always just pieces of uniform. Not specially drugged, but you could see that they had some kind of adrenaline coming out from the fact that they were within an armed group and they had a weapon."[84] The emphasis on children wearing "just pieces of uniform" instead of full military uniforms aptly captures what this modern binary child/adult has authorized in terms of understandings about childhood, a phase of life at which being a soldier is completely out of place, an abnormality. In a similar vein, the 2004 Human Rights Watch report "How to Fight, How to Kill: Child Soldiers in Liberia" also highlights that children rarely wear military uniforms, but rather T-shirts bearing the names of their fighting groups and sometimes their fighting slogan.[85] According to this logic, child-soldiers are an emergency insofar as they overflow both limits: of the ordered child and of the legitimate soldier.

Another element that plays a major role in the articulation of the child-soldier as a hapless victim is the use of drugs and how this relates to children's irrationality. Regarding the child-soldiers in the Central African Republic, for example, the program officer mentioned earlier also commented in the interview that "there was nothing to get out of them because they were completely drugged. The only thing that you want to get out of them is to ensure that they are not going to start shooting everywhere."[86] In a report on the armed conflict in Mali, Watchlist emphasized that armed groups gave illicit drugs to children, who, according to one witness, behaved in a "'high' manner, including shooting their guns up in the air 'just for fun.'"[87] According to Watchlist, "Armed groups use the administration of drugs to control children, for example by making them more obedient or by creating a dependency, that can have short- and long-term consequences including physical and mental harm, addiction, and increased vulnerability to exploitation."[88] These statements indicate that the use of drugs not only (re)produces the discourse of child-soldiers subsumed in a crisis situation but also articulates these children as dangerous beings who are completely out of control and may kill "just for fun." When faced with emergency situations like these, the desire to take immediate action to reinstate security is strong, irrespective of one's political, cultural, or moral position.

Despite the wider environmental conditions that shape child-soldiers' experiences and the particularities of age and culture, the image of the child as a victim rooted in the idea of childhood as a state of passivity and vulnerability tends to reproduce a pathological framework, which posits a direct and rather mechanical relationship between exposure to violent events and impaired mental health.[89] As such, the idea of a "lost generation"[90] is commonly used to describe child-soldiers, who are depicted as beings traumatized by their war experiences. In the words of another program officer of the Office for CAAC, "Most children actually are like crap. They were sexually violated, they didn't have a great time while in the force."[91]

While these articulations of child-soldiers as victims may help garner international attention to children's participation in wars, this international sympathy may be a double-edged sword, as it tends to regard this group of children as being "in recovery" from trauma but never fully "recovered." They are projected as being permanently vulnerable and banished from the right to self-government. The emphasis on victimhood may contradict children's own perceptions of themselves as capable actors and, as a consequence, can cause their own demands to go unheard. For example, in Northern Uganda, a study suggests a different construct for child-soldiers, in which the majority of children—both abducted and non-abducted—report low-level symptoms of psychological distress (e.g., aggressiveness and nightmares) in conjunction with high levels of prosocial behavior, such as political engagement.[92]

Furthermore, by invariably articulating child-soldiers as a problem in need of action by responsible protectors, not only are such children rendered as passive objects of the international gaze; their communities and nation-states are pathologized as dysfunctional and are politically delegitimized for their supposed inability to protect their most "precious resource." At the end of the day, as Lee-Koo summarizes, the image of the child-soldier as a hapless victim revolves around three themes: protection/rescue, innocence, and degeneracy. Together, she argues, "these three themes provide a moral foundation for conflict and project a familiar yet powerful metaphor for the claim that international order is the product of strong states, which protect vulnerable populations from abusive and ultimately illegitimate states."[93]

In stark contrast to the discourse of child-soldiers as victims is their image as dangerous and evil beings or simply as monsters, permanently lost in an endless cycle of unrelenting violence and irrationality.[94] It is as if by failing to meet the criterion of "innocence," these children are not only marginalized but actually demonized. This is clearly posed by Singer, when he refers to the participation of child-soldiers in ritualized killings of others as "the defining moment that changed their lives forever."[95] From the moment children cross the "ultimate moral boundary, they are made anathema to the only environment they knew."[96]

They become "killing machines" that do not have a sense of empathy for the civilian population.[97] As a child-soldier (age fifteen) confirms: "It's easier the second time [you kill]. You become indifferent."[98] This threatening image was similarly attached to the twin Htoo brothers—or "twin terrors"—who at age twelve controlled the God's Army, a Karen rebel group against the government of Myanmar.[99] As *Time* magazine described them: "One twin, Luther, shaves the front of his head, has a 1,000-yard stare and experiences psychotic mood swings that make him bark sharp reprimands at his followers like a sergeant major. The other twin, Johnny, has long hair, effeminate features and a beguiling smile that he maintains even when firing off a few rounds from his rifle."[100]

The photo by the Associated Press of the Htoo twins smoking cigars circulated globally: "the epitome of dangerous youngsters whose age and pathology appear to define them."[101] According to *Time*, the Htoo brothers "played with guns as if they were toys" and "had lost count of how many Burmese they had killed." The "more serious" of the two, then, tells the camera crew: "I have never cried. Why would a man cry?"[102] The childish aspects of the "normal" child disappear here: instead of happy-go-lucky, the Htoo twins are serious beings; instead of vulnerable, they never cry; and although they do enjoy playing, their plaything is a gun.

The 2013 Watchlist report about the armed conflict in Mali also portrays child-soldiers as potentially dangerous. By drawing on the testimonies of people from neighborhoods in Mali, it foregrounds the fear surrounding these children, even though they were *just* small boys: "We saw a young youth from our neighborhood, not older than fifteen years old. . . We didn't even want to look at him because we were afraid he'd kill us (for recognizing him). No one said anything. . . he was really a boy."[103] Another testimony says: "You didn't even want to look at them; they were really minors, small children. The guns they carried were too big."[104]

Despite their small size and "childish" biological features, child-soldiers, whose developmental process has been ruptured by their participation in war, induce feelings of condemnation as well as pity. The still uncivilized, savage child who is caught up by armed conflict is, according to the former French foreign minister Philippe Douste-Blazy, a "time bomb that threatens stability and growth in Africa and beyond."[105] A case in point is Dominic Ongwen, abducted at age ten, who became a senior commander in the Ugandan irregular armed group, the Lord's Resistance Army (LRA). From an innocent child who was forcibly recruited by the LRA when he was walking home from school, Ongwen was turned into a monster: "He is known as the most courageous, loyal and brutal of the men who serve Joseph Kony, the LRA's charismatic and ruthless founder," according to a *Globe and Mail* article from 2008 titled "The Making of a Monster."[106] Key among Ongwen's crimes is his leadership of abduction raids: "He would take small bands of rebels into Uganda, drive children from their homes or fields at gunpoint and march them back over the border to the camps in Sudan. None ever escaped on his watch."[107] A BBC report also writes that the brigade led by Ongwen was "responsible for some of the worst atrocities in the conflict that has ravaged Northern Uganda and has led to most of the Acholi people living in protected camps."[108] Furthermore, according to the *Globe and Mail* article, Ongwen refined Kony's signature messages of cruelty: "two of his former soldiers say Mr. Ongwen ordered people to be boiled alive in large cooking pots."[109] According to Kony, Ongwen is "a 'role model' among the child soldiers."[110] After this description, the article poses the following question: "How, in 11 years, did Dominic Ongwen turn from a boy too small to walk to the rebels' camp into one of their fiercest, most senior fighters?"[111] Incapable of answering it, the article retains the question mark in its title: Was Ongwen really turned into a monster? Or is he a child victim of war, like other child-soldiers who, as the article tells us, are "hauled into violent conflict before their own moral compass has developed [so that] they become unable to discern right from wrong"?

Together with three other LRA leaders, including Joseph Kony, Vincent Otti (who was supposedly executed by Kony), and Okot Odhiambo, Dominic Ongwen has been charged with seventy counts of crimes against humanity and war crimes by the International Criminal Court. As the BBC affirms, "He seems kind of dreamy in the news footage, this charming-looking man—but Dominic Ongwen is also probably the youngest man to be charged with war crimes," including child abduction, rape, and murder.[112] Ongwen is therefore the first person to be charged with the same war crimes that were committed against him: the conscription and use of children under the age of fifteen to participate actively in hostilities. Even if, on one hand, "dozens of witnesses stand prepared to testify at the ICC that they saw Mr. Ongwen rape, beat, torture and execute civilians, including hundreds of abducted children," on the other hand, "for every witness against him, there is one who could testify to the savage process of violence and psychological intimidation through which he was turned from child to killer."[113] At the time of writing, Ongwen, who pleaded not guilty to the charges, is still on trial, which started in 2016.

This very same dilemma is also present in the depiction of Omar Khadr by the international media, which tends to frame him either as an "innocent child" or as a "monster terrorist."[114] Khadr, now thirty-one, is a Canadian citizen who was held in Guantanamo Bay for eight years for allegedly throwing a grenade that killed a U.S. soldier in Afghanistan in 2002, when he was fifteen years old. Khadr is the first child in U.S. history to be tried for war crimes, including murder, conspiring with Al Qaeda, providing material support for terrorism, and spying on U.S. military convoys in Afghanistan. In 2013, he was transferred to a prison in Canada as a medium-security prisoner; then in 2015 he was released on bail on certain conditions, including that he wear an electronic tracking bracelet. Again, the same dilemma: "Who is the real Omar Khadr? Murdering jihadist, victim of circumstance or model-citizen-in-the-making?"[115]

This question brings to the forefront the ambiguities and complexities of childhood experiences. The competing narratives could not be more different, says Michael Friscolanti.[116] The only common thread is that all of them talk about a child, Omar Khadr, who defies definition under either of the static child labels of "good and promising" or "bad and risky," falling somewhere in between them. However, when the child-soldier is portrayed as a monster, the multiplicity of children's experiences is made invisible. The Ongwens and Khadrs of the world and countless other "dangerous children"—or monsters—are only seen for how they differ from the "correct child." As children who have *deviated* from the "normal" course of development and have been transformed into fierce combatants, child-soldiers are a threat to social stability. The monster is not merely an "other," but a category through which a multifaceted form of power operates. As such, the fusion of the dangerous, evil child-soldier with the child to be corrected—or restored—means that "discourses that would mobilize monstrosity on a screen for otherness are always involved in circuits of normalizing power as well."[117]

In one sense, these discourses that articulate the child-soldier either as a victim or as a monster take us back to the image of the boy-soldier from Liberia introduced at the beginning of chapter 1: the picture of the "vulnerable child" with no military uniform carrying a pink, fluffy, teddy-bear backpack merges with the picture of the dangerous being pointing a weapon toward the viewer.[118] The discourse of the child-soldier as an emergency is replicated in the two images that recur when a Liberian boy or any other child—especially a young one—is caught up in armed warfare. When child-soldiers invade the protected territory of the world-child and destabilize the boundaries that differentiate adults from children, the need to control them and the desire to restore them to their converse—the normalized child—become a matter of urgency. However, discourses of emergency cannot completely stifle otherness.[119] That is, the discourse of the child-soldier as an international emergency cannot fully curb the actions of "children with guns" who challenge the limits of the world and of the child within it. Therefore, instead of describing child-soldiers as the negative, voiceless counterpart of the positive, "normal" child, I prefer to speak of them as "children who soldier," who are multiple, complex political subjects.

While the images of both the victim and the monster are combined in formulating the child-soldier, the image of the "redeemed hero" is pinned on a group of children, once victims or monsters, who have had the chance to overcome extreme violence and great adversity, survive war, cast off the child-soldier, and reintegrate into civilian life. Different from the young "heroes" of the American Civil War, who are remembered as soldiers who fought with bravery, honor, and heroism, the contemporary former child-soldiers are considered heroes precisely because they survived the circumstances of war, were able to overcome their memories of fighting, and were thus able to "reset" their "natural" developmental course as children.

An obvious example of this construction is the case of Ishmael Beah: "while Beah's book has not been viewed as a simple, heroic tale, Beah's journey in and out of armed violence was documented by some journalists as a heroic transformation from violence to redemption."[120] This transformation process is translated into a picture of Beah wearing an Armani jacket and holding school books, while in the background there is an AK-47 inside a camouflage bag standing on the floor.[121] The picture is from a *Playboy* article about Beah's autobiographical book, in which ideas of victimhood, risk, and ultimately "redemption" and "salvation" are articulated. The happy ending is equivalent both to the exclusion of the camouflage bag with the AK-47 inside, which is left in the past, and to the inclusion of books as a signifier of school, a safe place where he can relearn how to be a child. The world-child as a norm operates here as the ultimate goal of the former child-soldier's reintegration into civilian life.

Within this formulation, one attribute of the child stands out: children's capacity to recover from adverse situations. In other words, children are articulated as (naturally) more resilient than adults. As Wessells argues, "children's identities—even more than the adults'—are multiple, fluid and contextual."[122] This idea is closely related to children's presumed malleability as they are in a process of development, maturing, and identity formation. Just as children are easily indoctrinated as soldiers, they can also easily become "normal" children again. [123] For example, Coomaraswamy concludes her statement at the Paris International Conference "Free Children from War," in 2007, making reference to Beah's resilience: "Terrible things have happened to children, but children are also resilient. They need encouragement, guidance and support; and with the proper care they can become outstanding members of society. Ishmael Beah, who is with us today, is a perfect example of this. This young man, a former child soldier from Sierra Leone, adopted by an American mother, went to school and university in the United States, graduating with honors."[124] In another event, also in 2007, Coomaraswamy sends the same message: "I often speak in these events about how I have learned from my field visits that children are resilient and a source of hope; they are not just victims."[125]

Child-soldiers are not *just* victims. If the child as a victim and monster is articulated as a target of intervention by evil recruiters—be they (illegitimate) nation-states or irregular armed forces—the former child-soldier as a redeemed hero is also a target of intervention, but this time one that is envisioned by international actors in the "best interests of the child." Put another way, with "proper care" and international guidance, former child-soldiers are able to recover from war and, like Beah, go to school and graduate with honors. Although these articulations surrounding the child-soldier may indicate paradoxical ideas—to be a child-soldier is to be innocent or to be feared—the logic of opposite extremes and the norm of the world-child combine and operate to (re)produce children as targets of intervention with no capacity for rational reasoning. While intervention in child-soldiers as victims or monsters is read as a form of "exploitation and abuse" by the adult recruiters, for the former child-soldier as the redeemed hero, (international) intervention operates as the only form of redemption and thus offers a rapid solution to the emergency.

Lopez Lomong, a South Sudanese–born American track and field athlete who told his story as a former child-soldier in *Running for My Life*, has also captured the public's attention and gained heroic status for his journey out of wartime violence. Lomong became famous when he was named the American flag bearer for the 2008 Olympic Games in Beijing. Describing his heroic passage from violence to civilian life and later to stardom as a U.S. Olympic athlete, his book cover reads: "One Lost Boy's Journey from the Killing Fields of Sudan to the Olympic Games."[126] Similarly, an article by CNN about Lomong's participation in the London Olympics in 2012 states: "From escaping bullets in Sudan as a young boy to becoming a track and field Olympics star, U.S. athlete Lopez Lomong has been running and defying odds nearly all of his life."[127] Both the autobiographical book and the CNN article construct Lomong's heroic trajectory through an extremist logic: from the "killing fields of Sudan," where the boy is lost amid a "barbarian" war, toward his participation in the Olympic Games, a safe and happy event that takes place outside South Sudan. It is possible to use the phrase "normalized presence/pathologized absence" to think about how the experiences of children engaged in armed conflicts are excluded, only to appear in association with "social problems" and for their lack of "normal" childhood qualities. This formulation fails to give voice to other South Sudanese child-soldiers who are also seen as heroes, but for quite a different reason: because of their contributions to the war efforts and, in many cases, because their army wages are an important source of income on which their families often rely for survival. Their demobilization from the armed groups and state forces is not necessarily welcomed by their communities, as it may represent a significant loss of income and their relegation from contributor to dependent.[128]

This contrast between these two understandings of the child-soldier as a hero calls attention to the risks of the discourse of the child-soldier that tends to frame these children within one of these three static and sometimes paradoxical images: the hapless victim, the monster, and the redeemed hero. These representations, when articulating the idea of child-soldiering as an emergency, silence the complexity and power dynamics that are involved when the world-child meets the deviant child-soldier.

In her book *Children's Rights in International Politics*, Anna Holzscheiter summarizes the various discursive strands that together form what she calls the "discursive ecology" of childhood: the depiction of the "irrational child," the "immanent child," the "innocent child," and the "evolving child" are complemented and (re)produced by particular norms and visions that articulate the conception of childhood.[129] By considering these four images and the discursive elements that articulate them—such as immaturity, irresponsibility, and irrationality for the "irrational child"; potentially valuable contributions to society for the "immanent child"; vulnerability, victimhood, apoliticism, and happiness for the "innocent child"; and autonomy and the right to speak for the "evolving child"—it is possible to glimpse some of the borders that (re)produce what I have termed the world-child. In order to shed light on the complexities and power relations involved in the articulation of the child-soldier as an international emergency, I suggest combining the images pointed out by Holzscheiter with those of child-soldiers identified by Denov, which operate as a mirror in which the world is able to affirm its own shaky order.[130] By doing so, it is possible to show how the discourse about the world-child related to normality and deviation simultaneously structures and is articulated by the idea of the child-soldier as a problem in need of an immediate solution.

The data presented in Table 1 clearly indicate the existence of a "politics on the line," since the ambivalent approach to the child, combining vulnerability and risk, generates huge challenges whenever or wherever (at the line/boundary) the world-child articulated as a universal form of the child and childhood clashes with the external conditions for its constitution—the deviant child-soldier—and also (equally importantly) with worlds that express the potential for difference, diversity, and plurality.[131] Affirming the universality of the world-child means (re)producing some kind of conditionality, or a relationship of "inclusive exclusion," between the world-child norm and the child-soldier deviation and thus authorizes boundaries of some kind. In the images of Holzscheiter's irrational child and innocent child, the risk—or emergency—arises precisely when the hyphen that connects the world-child is unmade. Put another way, in the absence of child protection practices, which operate as mechanisms for controlling and (re)producing the boundaries between the norm and its deviation, the monster and the hapless victim invade the secure, universalized (but not universal) world predicated on notions of progress and order in which differences must remain the same and must be excluded. It is as if the discourse of the child-soldier as an emergency articulated a "triple exceptionalism" that marks the limits of the modern individual, who corresponds to the "normal" child in the future.[132] Being a child is not enough when his or her

TABLE 1. Images of the World-Child and the Child-Soldier in International Politics

	Irrational child	Immanent child	Innocent child	Evolving child
Discourse elements of the "world-child"	immaturity	child as future	vulnerability —misery —suffering —happiness —playfulness —victimhood	individuality
	irresponsibility	valuable contribution to society	apoliticality (neutral zone) —immaturity —occupying a "carefree zone"	politicality —autonomy —right to speak out —social agent
	irrationality	uniform developmental stages		
		education as a means for personal development		
		progress		
		childhood as a transitory phase		
Discourse elements of the child-soldier	monster	redeemed hero	hapless victim	X
	threatening	malleable	exploited	
	dangerous	in the process of formation	abused	
	disorderly		subject to physical violence	
	representing a risk		vulnerable	

The table, based on Anna Holzscheiter's table of four child images and international politics in the twentieth century, represents how these particular narratives simultaneously articulate and are authorized by the three images identified by Myriam Denov within the prevailing discourse about child-soldiers. See Holzscheiter, *Children's Rights*, 137; Denov, *Child Soldiers*.

"normal" childhood has been lost. Secondly, this triple exceptionalism marks the limits of the modern state on the basis of its capacity to protect children. Being a state is not enough if its territory has been overrun by chaotic new wars. Finally, triple exceptionalism points out the limits of a world that keeps out children who fail to exhibit the features of the civilized world-child's world. The threat inherent to child-soldiers, whether they be victims or monsters or simply beasts, is that they might become "us," the modern world-citizens.

Faced with the emergency, the image of the redeemed hero hinged on the image of the "immanent child" operates as the promise of a good future or as the promise of *un*making the child-soldier and, in doing so, (re)building the hyphens between the world-child and the child-soldier. The report that celebrates the tenth anniversary of the Machel Report states: "In a globalized world, local and regional destabilization has global repercussions. Not only is responding to conflict a moral obligation; protection is in the direct security interests of all States."[133] The imaginary of the child-soldier as an emergency feeds the fear of a world *at risk* whose promise of a progressive future is under threat. As such, it reinforces the notion of risk, which immediately elicits the notion of risk management—that is, international intervention. The phenomenon of child-soldiers not only is depicted as a human rights violation but is included as a peace and security issue on the agenda of the UN Security Council. As a target of international intervention, no room is left for the "evolving child" as a political subject. Neither as a monster nor as a victim, nor as a redeemed hero does the child have any chance of autonomous decision making; they are either the objects of exploitation or the objects of salvation.

The next chapter turns the focus to international responses to this emergency—the mechanisms for restoring (but not changing) the linearity of the existing order. As the report *We the Children* has already warned, "there is no issue more vital to humanity and its future than the survival and full development of our children."[134] Conducted through official stories of protection and salvation, these interventions in child-soldiers (re)declare the very same boundaries that produce the category of the child-soldier as an exception to the norm of the world-child. In so doing, they are instrumental in (re)producing and propagating a particular version of the world, which, despite claiming to be universal, is actually an array of multiple inclusions and exclusions.

CHAPTER FOUR

(Re)Drawing Boundaries and Restoring International Order

The United Nations Intervenes to Protect Child-Soldiers

"The picture that you see is horrific. . . . These are kids, you know."[1] These were the words of a program officer of the UN Office of SRSG for CAAC when I asked him about the UN's high investments in tackling the child-soldier phenomenon. Since 1999, when the UN Security Council adopted the first thematic resolution on children and armed conflict,[2] twelve resolutions specifically addressing the same issue have been adopted, the latest one being UN Security Council Resolution 2427, which was passed in July 2018. By placing child-soldiers on its agenda, the Security Council is sending out an important message: children's participation in wars affects international peace and security or has the potential to do so. According to the British diplomat, there is no choice in the matter: "Especially on the child soldiers issue, you militarize the people who will run your country in the future. You're never going to find security, because your children don't know how to do anything but fight[. . . .] And if you're killing all your children, you'll also have no one to rule your country once the conflict is over."[3] A diplomat from Liechtenstein, who at the time of the interview was one of the members of the Group of Friends on Children and Armed Conflict at the UN General Assembly,[4] reinforced the same message: "When children are involved in armed conflict, you destroy the very basis of the social fabric of the society and kind of ruin generations. And like this you have the total breakdown of civilization and societies. And, of course, it's a threat to peace and security."[5]

Faced with these statements, the object of the protection—or salvation—contained in the UN Security Council resolutions may not be the child-soldiers themselves, but rather the promise of a progressive and ordered future not necessarily for these children in particular, but for the world. The potential scenario depicted by the interviewees is horrific, because the children are caught up in negative cycles of violence, and these very children, who know nothing but fighting and killing, may end up running their countries in the future. The adviser of the Child Protection Office at the UN Department for Peacekeeping Operations sums up their position in the following terms:

The entry point in the Security Council agenda was basically the children with guns who were mobilized to use violence and to destabilize some countries. The number of children being used was stunning. Armed groups were exploiting the most vulnerable as the cheapest form of renewable soldiers. In the immediate time children were being used, but there were also the long-term effects. It's really a loss of the future. If these children are mobilized, lose their prospect of education because they're fighting in war, what are their prospects in the future?[6]

Rather than an epistemological claim, the logic of this discourse that (re)produces the child-soldier as an international emergency is based on an ontological one, namely, that as child-soldiers are pathological in relation to what counts as the norm of the world-child, they pose a threat to international peace and security. Furthermore, when child-soldiers are framed as noncivilized or pathological becomings, this opens the way for them to be articulated as exceptions, thereby confirming the need for urgent interventions in the name of securing (not changing) the international order. Little time is given over to critical reflection on how to deal with emergencies: the problem has to be solved, and it has to be solved straight away. In the name of "the best interests of the child," a myriad of interventions has populated the international security and human rights agendas since the publication of the Machel Report in 1996. In 1998, the UN Security Council held its first Open Debate on Children and Armed Conflict. In his address, Olara Otunnu, the first special representative of the UN Office of SRSG for CAAC, proposed areas of engagement for the Security Council to move toward "prevention, protection and recovery."[7] In order to recover both the child and international security, interventions have been authorized through discourses of protection and development—on behalf of not only children but also the world. Such interventions have dismissed any idea that child-soldiers' past (dangerous) experiences could be anything but toxic, never a resource they could potentially draw on.

When these potentially dangerous children are normalized, the (docile) world-child is correspondingly (re)produced, instabilities are kept under control, and the promise of a progressive future for the world is renewed once again. At the end of the day, children's bodies and minds are supervised—or secured—internationally through the UN interventions so that a particular version of the world can be rescued. In face of its "grave concern at the harmful and widespread impact of armed conflict on children and the long-term consequences this has for durable peace, security and development," the Security Council "strongly condemns the targeting of children in situations of armed conflict, including [. . .] recruitment and use of children in armed conflict in violation of international law" and "calls on all parties concerned to put an end to such practices."[8]

In this chapter, some key international interventions in the sphere of child-soldiers will be analyzed, such as the thematic UN Security Council Resolutions and mandates, the UN Release and Reintegration programs, and the UN campaign "Children, Not Soldiers." In particular, this chapter explores how these practices—in their bid to save child-soldiers or to bring them back into the (civilized) world—have systematically overlooked the complex processes of exclusion that have enabled the emergence of official narratives of inclusion, marked by a discourse of care, protection, empowerment, and participation, in which the world-child is held up and (re)produced as a norm. In this sense, instead of the increasingly prevalent assumption that the world is becoming a universalizing space with a widespread sense of global continuity and unity, what emerges from this analysis is still a world of constitutive exceptions that shape, enable, and delimit what is possible in modern political spheres. Specifically, these interventions (re)produce the very same boundaries that frame and articulate the discourse of the child-soldier as an emergency, and in doing so prove the necessity for all "normal" children to live as they are supposed to live and for all those who deal with children to educate, protect, care for, and develop them as they should. These distinctions and borders become manifest in every instance of control and protection, in every child development action, in every practice designed to curb the use and recruitment of child-soldiers.

The two images of the child-soldier explored in the previous chapter—the hapless victim and the dangerous monster—make it possible to think about the international actions under analysis here as protection and development practices with two different foci or targets of intervention: the child-soldier per se and the recruiter, which could be either the state or irregular armed groups. Regardless of the kind of intervention, the main goal is made crystal clear by a program officer of the UN Office of SRSG for Children and Armed Conflict: "If you don't get rid of kids with guns, you're not going to have a peaceful transition."[9] His colleague in the same office concludes: "the child-soldier is not only a humanitarian issue, it's not only a human rights issue, it's a peace and security one."[10] At the core of both accounts of the problem of child-soldiers—as victims or monsters—is the notion of vicious or negative cycles of violence, whereby abnormal individual development portends and fosters the abnormal development of the world. Within this formulation, international interventions are the only mechanism through which child-soldiers, both as victims and as potential threats, can be deterred from suffering or committing violence again.

One example of this approach is the UN Release and Reintegration program, which invests in child-soldiers' transition and reintegration into civilian life by aiming to restore them to a "normal" course of development. Risks associated with deviation can be kept under control, and former child-soldiers can become "redeemed heroes." The Monitoring and Reporting Mechanism (MRM) on

Grave Violations Against Children in Situations of Armed Conflict, the "Children, Not Soldiers" campaign, and the ICC trials against armed groups members (to name but a few) are all initiatives designed to punish those who exploit children and prevent child recruitment. Notions of normality and deviation are extrapolated from these interventions in their aim to "save" child-soldiers, setting exceptions or boundaries that (re)produce a presence to be constantly enacted—the "normal" state of being for a child, a citizen, and a nation-state— and an absence to be constantly resisted. This raises some questions: In whose best interest are these international interventions carried out? The interests of the child? If so, what child? The interests of the world? If so, what world?

RESCUING THE WORLD, PROTECTING CHILD-SOLDIERS

At the first Open Debate on Children and Armed Conflict, held at the UN Security Council in 1998, Otunnu called on the council to invest in concrete initiatives to prevent the use of child-soldiers: "Words on paper cannot save children in peril." He then asked the council to "lead the way by sending forth a clear message that the targeting, use and abuse of children are simply unacceptable."[11] In the following year, Security Council Resolution 1261 was adopted, formally placing the issue of children affected by war on the council's agenda: "Expresses its grave concern at the harmful and widespread impact of armed conflict on children and the long-term *consequences* this has for *durable peace, security and development*."[12] It also identified and condemned "six grave violations" that most affected children in times of war, including not only the recruitment and use of children by armed groups but also killing and maiming, sexual violence, abduction and forced displacement, and attacks on objects protected under international law, including places that usually have a significant presence of children, such as schools and hospitals. The legal basis for these violations lies in applicable international law, which in turn encompasses international humanitarian law, international human rights law, and international criminal law. Two years later, in 2000, the second resolution on children and armed conflict, Resolution 1314, reaffirmed that the deliberate targeting of children constituted a threat to peace and security.[13]

A year later, in 2001, a much more powerful message was imparted to the UN member states through Security Council Resolution 1379, which requested "the Secretary-General to attach to his report a *list of parties to armed conflict that recruit or use children* in violation of the international obligations applicable to them, in situations that are on the Security Council's agenda or that may be brought to the attention of the Security Council by the Secretary-General, in accordance with Article 99 of the Charter of the United Nations, which in his opinion may *threaten the maintenance of international peace and security*."[14]

This list has come to be known as the "list of shame." Subsequent resolutions added four additional triggers for listing based on the six grave violations: sexual violence, killing and maiming, attacks on schools and hospitals, and finally the abduction of children.[15] Specifically, as established by the Secretary-General's Annual Report on Children and Armed Conflict, for a party to conflict to be listed for killing and maiming or rape and sexual violence, there must be sufficient information to demonstrate a "pattern," which implies a "methodical plan," "a system," and "a collectivity of victims."[16] Regarding attacks on schools and hospitals, there must be sufficient information to demonstrate a recurrence of violations (multiple violations). Moreover, this includes "direct attacks against [schools or hospitals] as well as indiscriminate attacks, resulting in damage to or destruction of these facilities or which have the effect of impeding the ability of a school or hospital to function and/or placing children at risk, and acts of looting of these protected facilities."[17] Ultimately, the list establishes and publicizes those states that do not conform to the models and standards for how they must behave.

The effectiveness of this mechanism lies precisely in its name: it is shameful to be included in the Security Council agenda. Or, as the British diplomat puts it, "if you're on the Security Council agenda, you're considered kind of a mess by the international community, so if you're a government and you respect yourself, you don't want to be on that list. There's an international demand for not recruiting children."[18] Similarly, the diplomat from Liechtenstein adds: "The listing of armed parties is an extremely successful thing. People don't want to be there. Even if you're a rebel group and know that you're listed, there is pressure to engage with the UN to be delisted."[19] These comments tend to suggest that the list of shame works by drawing a dividing line between the deviant states and parties to conflict that have not achieved a civilized status yet and the "normal" states that conform to basic standards of rights, in particular the respect and protection of child's rights. In this regard, the list can also be read as differentiating wars that are legitimate, where such violations are not committed, from wars that are illegitimate, or new wars, the primary symbol (and one of the most barbarous symbols) of which is the use of child-soldiers. The pressure to be removed from those annexes and gain access back into the (modern) world is thus very high. The delisting process was established in 2004 through Resolution 1539, in which the Security Council expressed "deep concern of the continued recruitment and use of children by parties mentioned in the Secretary-General's report in situations of armed conflict which are on its agenda." It then called on the listed parties to prepare, within three months, "concrete time-bound action plans to halt recruitment and use of children in violation of the international obligations applicable to them."[20] These action plans should lay out the concrete actions a party must take to end and prevent violations against children, such as issuing a military order to stop and prevent child recruitment, providing regular and unimpeded access to military camps and bases for child protection actors, developing release and reintegration programs for children, strengthening birth registration systems and national campaigns to raise awareness and prevent the recruitment of children, and prosecuting those violating the rights of children. Upon UN verification, a party to conflict is eligible for delisting when all activities have been successfully implemented. By the time of writing, twenty-nine Action Plans had been signed by twenty-eight listed parties to conflict, including eleven government forces and seventeen nonstate armed groups. Twelve of these parties had been delisted following the complete fulfillment of their commitments.

Also, in Resolution 1539 (2004), the Security Council expressed for the first time its intention to consider imposing targeted and graduated measures (sanctions) against parties and individuals if they fail to prepare an action plan or fail to meet the commitments in their action plans. These sanctions may include arms embargoes, asset freezes, travel bans, and financial or diplomatic restrictions. This commitment was reaffirmed in resolutions 1612 (2005) and 1882 (2009).[21] In tandem with these measures and with international efforts to end child recruitment, UN Security Council Resolution 1539 also called on the secretary-general to prepare a plan for a systematic and comprehensive reporting mechanism.[22] In response to that, the secretary-general's fifth report included an action plan for the establishment of a mechanism to monitor the six grave violations of children's rights in situations of armed conflict: (1) killing or maiming of children; (2) recruitment or use of child-soldiers; (3) attacks against schools or hospitals; (4) rape or other grave sexual violence against children; (5) abduction of children; and (6) denial of humanitarian access for children, the last of these being the only violation that is not a trigger for listing.[23]

Five months after this particular secretary-general's report was delivered to the Security Council and to the General Assembly, the Security Council adopted Resolution 1612 (2005), which called for the immediate implementation of the Monitoring and Reporting Mechanism (MRM) for situations that lead to state or nonstate parties being included in the list of shame.[24] The purpose of the MRM is to provide for the systematic gathering of information on the six grave violations committed against children in armed conflict. MRM information is collected by many actors on the ground, such as UN staff (especially child protection advisers and human rights staff) and national and international NGOs. It is then verified and compiled in a confidential database and analyzed by the Country Task Forces on Monitoring and Reporting, which are cochaired by the UNICEF representative and the highest UN representative in the country where the MRM is implemented. Then this information is included in the annual Report of the Secretary-General on Children and Armed Conflict and

country-specific reports, which in turn promote actions by the Security Council, governments, and other actors. The MRM also operates as a mechanism for
advocacy, for implementing programmatic measures directly linked to what has
been monitored and reported on the ground, and for prevention: "The prevention power of the MRM is that the threat to be listed would prevent countries
from taking actions that would result in them being on the list, which is a place
no country wants to be."[25]

The adoption of Resolution 1612 marks the transition to what has been
termed "the era of application." As Otunnu said in a press statement published
on the day of the UN Security Council vote, "for the first time, the UN is establishing a formal, structured and detailed compliance regime of this kind [. . .].
This is a turning point of great consequence."[26] More specifically, a UNICEF
adviser at the Child Protection in Emergencies unit celebrated the MRM apparatus for being a significant change, since it "made children know that they
can be helped as well and it is not only the will of one person but of the entire
international community."[27] In addition to the implementation of the MRM,
Resolution 1612 is also internationally recognized as a watershed in the process
of addressing the phenomenon of child-soldiering because it establishes a sub-
sidiary body, the Working Group on Children and Armed Conflict. This group
is responsible for reviewing parties' development and implementation of their
action plans. Based on MRM information, the group also recommends actions
to the Security Council and makes requests to other bodies within the UN system to support the resolution's implementation. These two mechanisms—MRM
and the Working Group—are still highly celebrated among the members of the
UN system engaged in tackling the issue of child-soldiers. UNICEF representatives, for example, emphasize that the message these two tools give is that "if
we want peace and security, we need to deal with grave violations committed
against children in armed conflicts."[28] As a UNICEF adviser at the Child Protection in Emergencies unit says, "this [MRM] is brilliant because the Security
Council knows what is going on in the country way down to the community
level. I mean, there aren't many other thematics that you can think of where
information can go so fast."[29] However, in an interview, the director of an NGO
that works on the issue of children and armed conflict cast the information-
gathering process into question, as the percentage of violations committed
against children that appears in the official reports is usually lower than the
percentage actually seen on the ground.[30] This lack of precision in relation to
data, according to the NGO's director, makes it hard to develop "appropriate responses" to these violations against children affected by armed conflicts. Understanding why violations occur, for example, is essential when trying to address
them in the long term.[31] Nevertheless, the UN's answer to this apparent flaw is
always the same: regardless of the registered number of children who have been

gravely violated, the MRM's most important role is its capacity to identify that these crimes are indeed being committed, and thereby substantiating the listing of the parties to the conflicts in question.[32] This conversation reinforces the questions posed earlier in this chapter: Who or what is the target of these international interventions"? Every child whose rights have been violated? The idea of a "normal" childhood in which certain life experiences are not acceptable? Or the (uncivilized) parties, which must be kept outside the (civilized) world?

Branded as perpetrators, listed parties are temporarily excluded from the group of modern states; that is, states that are deemed capable of regulating and protecting their own territories and populations in such a way as to avoid instability and risks. In other words, in the name of securing the international political order, these parties are labeled as shameful (or "kind of a mess"), the exception to the norm of the modern state is (re)declared, noncivilized parties, including state governments, take (urgent) steps to be delisted, and ultimately modern categories of the child and the nation-state are repeatedly enacted while all deviations are consistently challenged. As a result, a particular version of the child and a particular version of the world may be saved, but not just any child or any world.

In a similar vein, the Special Court for Sierra Leone also aimed to punish the recruiter, who in this particular case was the former Liberian president Charles Taylor.[33] In April 2012, Trial Chamber judges convicted Taylor of war crimes and crimes against humanity, including conscripting or enlisting children into armed forces or groups and using them to participate actively in hostilities. He was sentenced to a fifty-year jail sentence. In September 2013, Appeals Chamber judges upheld both Taylor's conviction and his sentence. He is now serving his jail sentence in a British prison. The Report of the Special Representative of the Secretary-General for Children and Armed Conflict that celebrates ten years of the Machel Report highlights the importance of this trial: "This action against a former President sends a clear message that no individual is beyond the reach of justice for crimes against children."[34] From these different forms of intervention, it is possible to see how the discourse of emergency operates: the recruitment of child-soldiers is articulated as an unpredictable abnormality, a war crime, or a grave violation, which has considerable capacity to command international attention and mobilize resources because it inspires such an urgent need to restore security and peace.

Resolutions 1882 (2009) and 1998 (2011) both reinforced the international measures already adopted in earlier resolutions and added two new criteria for listing and delisting parties: first, parties who kill and maim children and who commit rape or sexual violence against children in armed conflict situations; second, in 2011, attacks against schools and hospitals or education and medical personnel. In 2012, Resolution 2068 reiterated the Security Council's readiness to adopt sanctions against persistent perpetrators of grave violations against children.[35] However, when it came to passing the resolution, it proved harder than for any previous resolution on children and armed conflict, attracting abstentions for the first time. As the diplomat from Liechtenstein puts it, passions were stirred: "There was a huge debate about why the Security Council was dealing with the issue of children and armed conflict. Some countries believe that the SRSG is stepping in the mandate by listing situations that are not on the agenda of the Council."[36] In a study of the subject, Ingvild Bode identified the composition of the Security Council Working Group as one of the main reasons why 2012 became the "annus horribilis for the CAAC agenda": its membership was made up of critics, a handful of disinterested or silent members, and almost no supportive states.[37] Additionally, some state and nonstate parties of three elected members—Pakistan, India, and Colombia—were either mentioned or listed in the special representative's 2012 report.[38]

Commenting on these challenges and the ever-increasing list of triggers for listing, a program officer of the UN Office of SRSG for Children and Armed Conflict asked the following question in our August 2012 interview: "How much will we be able to be protective of that? Will we have at some point to narrow the agenda again to child soldiers as children carrying weapons? Or will we be able to continue expanding it as much as we can in terms of protection?"[39] Instead of asking *which* child-soldier the International is able to protect, the question should be directed toward what violations are grave enough to be articulated as "international emergencies" that automatically trigger strong demands for intervention. Is the recruitment and use of children the only violation, or deviation, to be considered grave enough, or pathological enough, to jeopardize international stability and peace? If not, the list of violations may continue to grow, including other "deviations" from the world-child's childhood, such as forced labor, child detention, and the displacement of children, addressing them as things to be treated, resisted, or cured. Either way, international interventions are continuously at play: in their response to the problem of children engaged in war, the Security Council resolutions keep framing it as a deviation from the norm of the world-child, thereby reaffirming what is articulated as a "normal" child in a "normal" world, despite the existence of so many exceptions.

In March 2014, a decade after the adoption of Resolution 1349, which establishes the mechanism for listing parties to conflict for recruiting and using child-soldiers, the special representative jointly launched a campaign with UNICEF to end and prevent the recruitment and use of children by national security forces by 2016, titled "Children, Not Soldiers." The campaign received immediate support from member states, the UN, NGO partners, regional organizations, and the general public. The UN Security Council, through its Resolution 2143 (2014), welcomed "Children, Not Soldiers" and requested regular updates through the special representative's reporting.[40] At the time of the launch, the countries that were the focus the campaign were Afghanistan, Chad, the Democratic Republic of the Congo, Myanmar, Somalia, South Sudan, Sudan, and Yemen. Representatives from each of these states attended the launch event and pledged their full support in reaching the objectives of the campaign. In the words of a UNICEF senior adviser at the Child Protection in Emergencies Unit, who was at the launch event, it was "frankly not shocking, but surprising" to see all eight countries taking the microphone to welcome the campaign: "They said that welcoming the campaign was a way for them to advance their efforts to prevent child recruitment because no one wants to be listed. They want to be professional armies, they don't want children in their ranks."[41] At the time of writing, all the governments targeted in the campaign are engaged in an Action Plan process mandated by the Security Council. Chad and the Democratic Republic of Congo have put in place all the measures needed to end and prevent the recruitment of children in their armed forces and are no longer listed.

In the poster campaign, the insurmountable barrier between the child and war is presented as a given. The diversity of child-soldiers' war experiences is silenced when children, in this particular campaign, are articulated within the static framework of victimhood. "They" (children) ask "us" (viewers) to tell the world what is happening to them. However, what story can be told within such a framework? Is it just the story of children who are too vulnerable and too small to wear (adult size) military boots and a helmet? The contrast between the cartoon character of the child and real warfare, represented by the pair of boots and the helmet, (re)produces the paradox of the child dressed in pieces of military clothing not for fun or play, but in readiness for actual combat. Deviant child-soldiers are made visible only as "the threatening exteriority of the not yet, not quite human" in the form of hapless victims who are in need of help not only from nation-states, which must learn how to behave according to the Security Council's action plans, and international organizations, but also from "us."[42]

In the year after the campaign launch, the Security Council, faced with mass abductions of hundreds of children by Boko Haram in Nigeria and the actions of other parties to conflict in the Middle East and Africa, adopted Resolution 2225 (2015), again expanding on the triggers for listing by including the abduction of children in situations of armed conflict.[43] While the expansion of the triggers for listing enables the MRM to bring to the forefront some accurate accounts of children's experiences in conflict zones dominated by the ravages of war, it still focuses solely on children's victimhood and vulnerability. In fact, each grave violation brings with it a set of nonproblematized ideals about childhood, conflict, and the role of the international community to mediate

Figure 2. Poster available at the official UN Office of SRSG for Children and Armed Conflict website. United Nations/Graphic Design Unit.

the two.[44] Based on the six grave violations, the only possible narrative about children is their being caught up in negative cycles of violence, which they are unable to shape, withstand, or mitigate. However, child-soldiers' lived realities point toward the impossibility of the modern claims that children should be kept from engaging in political violence.[45]

Referring specifically to the UN reports on children affected by the war in Afghanistan, Lee-Koo states that they can only offer a "one-dimensional, extreme and unfettered view of the experiences of children in conflict zones."[46] Within this story, very limited space is left for thinking about and exploring the nuances of children's agency in conflict. However, analyzing children's experiences in the war in Afghanistan and in other armed conflicts—providing care for their family and community members, running households, providing income for their family, joining armed forces, resisting political oppression, and building networks with other children across conflict fault lines—can offer a more robust and nuanced understanding not only of how children survive in conflicts but also of their capacities and competencies to help rebuild their own societies.[47]

To date, in order to fulfill its main goal of promoting international peace and security, the UN Security Council has adopted twelve thematic resolutions over a period of almost twenty years. In July 2018, Resolution 2427 was unanimously adopted with the goal of further crystalizing the protection of children in armed conflicts, emphasizing that children associated with armed forces accused of committing crimes during wars should be treated primarily as victims. In this regard, the resolution "urges Member States to consider *non-judicial measures as alternatives to prosecution and detention* that focus on the rehabilitation and reintegration for children formerly associated with armed forces and armed groups taking into account that *deprivation of liberty of children should be used only as a measure of last resort and for the shortest appropriate period of time*."[48] Following the same line as the previous CAAC resolutions, this latest one is also a product of three imperatives: "international legal responsibilities to uphold children's right to be free from violence, moral obligations to protect children from violence, and—importantly—instrumentalist claims that children's protection is a tool in the maintenance of peace and security."[49]

As the British diplomat comments, "we braided the normative framework in a sense that child-soldiers are an international peace and security issue. And it's a matter of concern of the whole community and not only a matter of concern of state governments. So we can and we will come in. In this way, I think it's a very powerful statement."[50] A circular movement can be seen in the UN Children and Armed Conflict agenda: by aiming to immediately resolve the problem of child-soldiering, these international interventions (re)produce the very same boundaries between the norm of the world-child and the deviant child, by which the child-soldier is then framed as an international emergency for which urgent action is an imperative. As R. B. J. Walker puts it in his discussion on the modern International, "we have not all come inside."[51] There are always the exceptions—the nonmoderns, the noncivilized, the failed states, the child-soldiers—which must be excluded so as to permit the modern self to know itself. The child-soldier, thus, is not only a threat to the child but a threat that defines the child. By saving the world and safeguarding the promise of a progressive future, the norm of the world-child is permanently (re)produced, while many children are consistently excluded or silenced through the different "rescue mechanisms."

In the next section, I explore in more depth one of the main rescue mechanisms devoted to child-soldiers: the UN Release and Reintegration program. As the Executive Director of UNICEF, Anthony Lake, stated in an official meeting in 2010, "If we do not succeed in reintegrating these children into their communities and supporting them once they return, we cannot hope to break the cycle of violence."[52] An analysis of the components of this program shows how it operates as a "site" for declaring and (re)producing exceptions to the norm of the world-child. In this sense, the Release and Reintegration programs do not offer a way for the child-soldier to transit from one way of being a child to other multiple forms of experiencing childhood. Rather, what happens is an intensification, augmentation, and general proliferation of practices that (re)produce the boundaries between the single "normal" child and the many deviant others.

RESCUING CHILD-SOLDIERS, PROTECTING THE WORLD

In response to new commitments from every continent to endorse the Paris Principles to end the use of child-soldiers, Anthony Lake has declared: "The Paris Principles reaffirm our collective commitment to protect the most fundamental right of a child: To *be* a child."[53] Surely, however, it is fair to wonder what is meant by the right to "be a child," which seems to be deemed so natural that it does not call for any further qualification or clarification. Regardless of its conception, the idea of the child-soldier as a deviation is undisputed. The goal of reintegrating child-soldiers into civilian life is intended to return lost childhoods through a "machine" that puts child-soldiers in one end and produces a particular model of the child and its childhood at the other.[54] From monsters or hapless victims, they become redeemed heroes, who, after leaving their armed group and receiving training at an international rehabilitation center, are then capable of choosing what they want to be and doing something forward-looking or, to put it simply, are capable of being a "normal" child. Within this formulation, the "ideal trajectory in the life course of a child-soldier" would be "normal village life, abduction, 'in the bush' (fighting), demobilization, rehabilitation, family tracing and reunification, reintegration (and therefore back where he started)."[55] The focus of this section turns precisely to the complexities of this desirable process of return to a supposedly normal life before abduction, which operates as a productive site in which the norm of both the child and childhood are the locus for a particular political struggle, namely, the articulation of a specific version of the world and its claim for progress. In this sense, it is actually the idea that "children are our future," which may be made less rosy by the experiences of child-soldiers, that is the focus of international "salvation."

The first UN resolution on the issue of children affected by armed conflict (s/RES/1261) already "urges States and the United Nations system to facilitate the disarmament, demobilization, rehabilitation and reintegration of children used as soldiers in violation of international law."[56] In the same year, Sierra Leone made explicit provisions to ensure the inclusion of child-soldiers within the Disarmament, Demobilization and Reintegration (DDR) process initially developed for adult soldiers, which has come to be known as the first child DDR. According to the Lomé Peace Accord, "the Government shall accord particular attention to the issue of child soldiers. It shall accordingly mobilize resources, both within the country and from the international Community, and especially through the Office of the UN Special Representative for Children and Armed Conflict, UNICEF and other agencies, to address the special needs of these children in the existing disarmament, demobilization and reintegration process."[57]

The only prerequisite for being included in Sierra Leone's DDR program was that the child should have engaged in war as a combatant. Denov explains that the eligibility criteria for proving child combatant status required that the child be between the ages of seven and eighteen, had learned to cock and load a weapon, had been trained in an armed group, and had spent at least six months in an armed group.[58] These criteria, however, go against the trend in child rights to expand the concept of child-soldier in order to protect not only child combatants but also children who participate in hostilities in other roles. The Sierra Leone DDR experience and others, which were basically an adaption of the DDR model developed for adult soldiers, such as in Liberia, Burundi, and Angola, prompted UNICEF to start a review process for such programs, which culminated in the adoption of the Paris Principles.[59]

The change was made explicit in the program name by eliminating the first two Ds, which were considered inappropriate for addressing the issue of children engaged in armed conflict situations. Instead of disarmament, demobilization, and reintegration, the program specifically for child-soldiers must be called "Release and Reintegration." A UNICEF senior adviser at the Child Protection in Emergencies Unit, who at the time of the interview was also cochairing the Paris Principles Steering Group with the NGO Save the Children, explained the rationale behind the name change.[60] First, to be eligible for a DDR program, a child simply has to show up. No proof of membership or weapon is required, since some of them will not have taken part directly in combat. Then, she explained, demobilization is a concept that does not make sense for children, because they are not *formally* mobilized to participate in war as adult soldiers are. "Children have actually been either mistakenly or deliberately or forcibly taken, because they [armed groups] didn't know the children's age or they just didn't care."[61] Within this formulation, no account is taken for autonomous decisions taken by children. Unlike the (legitimate) adult soldier, who may choose to be a combatant and be decorated for valor and bravery, child-soldiers are primarily victims who are forced to join armed groups. As the program officer of the UN SRSG Office for Children and Armed Conflict has summarized, child-soldiers do not even wear a full uniform, just pieces.[62] The UNICEF representative understands child-soldiers' participation in Release and Reintegration programs as their right: "children are entitled to be released and to receive the reintegration package."[63] Article 39 of the CRC formalizes this particular right: "States Parties shall take all appropriate measures to promote physical and psychological recovery and social reintegration of a *child victim* of: any form of neglect, exploitation, or abuse; torture or any other form of cruel, inhuman or degrading treatment or punishment; or armed conflicts. Such recovery and reintegration shall take place in an environment which fosters the health, self-respect and dignity of the child."[64] For the CRC, children are also innocent victims.

Peace, development, and protection. This is the triad of priorities—not necessarily in this particular order—advanced by the United Nations Release and Reintegration programs for child-soldiers around the world. Michael Wessells, former cochair of the Inter-Agency Standard Committee (IASC) Task Force on Mental Health and Psychosocial Support in Emergency Settings, makes a connection between these three points when justifying the importance of former child-soldiers' successful transition into civilian life to break cycles of violence and build peace. In his words, "The urgent link between reintegration and development is clear: war shatters economies, robs children of education and skills they need to become effective civilians, and creates instability that undermines economic well-being. Reintegration also connects intimately with protection. Children who transition successfully into civilian life are less likely to continue the life of the gun, with its inherent dangers."[65]

From this particular statement, child-soldiers go from one type of space to another: *there*, "the life of the gun," where children, robbed of their right to school education, are capable only of imperfectly perceiving the world around them, and *here*, after the process of reintegration, where they learn the skills they need to operate within the codes of prescribed social behavior, eliminating any inherent dangers they may bear in virtue of their life experiences in war. The assumption, as the anthropologist Susan Shepler argues, is of a "clear break, yet in many ways, in practice, the break is not that clear."[66] When the UN program sets a certain destination to be reached (i.e., the child-soldier's transformation into the model of the civilian world-child), the various and obscure courses children take during the process of Release and Reintegration are silenced or articulated as unacceptable. In this regard, as Wessells argues, reintegration could be seen as being intimately connected to international protection and development practices.[67] Their focus, though, is not necessarily on children engaged in war, but a particular construct of the child and of the world, whose limits are (re)drawn with such elegance and such violence.

The Release and Reintegration process starts with UNICEF trying to negotiate the release of children from armed forces and groups. As the Paris Principles state, "Children should be rapidly separated from adult fighters and handed over to an appropriate, mandated and independent civilian process."[68] Once released, former child-soldiers are accommodated in "transitory centers," which are understood as an efficient manner for separating child-soldiers from military authority and preventing them from being re-recruited.[69] While children are in these centers, which are usually run by UNICEF together with an NGO partner, their families are traced so their reunification can happen as soon as possible.

Ideally, according to a UNICEF senior adviser, children should not stay longer than three months in these centers.[70] There, children first go through a screening process, in which UNICEF representatives ask their age, ask them about their war experiences, and try to identify what kind of psychosocial, mental health, and social needs they might have. In order to prepare these children for reintegration into civilian life and a return to family life, psychosocial support activities begin immediately at this stage. This process of "going back" to their lives before they were recruited can be very hard "for kids who have gone through so much and then all of a sudden they have to try to be normal in their family and in their community."[71] Similarly, Wessells argues, "The children need to learn to let go their soldier identities and envision their future as civilians[. . . .] A high priority is to express pent-up feelings and release the energy associated with their war experiences."[72] This process can be accomplished, for example, through "cultural activities, spiritual initiatives, sports, individual guidance, and peer-group activities."[73] Also, in the centers, children have access to catch-up classes in order to "re-stimulate them in going back to school."[74] What is at stake here is the development of a new, "normal" identity for the former child-soldiers, one that is associated with very specific childhood spaces far from the context of war: family, community, and school. In this case, the idea of "new" does not mean an opportunity to build something different, but a return to a supposedly "normal" and desirable childish *past* life that may never even have existed. Within this formulation, if child-soldiers manage to "release the energy associated with their war experiences" and go back to where they started as supposedly "natural children," then their childhood may be recovered. Likewise, reintegration is presented as a natural obligation of their families, and the fact that child-soldiers have often committed acts of violence against their own family members is simply not considered.[75]

Within this set formula of activities, transitory care centers turn out to be a great opportunity to discuss with children what they want to do when they return to civilian life so they can start learning the basic skills. The importance of learning not only professional skills but also how to behave as a child civilian is highlighted by the child protection consultant Beth Verhey, given that in war the children "have learned to rely on aggression to meet needs and solve problems. In some cases, child soldiers have stolen material goods from centers or returned to the military to obtain drugs or seek sexual partners."[76] Without wishing to diminish in any way or to call into question how challenging it must be to deal with children in these centers, I would like to shed light on how these constructs about the process of release from armed groups and reintegration into civilian lives must themselves involve a rupture from an exclusively negative military past life that must be overcome to a life where (good and healthy) dreams may come true. The possibility of *learning* how to be a child through *international instruction* is a crucial step. In this regard, the UNICEF senior adviser highlights the process of questioning children not only about "their war experiences, but also about their aspirations and their hopes. They should be able to choose from the kinds of training activities[. . . .] We can't give them the world, but we can try to make their next step as positive as possible."[77] In a similar vein, another UNICEF representative at the Child Protection unit explains how children are consulted about their needs and expectations. However, "if we see that the things they want are wrong, we try to show them, through social workers, the consequences of what they want and work with them."[78] In the same vein, when I asked the UNICEF senior adviser about children who preferred to remain part of the armed group, she told me about a Congolese boy who at the time was sixteen years old: "I remember he clearly liked the power of being part of this group. He had no interest in leaving. He was being quite aggressive even and not cooperative. But the local staff that worked in this area had to be very skilled, remaining calm, knowing what to say to children and addressing their needs, their kinds of concerns, but also doing it in a positive way."[79] The discourse, she explains, is as follows: "This [the army] is not the place for you right now, but if you decide when you're eighteen that you want to join the army, this choice is going to be open to you. And in the meantime there are many other things to be exposed to."[80] Or, in a more straightforward way, the British diplomat affirms "that's where the boundaries come in. We don't give the right to choose to fight to children under eighteen."[81]

The "other things" available to these former child-soldiers do not, for instance, include the possibility of girl soldiers choosing to stay with their "bush husbands" with whom they have children. According to Afua Twum-Danso, although some girls were coerced into remaining with their commanders, others formed strong bonds and claimed to be in love with them.[82] Another example is given by the UNICEF senior adviser regarding her experience in Nepal and how difficult it was to convince girls to break away from the Maoist group: "The girls had more power and they were perceived more equally when they were with the Maoists than they would be when they returned home to their communities, because Nepali society is very traditional in the rural areas and girls are second-class citizens. These girls, some of them, were like commanding men. They were leading companies of men. They were very, very unhappy to be having to disassociate themselves, and no doubt it was a difficult job for us."[83] Finally, the harrowing words of a fourteen-year-old boy from the DRC who became a child-soldier at the age of eleven challenge many (stable) ideas, including the one that their military past is meaningless and must be forgotten for them to move toward a progressive future as a civilian child: "When I was in the militia I was used to being alone and being independent. It's hard to go back living with parents after that. I didn't like living with my parents. I'm a child, yes, in age, and in size I'm still small, but *I know so many things about the world that nobody can joke with me or tell me what to do*. I'm young in age and you can see that I'm small in size, but *I'm not just a child*. I know so much. *Nobody can play with my life*. I always go off on my own and survive. I don't care."[84]

However, these experiences are less explored while stories of child-soldiers as innocent, blameless, unknowing victims are (re)produced internationally. Even the UNICEF senior adviser, who had had the opportunity to meet many children with different life experiences, says: "I never really accept the true voluntariness of those choices, because children in those circumstances often have no choice. I mean, is it really voluntary when you have no food at home, there's no money to go to school, or you've just watched your whole village get attacked by this rebel group and family members have been killed and raped? I mean it's not really voluntariness under those circumstances."[85] This statement resonates within the bounded conception concerning not only childhood but also specific ideas about the child and the child-soldier, which exclude the possibility of holding the child accountable and responsible for their own actions.

Whether as victims or as monsters, these diametrically opposed constructs of child-soldiers depoliticize children and consistently deny their agency and their particular experiences and perspectives. Even when these children are supposedly *free* to present their expectations and desires in relation to their (new) civilian lives, some options may not be internationally accepted because, in a nutshell, they are "wrong": "The child will say that there is nothing to go back to, this is their family, they want to stay, the commanders are taking better care of him. And it's very challenging, but we cannot accept it as a reason for them to stay."[86] While the denial of children's agency and capacity to take autonomous decisions may be motivated by high ideals to protect children against exploitation or manipulation, it risks opening the door to new problems in children's lives and also reveals, as Karl Hanson argues, some of the weaknesses in the concept of agency itself, which, based on a presumed shape and content, covers issues about what is considered "right" or "wrong" in relation to children.[87] In this relationship between former child-soldiers and UNICEF representatives, children's diversity and agency are indeed permitted, but within a single format, which is framed or bounded by the contours of a "normal" or *world*-childhood. In fact, what constitutes difference between children is emptied out of any historical or political content. Ultimately, differences that go beyond or defy the limits of childhood "diversity" are homogenized so that relations between different children are represented not as asymmetrical and hierarchical, but as relations between separate but nevertheless equal subjects of the *same type*, with the *same childhood*, who inhabit the *same humanity*. In other words, while each child may be unique, their differences are all of the same kind, which fit within the limits of a particular world.

A special report published by *Newsweek* in August 1995 titled "Boy Soldiers" purported to tell the story about child-soldiers from Liberia but actually stripped their war experiences of any real substance by subsuming them all in an essentially negative process that turned them into "willing, ruthless warriors."[88] At the end of the report, the journalist asked: "Robbed of a normal childhood, what will the child soldiers become?" Then, to exemplify—and support—his concern, he described the daily life of one of the former boy soldiers he met: "He still eats alone, keeps to himself and lives in terror that one of the other boys from a rival Liberian militia will kill him. And he's without remorse. 'I liked the sound of the gun,' he says." Child-soldiers exemplified by this particular account are not only victims but traumatized victims, whose war experiences cause dysfunction and social instability. Long-term reintegration is, then, the only route through which children can build a new identity, one that renounces violence and embraces skills necessary for civilian life, such as decision making, coping mechanisms, and peaceful means of resolving conflict.[89] Psychosocial support is one of the three fundamental pillars of successful reintegration into civilian life, according to the Paris Principles, together with two other components: family reunification and opportunities for education and livelihood.[90]

From the understanding of protection as *tutore* ("to look after"), the reintegration process as a form of protection both delimits spaces where the protected former child-soldier must be placed, such as in school and in the family sphere, and also organizes and monitors children's experiences in the present, while preparing—or directing—them toward their future as productive adults.[91] However, unlike the progressive time of the world-child, who must enjoy a linear course of development toward adulthood, the time of (deviant) child-soldiers is one of *redemption* and does not follow a single direction pointing toward the future. In fact, in order to be able to move forward and become a (normal) adult in the future, the child-soldier must go back to the (idealized) childish past before he or she was diverted into participation in war. This return is only possible through a reintegration process, in which the child-soldier may acquire the status of *former* child-soldier. The lost childhood is recovered, and the child can be prepared for (a particular version of) the future by returning to his or her "normal" process of development. Once victims or monsters, former child-soldiers are *redeemed* heroes as they continuously overcome all their past traumatic events. As Fionna Klasen et al. conclude from their research about former Ugandan child-soldiers, "One of the most impressive phenomena of child development is the ability of many children to develop into healthy, well-adapted adults despite adversity and trauma."[92]

According to the Paris Principles,[93] the process of reintegrating former child-soldiers into civilian life is a long-term process that requires at least three years and includes the following five components:

1. Family reunification.
2. Educational opportunities so they can "gain the skills and knowledge they missed out on when they were soldiering instead of attending school."[94] Indeed, a senior adviser at UNICEF highlights that "education is a top priority for boys and girls who have been released from the armed groups. Their desire for education trumps everything else, because they don't want to be left behind, they don't want to be rejected. For example, in Sierra Leone, children made education their number one recommendation to the Truth Commission. They wanted to be able to contribute to their society. They wanted to become their dream. They saw education as their opportunity for that."[95]
3. Psychosocial supports, which "help quiet their memories of the furies of war and construct civilian identities and roles."[96]
4. Training in vocational skills.
5. Community mobilization to receive former child-soldiers.

Specifically on this last point, another senior adviser at UNICEF explains that "communities need to protect their children as well, and helping communities understand how to do that and what the risks are, those are all the kinds of things that we try to promote."[97] In this setting, the protector (UNICEF) is understood as having the capacity to know children's needs and teach them better than their own communities.

At the end of the whole process, if it is successful, former child-soldiers will have learned how to be and behave in accordance with the norm of the world-child, which is not only a valuation that contains a judgment but also a prescription of a goal to be achieved. This particular model of childhood enacts the classification and hierarchization of the categories of the child and the deviant child-soldier, of the correction of pathologies, of the making of the "normal" child, and finally, of the (re)production of the very same norm of the world-child. Wessells illustrates this disciplinary process by emphasizing the importance of livelihood interventions, such as skills training: "Having an income enables them [child-soldiers] to enter and to succeed in *normal civilian roles* such as husband, wife, mother, and worker. To take on such roles is to become *functional* in civilian life and to be seen as a *responsible citizen* rather than a troublemaker or misfit."[98] With this, not only are the potential risks associated with child-soldiers as "little devils" put under control, but (and equally important) the norm of the responsible, working adult citizen is also (re)produced when the possibility of the children becoming adult troublemakers is ruled out. The British NGO War Child, in a report about the future of war and its impact on children titled "War: The Next Generation," puts this very idea in the following terms: "Lack of investment in education and livelihoods for children can destabilise societies in the future when they become adults."[99] Within this formulation, it is worth asking whether the report is really about the "next generation." If so, who inhabits this "next generation"? Or, as the Mental Health Foundation suggests, although we claim to be a child-centered society—in this particular case, focused on the "next generation"—there is scant evidence that we are: "In many ways we are a ruthlessly adult-centred society where children are defined almost exclusively in terms of their impact on adult lives."[100]

Child-soldiers' emotional scars, their sense of despair and helplessness, trigger contradictory reactions, drawing attention to a moral obligation to rescue children at risk, while at the same time raising alarms about the dangers posed by these children who have deviated from the normal course of development. Child-soldiers are seen as an international emergency, and their relationship with the world is always dubious and potentially volatile and must be controlled. In this regard, psychosocial interventions in child-soldiers, in particular, may be read as mechanisms for managing the risks inherent to the ambivalent meaning of the child or, as Pupavac has termed it, "therapeutic governance."[101] According to the Paris Principles, psychosocial support should be incorporated into the release process at the earliest stages and into all stages of reintegration in order to encourage and facilitate "children's active participation in developing responsive and sensitive activities and programmes."[102] The term "psychosocial" underlines the dynamic relationship between psychological consequences, such as changes in emotion, behavior, thoughts, memory, learning ability, perceptions, and understanding, and social consequences, such as altered relationships following death, separation, estrangement and other losses, family and community breakdown, damage to social values and customs, and the destruction of social facilities and services.[103] Under the psychosocial label, activities focus on restoring connections with families and communities, re-creating social networks, and providing children with greater capacity to deal with the challenges of reintegration. Actions ranging from trauma counseling to sports and games to develop life skills and coping mechanisms support initiatives that build resilience and self-esteem. Likewise, it is possible to help children develop and build their "strengths and resilience" and to reduce their vulnerability.[104] In addition to psychosocial interventions, clinical mental health interventions are made for former child-soldiers who continue to demonstrate mental health distress or impairment following front-line normalizing psychosocial activities. Such interventions are usually tailored to a child's individual trauma history and target specific psychopathologies through individual or small-group counseling designed with a particular therapeutic goal in mind.[105] According to the Guidelines on Mental Health and Psychosocial Support in Emergency Settings, developed by the IASC, it is best to take a holistic approach, so these two approaches are seen as complimentary, offering support that meets the needs of different groups of children and adolescents.[106]

Implicit in this process of "going back to a normal/lost childhood" is the association of children's (natural) resilience with the idea of the child as a *malleable* becoming in the process of turning into a "normal" adult. As a program officer of the UN Office of SRSG for CAAC says, "Children are very resourceful when it comes to just forgetting about something, they're very resilient. I think that is true for most of them, but it's never easy because you can see that they're broken inside anyways. They've gone through situations that are very difficult."[107] Thus, former child-soldiers are depicted as "traumatized," "psychologically scarred," or "emotionally damaged" beings, but also as passive objects in need of external help and guidance and equally as resilient becomings who are capable of overcoming their war experiences and doing the right thing. In this regard, Theresa Betancourt et al. highlight how important it is to recognize the role of protective factors that may mitigate the effects of potentially harmful experiences, such as the support of family, community, and peer groups, educational and livelihood programs, and traditional healing ceremonies, which "may all help former child-soldiers maintain moderate to high levels of functionality."[108]

Regardless of the IASC guidelines' recommendation of a holistic approach to dealing with former child-soldiers' experiences, scars, and demands, and regardless of the plurality of the stories they tell, such interventions still tend to address their military past as a single *event*, one traumatic moment, which ruptures or destabilizes the children's mental health and their "normal" course of development. To put it another way, in the translation of children's acts of re-sistance and suffering into symptoms of trauma, something of the meaning they intend to give to their lives and something of the humanitarians' potential un-derstanding of the situation is lost. For example, Neil Boothby, a former senior coordinator for the USAID administrator on children in adversity, emphasizes the traumatic state of former Mozambican boy-soldiers, which he sees as being related to the length of time the children spent with Renamo (the Mozambican National Resistance).[109] His study of thirty-nine male former child-soldiers over a period of sixteen years (from 1988 to 2003) found that they had all manifested at least one "post-traumatic shock symptom," such as recurrent thoughts or memories of traumatic events (100 percent of the boys), recurrent nightmares (52 percent), and inability to remember parts of the most hurtful events (61 per-cent).[110] The ones who "spent six months or less with Renamo (72 percent) ap-peared to emerge with their basic trust in human beings and social values more or less intact. Although all of the boys had been exposed to severe trauma and some had also participated in abuse and violence, members of this group de-scribed themselves as victims rather than members of Renamo."[111] In contrast, Boothby states that boys who had spent longer than six months with Renamo continued to display disobedient and uncooperative behavior during the first three months at the center. For example, "despite their ability to articulate the belief that violence was wrong, these boys continued to use aggression as a principal means of exerting control and social influence."[112] At the end, although a majority of the sample of former child-soldiers made significant progress in returning to civilian life, none were able to fully escape their violent pasts.

Within this particular study, child-soldiers' "psychological problems" after the release process were classified according to a diagnostic assessment tool called the Trauma Symptom Checklist for Children, which is widely used in clinical research.[113] In particular, because they are seen as part of an emergency, child-soldiers' experiences (both during and after conflict) are relocated from the social to the biomedical realm, thus suspending their individual and collec-tive times and divesting their behavior of any political significance. However, it is not just about biology, but also a matter of biography.[114] This silencing of their personal stories is even reinforced in the correlation Boothby draws be-tween children's disobedience or uncooperativeness and the length of time they spent with the armed group. Likewise, not only is children's participation in war (re)produced solely as a bad experience that diverts the child from being "socially accepted," but children's varied experiences in situations of war are left unheard. As Derek Summerfield notes, this is the "objectification of suffering as an entity apart."[115] Child-soldiers' experiences are translated into "meaning-less symptoms" to which technical solutions are supposedly applicable.[116] Here, the technical approach derives primarily from a "universalist" and "essentialist" position; universalist because the categories and assumptions that construct child-soldiers as pathological beings in need of care and therapy by an intervening subject are considered appropriate regardless of the context, and essentialist because of the idea that the core dysfunction of former child-soldiers will then take a similar course of development, with a uniform prognosis and a uniform response to treatment.[117]

Because children are resilient, former child-soldiers should not be seen as a "lost generation" or as "future barbarians." As Boothby argues, "once they are submitted to psychosocial interventions such as traditional cleansing ceremonies and trauma counseling, the majority of this group of former child-soldiers have become productive, capable and caring adults."[118] So within this setting, resilience means children's capacity to go back to where they were before they took part in war and to follow a "normal" course of development toward adulthood, in the hope that their varied experiences as soldiers—which tell different stories of oppression, participation, and resistance—will be erased or forgotten. Yet in what way can reintegration (or redemption) be regarded as successful when its success is predicated on a return to a supposedly positive childish past? And, more importantly, how does it tie in with the children's own demands and ideas of what success and a happy ending might be?

The journey out of war for many former child-soldiers does not necessarily coincide with the end of violence in their lives, the challenges of which continue long after the end of the UN Release and Reintegration process and the formal establishment of peace. Faced with the persistent prevalence of violations against children, a senior adviser at UNICEF, who started working at the UN agency in 1995, concludes:

> We would never have imagined that we could get all countries, every armed force in the world, to embrace the straight-18 ban to end the use of child soldiers. That's been an amazing achievement. Still, you can criticize its implementation and say that it's far from having reached the goal, but at least there is a consensus about the goal. This is remarkable. However, it does not mean to say that the world is safer. That remains an urgent question. We've made so much progress, but at the same time we see tremendous threats against children. We still have a lot of work to do.[119]

To a certain extent, these narratives about former child-soldiers as traumatized beings, but also as resilient becomings who can be "saved" through international interventions, (re)produce the discourse of the child-soldier as an international emergency by which children's participation in armed conflicts is seen as both wrong and abnormal and in need of rapid and technical solutions. Along these lines, through "humanitarian reason"—that is, when moral sentiments enter the political sphere—the threatened and threatening lives of former child-soldiers are brought into a specific existence as intolerable objects in need of protection.[120] Meanwhile, by adopting a particular, limited political approach, the UN reintegration process makes the intolerable minimally bearable: it normalizes (deviant) children and provides the instruments for the construction of their new (civilian) identity. The boundaries between the normal child and the deviant other, whose behavior is "psychiatrized" or placed outside the norm of the world-child, are thus (re)produced.[121] In other words, when child-soldiers are submitted to the international interventions analyzed throughout this chapter, it is the multiplication and proliferation of boundaries, not the disappearance of exceptions, that is (re)produced, reinforcing the norm of the world-child as the optimal model to be used to evaluate what is "natural and healthy" and what is not.

By (re)drawing the boundaries of the discourse of the child-soldier as an emergency, these international interventions (re)produce the triple exceptionalism that marks the limits of the modern individual, the modern state, and the world, since three points are constantly enacted: the child is not evil, the child is not an adult, and the child is indeed a symbol of a progressive future. In 2009, the NGO Save the Children articulated these boundaries in an exhibition in Australia against the use of child-soldiers, setting the tone of the campaign by proclaiming that "we must make this a thing of the past." Specifically, one of the billboards for the campaign showed a picture of a young African boy wearing old military clothes and trainers set inside a glass case (or cage) in an empty, arid place that seemed to be devastated by war.[122] Unlike Beah, depicted in the *Playboy* magazine article, this boy still carries a big gun like an AK-47.[123] A small plaque outside the case just says "Democratic Republic of Congo." Just below the name of the country, there is a small drawing of the map of Africa, in which there is an indication of where the distant—and barbaric—DRC is located. The child, whose name the viewers do not know and whose voice the viewers cannot hear, is kept under control behind solid boundaries like a museum exhibit. He cannot move. He cannot become a threat to the world. As an international emergency, the child-soldier phenomenon must be urgently "resolved." He, the child-solider, must be relegated to an uncivilized past so that the promise of a progressive future for "all" humanity can be renewed.

What would happen, then, if instead of affirming the world-child through absolute negations or exceptions, notions of childhood—and adulthood—were destabilized and politicized? The next and concluding chapter, rather than thinking about child-soldiers in terms of "children without childhood," discusses the idea of what I call "children *between* boundaries," in which the limits of childhood are not only permeable but are also constructed *for* and *by* the children themselves—that is, by children who do not escape from the limits of "normal" childhood but challenge them. Rather than being wiped out or muted, the boundaries can be politicized, thereby bringing forth the enormous complexity of what have come to be treated as the simplified—even natural-ized—ideas of the particular child, the particular adult citizen, and the particu-lar world. No fixed truth is to be gleaned from such a process. Rather, as Walker suggests, the challenge is "to reimagine the potentials that might be created in a sustained politicization of the boundaries, borders and limits of modern polit-ical formations," when there may or may not be perfect synchronicity between real children's childhoods and the one prescribed by the world-child.[124]

Neither "Beyond" nor "Behind"

Child-Soldiers as Children between Boundaries

One of the most famous soldiers of the American Civil War is John Lincoln Clem, who became known as the "Drummer Boy of Chickamauga." At the age of ten, Clem ran away from home to serve in the Union Army. He started his military career as an unofficial drummer boy but became a national celebrity after the Battle of Chickamauga, when, armed with a musket, he shot a Confederate colonel who told him to surrender. For his actions and bravery, Clem was promoted to sergeant, making him the youngest soldier ever to become a noncommissioned officer in the U.S. Army. Clem died in 1937 with the rank of major general and was buried with full military honors at the Arlington National Cemetery in Washington, D.C.

Estimates suggest that of the 2.7 million soldiers who served in the American Civil War—or "The Boys' War"—Clem was just one of over a million who were aged eighteen or under and one of about one hundred thousand aged fifteen or under.[1] The American Civil War was not an exception, but actually the rule: The armed groups and armed forces that engaged in the French Revolution and the World Wars in the first half of the twentieth century all had children in their ranks.[2]

The historian Tim Cook calls attention to the fact that as many as twenty thousand underage Canadian soldiers served overseas during the First World War.[3] Most of them were sixteen or seventeen years old: "A sense of adventure, peer pressure, and fierce patriotism impelled young and old to serve."[4] For those parents who did not want to let their children go to war, shaming techniques based on patriotic discourse were used to convince them not to hold their children back. A poster aimed at the "Women of Canada" demanded: "When the War is over and someone asks your husband or your son what he did in the great War, is he to hang his head because you would not let him go?"[5] Stories of patriotism and fear permeate the testimonies of the Canadian children who went to war. A letter from John Write to the Canadian prime minister, Sir Robert Borden, sheds light on the children's motivations:

> I am only a boy of 16 years and want to give my life for my country[. . . .] I am strong and healthy, I have never had any sickness in my life. I was just reading the

paper this morning and saw that you said 'Canadians must hold the line.' They cannot do it without men. Please will you give me a position in that line. *I don't call myself a man but I might help to hold that line.* So please give me a chance, the line is more valuable than my life.[6]

Private J. D. Thomson, who had enlisted at sixteen and was fighting in the trenches by seventeen, highlights in his letter how frightening and foreign the trenches were, but he also adds: "I am a mere boy, but I thought I was a man, and now I know I have to stick to it," signing his letter, "Not a Hero."[7] Cook concludes from this that although Thomson might not be a hero in the conventional sense, his behavior was heroic: "The quiet courage of doing one's duty while sick with fear was a trait not unique to underage soldiers, but countless references bear witness to how adolescents stuck it out."[8] It is worth noting how both testimonies articulate soldiering as an adult activity, but that when children assume this role, it does not necessarily indicate any pathology on their part, but rather heroism.

Before the Second World War, in 1922, the Nazis had already created the organization that in 1926 was renamed the Hitler Youth. Its camps served as places where young people could learn how to use weapons, build their physical strength, and learn war strategies, and where, from 1933 on, they were also indoctrinated in anti-Semitism.[9] Meanwhile, virtually every partisan and resistance movement had children among their ranks. David Rosen writes specifically about the groups of Jewish partisans who played a major role in the resistance against Germany's policy of genocide.[10] While some children served as couriers, helped manufacture crude weapons, distributed resistance publications, or delivered basic support services such as making food or taking care of animals, in most instances children were directly involved in combat. As Rosen emphasizes, joining the armed resistance was a matter of life or death: "Under such conditions, the conventional thinking that child soldiers are victims of their recruiters is turned on its head. The recruiters may be their only saviors."[11] The testimony of Misha Melamed, commenting on the day five partisans from the Stalin Brigade under the command of Yasha Horoshayev came to the house where he was hiding with his family, is very illustrative. He was fifteen years old when the war broke out:

> Efraim and I immediately joined Horoshayev's company and my father was appointed the head doctor of one of the battalions of the Stalin Brigade. Efraim received a rifle immediately as he had undergone pre-army training in the Vilna Gymnasium. There was no limit to my joy when I received, after a short period of training, a rifle with fifty bullets. After physical and spiritual humiliation, after [the] beating and murdering [of] my fellow Jews, I was able to fight and take revenge. I was willing to sacrifice my life in the struggle against the Nazis. I was free, a partisan with a rifle, thrilled and ready for any battle.[12]

The stories of Melamed and other child partisans are constantly retold on Holocaust Remembrance Day around the world. These children are remembered as people who made dignified and honorable choices when there were no places of safety, challenging the authority of a frightened and oppressed adult society that labeled armed resistance dangerous and criminal. Here, the voluntary nature of their acts is not questioned. In fact, children's decisions to join the armed resistance are justified precisely because they were living in oppressive circumstances. Ultimately, it was a rational choice to have a rifle in their hands in order to survive.

From this particular narrative and the other accounts presented here about children's engagement in war, it is possible to look at their experiences from a perspective that does not necessarily pathologize their childhood. In fact, examples of heroism, patriotism, and bravery are emphasized when children decide to fight either to defend their country or to save their own lives. Put simply, these children are not (re)produced as deviant child-soldiers. Although there may seem to be much in common between Melamed's, Thomson's, and Clem's stories and the many other experiences of children engaged in wars presented in this book, their deviations from what counts as the norm of the world-child are not seen as necessarily pathological or an emergency that warrants urgent international control and response.

By turning the focus to the contemporary militarization of childhood beyond the Global South, Macmillan questions the discourse of the child-soldier as a deviation, exploring how the trope of developmentalism has been appropriated by the military in the English-speaking world (Australia, Canada, the United Kingdom, and the United States). The recruiting message is that the lifestyle promoted by the armed forces is "*preparatory* for adulthood and provide[s] choice and prospects."[13] According to this logic, harm to children's development can be avoided by keeping them out of direct participation in armed conflict, but their experience of hardship and even danger during training and service can be both mentally and physically *challenging*, rather than *threatening*. Following on the same criticism, Lee-Koo demonstrates the different constructions of the child-soldier and the militarized child in Australia: while the former immediately evokes images of horror, disgust, and pity, "the Australian boy is presented as school-educated, white, male but, more significantly, a promising candidate for the future opportunities and responsibilities of adulthood."[14] The author concludes: "If examined in unison, the matching of youth with militarism seems to celebrate the coming of age in the global North, while mourning the loss of innocence in the global South."[15]

Children's participation in armed conflicts in the past and the current military recruitment of children in some countries in the Global North are not cited here with a view to defending the idea that a toy can or should be exchanged for a rifle, nor to indicate that certain causes may be legitimate enough for a child (soldier) to die for. Rather, through these historical examples, the idea is to show that children's engagement in war, whether "voluntary" or "forced," does not necessarily imply turning a human being into an apolitical object of protection—or control. Similarly, I do not intend to question UN officials' good intentions toward children who are soldiering in wars in different parts of the globe today. And, of course, the children concerned deserve the attention paid to them. The way the figure of the child-soldier is articulated in relation to what is (re)produced as the "normal" child does, however, call for critical analysis. What I argue throughout this book is that (re)producing the child-soldier phenomenon as an international emergency that needs to be urgently resolved by external others is not necessarily the best or only way of respecting these children, engaging with them, or, indeed, rescuing them.

In fact, the way these previous examples are articulated opens room for problematizing and critically reflecting on children whose life experiences challenge the bounded ideas held up as universal. My ultimate goal has thus been to think about childhood, children, child-soldiers, and the world in ways other than the modern International's strict logic of exclusion when fixed boundaries and normalized categories become contingent and permeable. This exercise raises many questions, but not necessarily any answers. But as Olga Nieuwenhuys reminds us, mixing up some (stable) ideas might ultimately be the best source of inspiration.[16] This leads to a number of questions: What is implied by labeling and (re)producing children's experiences in wars as "child-soldiering"? What happens when different imaginations of childhood and (ideal) paths toward securing children and their futures collide? Why can being recruited by a "civilized" armed force in the Global North be seen as a step toward children's fulfillment of their potential as contributing members of society, but their engagement in a new war as inevitably damaging their progress toward becoming full (adult) citizens? What is being articulated in terms of the international order when some children engaged in war are pathologized while others whose life experiences are militarized are not? Why are child partisans remembered as heroes while the boy without an authentic military uniform from Liberia is *just* a "child-soldier"? Why is Ishmael Beah articulated as a hero because he survived the extreme violence of contemporary war, while John Lincoln Clem is held up as a national American hero precisely because of his actions *in war*? And, finally, what world is this that celebrates and remembers some stories of children's participation in war while at the same time relegating others to somewhere outside the bounds of normality?

In February 2014, the NGO Save the Children posted a picture on its Twitter account in which an African baby being held by a woman (probably his mother) is looking over her shoulder into the distance, or looking into the (promised) future ahead of him.[17] The phrase posted next to the baby is quoted at the opening of the book *The Disappearance of Childhood* by Neil Postman: "Children are the living messages we send to a time we will not see."[18] However, no further clarification is given as to what that message and what that future, which are open to different interpretations and could serve different ends, will be in years to come. In this particular post by the NGO Save the Children, children, in their process of being, inescapably signify and embody futurity. It is as if "children can never simply stand for themselves as individuals in the here and now of the observational present."[19] One object of investigation in this book is the discourses that frame and (re)produce the norm of the world-child, articulating a single, specific message about the child, about its future profile as a world-citizen who will live in "a time we will not see," and about the world and its (promise of a) progressive future. The moral virtue this model represents has made it all but untouchable. Meanwhile, I have also tried to de-stabilize this message by problematizing the discourse about the child-soldier as essentially deviant in relation to the norm of the world-child. Between the child as a victim of adult abuse, the child as a dangerous becoming who is depicted as a risk to the world, and the child as a redeemed hero, there are a great many children who participate in wars whose stories about their child-hood experiences, about who they are and who they might become, do not necessarily fit into the trajectory of redemption envisioned by the UN through its international interventions. The messages that these children bear are not necessarily the one the world-child suggests and prescribes, and this offers a chance to think about "other ways of becoming otherwise in worlds that do not end where we have learnt to draw the line with such elegance, and with such violence."[20] Both categories—the world-child and the child-soldier—operate in this book as "analytic prisms" through which to explore their constitutive capacity and also the contradictory practices they allow and enable.[21] They have emerged as one of the many battlefields in which a particular version of the world that seems particularly well equipped to produce and exclude its many exceptions may be contested.

The first chapter of the book starts with the description of a picture of a child-soldier from Liberia from a BBC news story.[22] Besides learning that he is a child who carries a weapon in the context of an armed conflict, we, the viewers, are not told anything else about him. He is nothing but a victim or a potential threat to the world. In this regard, one question still remains: Does the (re)production of the International call for—or depend on—more information about this boy in particular, or is classifying him as just a "child-soldier" enough? More specifically, is it enough to define and authorize the child-soldier as deviant and, thereby, the mechanisms to set him back on the path of "normal" childhood, which implies providing resources for his development toward adulthood? In chapter 1, the prevailing discourse about the "phenomenon of child-soldiers" is presented according to the main ideas or explanations concerning the participation of children in contemporary armed conflicts. However, it also brings certain arguments from childhood studies to the forefront, which question the notion of the natural and universal child, allowing room to destabilize both the norm of the world-child and the pathological status of the child-soldier.

In chapter 2, the focus turns to the (re)production of the model of the world-child by investigating the "children's rights milestones" through two interrelated key themes: protection and development. I discuss how the various international efforts have, over time, determined, arranged, and defined the boundaries and dimensions that articulate a particular idea of the child and its future profile as a world-citizen. The children's rights milestones are instrumental in promoting and (re)producing not only notions of what is good and bad or what is right and wrong in relation to certain conceptions of children but also the limits of a particular version of the world predicated on assumptions of order, security, and progress. Among the "bad" and "wrong" conceptions of children, the child-soldier emerges as an illustrative example of the figure of what is certainly not "our children." Furthermore, because these children are not "ours," they do not promise or portend "our" desired future.[23]

In chapter 3, the focus falls squarely on the discourses—of the law and of the norm—that articulate child-soldiers as a pathological other in relation to the "normal" child, or as an international emergency that the world is busy trying to resolve. Specifically, through the analysis of international practices that articulate the participation of children in war as something wrong that must be banned according to international law and the examination of policy and media narratives about children engaged in wars, the discourse of the child-soldier not only articulates these children in particular as abnormal but also enables the (re)production of the model of the world-child. In the face of child-soldiers—those children who emerge from "dangerous places" and present the modern International with challenging behavior—interventions are urgently called for, and increasingly complex and far-reaching means of control are constantly authorized.

Chapter 4 explores United Nations interventions, which are authorized in the name of saving children's lives and alleviating their suffering. However, by insisting on the deviant and pathological nature of child-soldiering, these international interventions ultimately (re)declare child-soldiers as exceptions and thereby contribute to the (re)production of the "normal" child and, in binary thinking, the future "normal" adult as universal bounded categories. The risks inherent to the ambivalent meaning of the "normal" child are put under control and the promise of a progressive future for international relations is safeguarded and repeatedly renewed. Put another way, in the name of securing (not changing) a single world articulated in the model of the world-child, many worlds and childhoods are constantly excluded—or silenced—through stories of protection, care, development, and, ultimately, salvation championed by international interventions.

At the end of this analysis, what becomes clear is the urgent need to challenge an overwhelming focus on childhoods defined by what they lack and what they put at risk and to move toward considering a multiplicity of childhoods and children that do not fit the models assigned to them. In such an approach, "to stress that children are important actors in society is not to say that they act like adults or that the differences between children and adults are minimal."[24] Furthermore, by recognizing that children—as well as adults—are in a constant state of simultaneous being and becoming and that there is no point of complete separation between childhood and adulthood, it might be possible to move, as Foucault suggests, beyond the outside-inside alternative: "We have to be at the frontiers. Criticism indeed consists of analyzing and reflecting upon limits."[25]

I conclude this book by talking and thinking about child-soldiers as neither *behind* nor *beyond* normalized boundaries, but as "children *between* boundaries," who do not so much escape from as defy the limits of "normal" childhood. Instead of looking at child-soldiers' "transgressions" as disruptions of a proper normative international life that must be urgently treated and thus eliminated, seeing them as children between boundaries allows many possible critiques of the current international political order. Specifically, once the limits between child and adult, "normal" child and "deviant" child, are problematized, it is possible to explore child-soldiers not as risks to the prevailing international order but as potential ways of (re)thinking this order and its naturalized categories. I do not mean to envisage a complete switch from today's political circumstances to something else or to construct a completely new form of human being, but rather to insist on exploring the already complex politics of boundaries that express and enable some of the most pervasive constructs of modern life, such as the model of the world-child, and their exceptions or deviations, such as the child-soldier. That is, instead of reifying the boundaries between childhood and adulthood, between the normalized and the deviant child, the effort here is to grapple with the contradictions and limits inherent to the ideas of the world-child and the child-soldier, both of which sustain and can be made to challenge the proliferation and normalization of the processes by which a particular version of the world is ordered.

Finally, the choice of the word "children" instead of the singular "child" followed by the preposition "between" is not unintentional. The expression "children between boundaries" denotes that it is exactly by challenging the boundaries between here and there, self and other, normal and pathological, particular and universal, that it may be possible to consider *encounters*—instead of exclusions/inclusions—between differences. Encounters that may happen through many varied and winding paths that do not necessarily lead toward a single, stable endpoint portrayed as progress. After all, what makes humanity unique is its extraordinary plurality.

NOTES

INTRODUCTION

1. This description refers to a piece of graffiti art by Banksy called "Child Soldier," available at https://theartstack.com/artist/banksy/child-soldier-8.

2. James and Jenks, "Public Perceptions," 315.

3. MacVeigh, Maguire, and Wedge, *Stolen Futures*.

4. Machel, *Promotion and Protection*.

5. Watson, "Children and International Relations," 239.

6. D. T. Cook, "When a Child," 9.

7. D. T. Cook, "When a Child," 9.

8. For "human security" see Commission on Human Security, *Human Security Now*; Human Security Report Project, *Human Security Report 2005*; and UNDP, *Human Development Report, 1994*. For the other two terms see Kaldor, *New and Old Wars*; ICISS, *Responsibility to Protect*. See also Jacob, "Children and Armed Conflict."

9. For global politics see Brocklehurst, *Who's Afraid of Children*; Holzscheiter, *Children's Rights*. For the international political economy see Watson, *Child in International Political Economy*. For security studies see Wagnsson, Hellman, and Holmberg, "Centrality of Non-Traditional Groups"; Watson, "Children and International Relations"; Jacob, "Children and Armed Conflict"; Huynh, D'Costa, and Lee-Koo, *Children and Global Conflict*.

10. In 2015, a special issue of *Critical Security Studies* (vol. 3, no. 1) was published on the intersections between children, childhood, and security, complexifying our ideas of security and the universalized child as an object of international protection. Later, in 2017, the articles were published as a book, *Childhood and the Production of Security*, edited by J. Marshall Beier. Another example following in the same academic vein is the special issue of *Global Responsibility to Protect* (volume 10, issue 1–2) that came out in early 2018 with the aim of engaging in critical dialogue about whether current forms of international cooperation and global governance are well equipped or ill adapted to meet the challenges of child protection.

11. Watson, "Children and International Relations," 241.

12. Malkki, "Children, Humanity."

13. Malkki, "Children, Humanity," 60.

14. For views of children in other fields of knowledge see, for example, Ariès, *Centuries of Childhood*; Stephens, *Children and the Politics*; Jenks, *Childhood*; and James and Prout, "New Paradigm." Their arguments and debates are further analyzed throughout this book, especially in the next chapter. For accounts of children in international relations see Archard, *Children*; Pupavac, "Misanthropy without Borders."

15. Watson, "Can There Be."

16. Berents, *Young People and Everyday Peace*; Pruitt, "Fixing the Girls."

17. For anthropologists see, for example, Rosen, *Armies of the Young*; Shepler, *Childhood Deployed*; Denov, *Child Soldiers*. For other power relations see, for example, Macmillan,

"Child Soldier"; Lee-Koo, "Horror and Hope." See also Beier, "Children, Childhoods, and Security Studies."

18. Huynh, D'Costa, and Lee-Koo, *Children and Global Conflict*.

19. Jacob, *Child Security in Asia*, 54–77.

20. Beier, "Children, Childhoods, and Security Studies," 2.

21. Brocklehurst, *Who's Afraid of Children?*, 174.

22. Beier, "Children, Childhoods, and Security Studies," 10.

23. Walker, "Double Outside," 57.

24. Walker, "Double Outside," 57.

25. Walker, "Conclusion," 248–49.

26. Walker, "Lines of Insecurity."

27. Walker, "Lines of Insecurity," 70. The other rules, according to Walker, are (1) no empires; (2) no religious wars, and (3) keep political life inside the sovereign nation-state.

28. Walker, "Lines of Insecurity," 70–71.

29. Esteves, "Unfolding the International," 21.

30. Walker, "Lines of Insecurity," 71.

31. Walker, "Double Outside," 58.

32. According to UNICEF's website, the School-in-a-Box is used in many back-to-school operations around the world. The kit is supplied in a locked aluminum box and contains materials for a teacher and up to forty students. With this kit, UNICEF intends to provide the continuation of children's education within the first seventy-two hours of an emergency. Information is available at https://www.unicef.org/supply/index_40377.html.

33. Bartelson, *Genealogy of Sovereignty*.

34. Jenks, *Childhood*, 42.

35. Shapiro, *Reading Postmodern Polity*, 12.

36. Brocklehurst, "State of Play," 32.

37. Foucault, "Practicing Criticism," 155.

38. Linde, "Globalization of Childhood"; Beier, "Children, Childhoods, and Security Studies," 3.

39. Hansen, *Security as Practice*.

40. Hansen, *Security as Practice*, 49.

41. Hansen, *Security as Practice*, 49.

42. Hansen, *Security as Practice*, 49.

43. Foucault, "Order of Discourse."

44. Foucault, "Truth and Power," 117.

45. Jabri, *War and the Transformation*, 9.

46. League of Nations, Geneva Declaration; UN General Assembly, Declaration of the Rights; UN General Assembly, International Year of the Child; UN General Assembly, Convention on the Rights—at the time of writing, there are 140 signatories and 196 parties to the Convention on the Rights of the Child; UN General Assembly, World Declaration; ILO, Convention concerning the Prohibition; UN General Assembly, World Fit for Children; UN General Assembly, Declaration of the Commemorative.

47. UN General Assembly, Universal Declaration of Human Rights; ILO, Convention concerning Minimum Age.

48. Moeller, "Hierarchy of Innocence," 53.

49. ICRC, Additional Protocols; UN General Assembly, Convention on the Rights; UN General Assembly, Rome Statute—at the time of writing, there are 139 signatories and 118 ratifications to the Rome Statute; OAU, African Charter; ILO, Convention concerning the

Prohibition; UN General Assembly, Optional Protocol—at the time of writing, there are 129 signatories and 152 parties to the Optional Protocol to the Convention on the Rights of the Child on the involvement of children in armed conflict; the treaty was adopted by Resolution A/RES/54/263 of 25 May 2000 at the fifty-fourth session of the General Assembly of the United Nations and entered into force on 12 February 2002; UNICEF, Cape Town Principles; UNICEF, Paris Principles.

50. Denov, *Child Soldiers.*

51. A-J Lee, "Understanding and Addressing."

52. Martins, "Dangers of the Single Story."

53. Foucault, "Order of Discourse," 67.

54. Foucault, "Order of Discourse," 73; emphasis in the original.

55. Denov, *Child Soldiers.*

CHAPTER ONE. "CHILDREN WITHOUT CHILDHOOD"

1. Doyle, "Call to Help."

2. Doyle, "Call to Help"; emphasis added.

3. This sentence makes reference to Graça Machel's report on the impact of armed conflict on children, which sets forth the main ideas that constitute the discourse about the child-soldier. There, the author says: "Children [child soldiers] are dropping out from childhood" (Machel, *Impact of War on Children*, 57).

4. McGregor, "With Your Help."

5. Holt, *Escape from Childhood*, 22.

6. ILO, *Wounded Childhood*; Vallely, "Childhood Violated"; and Barnett, "Ex-Child-Soldier."

7. Boyden and de Berry, Introduction to *Children and Youth*, xii.

8. Chin, "Children out of Bounds."

9. D. T. Cook, *Commodification of Childhood.*

10. Higonnet, *Pictures of Innocence.*

11. Higonnet, *Pictures of Innocence*, 85.

12. Higonnet, *Pictures of Innocence*, 15.

13. Ariès, *Centuries of Childhood.*

14. UN General Assembly, Convention on the Rights.

15. Ryan, "How New Is the 'New'?"

16. Jenks, *Childhood*, 4.

17. Stephens, introduction to *Children and the Politics*, 14.

18. Boyden, "Childhood and the Policy Makers."

19. Hockey and James, *Growing Up and Growing Old*, 60.

20. Jenks, *Childhood*, 123.

21. Hockey and James, *Growing Up and Growing Old.*

22. Qvortrup, "Varieties of Childhood," 5.

23. James, Jenks, and Prout, *Theorizing Childhood.*

24. James, "Understanding Childhood," 33; emphasis added.

25. UN General Assembly, Convention on the Rights.

26. Wyness, *Childhood and Society*, 14.

27. Jenks, *Childhood*, 8.

28. N. Lee, *Childhood and Society*; Qvortrup, "Waiting Child"; Qvortrup, "Childhood as a Structural Form."

29. Burman, *Developments*, 11.

30. Jenks, *Childhood*; Ryan, "How New Is the 'New'?"

31. Rasmussen, "Places for Children."

32. Kovarik (1994), quoted in Jenks, *Childhood*, 76.

33. Jenks, "Journeys into Space."

34. Jenks, *Childhood*, 76.

35. Hockey and James, *Growing Up and Growing Old*.

36. Jenks, *Childhood*; Burman, *Deconstructing Developmental Psychology*.

37. Woodhead, "Psychology."

38. James and Prout, "New Paradigm," 10.

39. The expression "in their best interests" is inspired by the formulation "In the Best Interests of the Child," which was used for the first time in the Declaration of the Rights of the Child (UN, General Assembly), and it was then repeated by the UNCRC.

40. Mills, "'Special' Treatment."

41. Foucault, "Order of Discourse."

42. Burman, "Developmental Psychology," 140; emphasis in original.

43. Woodhead, "Child Development."

44. Kofsky Scholnick (2000), quoted in Burman, *Deconstructing Developmental Psychology*, 7.

45. Cunningham, *Children and Childhood*.

46. Woodhead, "Child Development."

47. Rose, *Governing the Soul*, 145.

48. Burman, *Deconstructing Developmental Psychology*.

49. Ryan, "How New Is the 'New'?"

50. Rose, *Governing the Soul*.

51. Ryan, "How New Is the 'New'?"

52. Woodhead, "Child Development," 49.

53. Burman, "Developmental Psychology."

54. Woodhead, "Child Development," 49.

55. Woodhead, "Child Development," 49.

56. Corsaro, *Sociologia da Infância*.

57. Jenks, *Childhood*, 22.

58. Corsaro, *Sociologia da Infância*.

59. Singer, *Children at War*, 70.

60. Human Rights Watch, *"My Gun Was as Tall,"* 6.

61. For a key analysis on the participation and involvement of children in warfare throughout history, see Rosen, *Armies of the Young*.

62. Denov, *Child Soldiers*; Honwana, *Child Soldiers in Africa*; Wessells, *Child Soldiers*.

63. Machel, *Promotion and Protection*; Kaldor, *New and Old Wars*; Singer, *Children at War*.

64. Wyness, *Childhood and Society*.

65. UNICEF, Paris Principles; ICRC, Additional Protocols.

66. UNICEF, Cape Town Principles; UNICEF, Paris Principles, 7; emphasis added.

67. Rosen, *Child Soldiers*.

68. A-J Lee, "Understanding and Addressing."

69. Rosen, *Armies of the Young*.

70. Ariès, *Centuries of Childhood*.

71. Rosen, *Armies of the Young*, 14.

72. Machel, *Promotion and Protection*.

73. Machel, *Promotion and Protection*, 6; emphasis added.

74. Machel, *Promotion and Protection*, 11.

75. Rosen, *Child Soldiers in the Western Imagination*.

76. A-J Lee, "Understanding and Addressing."

77. Watchlist on Children and Armed Conflict, *Where Are They*, 18.

78. Watchlist on Children and Armed Conflict, *Where Are They*, 18; emphasis in the original.

79. Rosen, *Armies of the Young*, 134.

80. Machel, *Promotion and Protection*, 12.

81. Machel, *Impact of War*, 11.

82. Watchlist on Children and Armed Conflict, *Where Are They*.

83. Interview 1, UNICEF senior adviser.

84. Lorey, *Child Soldiers*, 17; emphasis added.

85. Brocklehurst, *Who's afraid of Children?*

86. Brocklehurst, *Who's afraid of Children?*, 35.

87. Macmillan, "Child Soldier."

88. Human Rights Watch, *Scars of Death*, 5.

89. Wille, "Children Associated with Fighting Forces," 204.

90. Singer, *Children at War*; Machel, *Promotion and Protection*.

91. Honwana, *Child Soldiers in Africa*.

92. Honwana, *Child Soldiers in Africa*, 72.

93. UNICEF, *Will You Listen?*, 4.

94. Macmillan, "Child Soldier."

95. Boothby, "Mozambique Life Outcome Study," 234.

96. Machel, *Promotion and Protection*, 11.

97. Radio Netherlands Worldwide, cited in Singer, *Children at War*, 83; emphasis added.

98. Machel, *Promotion and Protection*, 57.

99. Briggs, *Innocents Lost*; Images Asia, *No Childhood At All*.

100. Kaldor, *New and Old Wars*; Münkler, *New Wars*. In addition to Kaldor's analysis, many scholars have discussed the possibility of a new kind of warfare, such as Holsti (*State, War; Peace and War*), who classifies the new forms of armed conflicts within states and between communities as "wars of the third kind." Although Holsti and Kaldor agree in terms of an increasing deinstitutionalization of war, Holsti affirms that wars have undergone significant changes since the Second World War, and these modifications are closely related to the processes of decolonization in the African and Asian continents, while Kaldor focuses on the post–Cold War period. For "fractured states," see Gates and Reich, *Child Soldiers*.

101. Kaldor, *New and Old Wars*.

102. Kaldor, *New and Old Wars*, 20; Holsti, *Taming the Sovereigns*.

103. Singer, *Children at War*, 53.

104. Machel, *Promotion and Protection*, 9.

105. Machel, *Promotion and Protection*, 9–10.

106. Malesevic, "Sociology of New Wars?"; Newman, "'New Wars' Debate."

107. Newman, "'New Wars' Debate."

108. Jabri, *War and the Transformation*.

109. Rosen, *Child Soldiers in the Western Imagination*.

110. Jabri, *War and the Transformation*.

111. Wessells, *Child Soldiers*.

112. Machel, *Promotion and Protection*, 10.

113. Machel, *Promotion and Protection*, 10; emphasis added.

114. Small Arms Survey, *Small Arms Survey 2008*, chapter 1, 7.

115. Machel, *Promotion and Protection*, 10.

116. Rosen, *Armies of the Young.*

117. Rosen, *Armies of the Young.*

118. Rosen, *Armies of the Young.*

119. Macmillan, "Child Soldier," 36.

120. Machel, *Promotion and Protection*, 6.

121. D. T. Cook, "When a Child."

122. Burr, *Vietnam's Children.*

123. Burr, *Vietnam's Children*, 101.

124. Cheney, *Pillars of the Nation*; Nieuwenhuys, "Global Childhood."

125. Nieuwenhuys, "Global Childhood," 4.

126. In 1991, James and Prout wrote a chapter titled "A New Paradigm for the Sociology of Childhood?" in which they suggest and question the possibility of a new paradigm based on six "rules" or principles mentioned in the text. In this book, I use the expression "childhood studies" to refer to this project, which, in my point of view, guides the interdisciplinary effort that propounds a different way of analyzing and studying children and childhood.

127. James and Prout, "New Paradigm."

128. In addition to Ariès's *Centuries of Childhood*, a trio of books are often grouped as marking the particular approach to the history of children and childhood: Lloyd de Mause, ed., *The History of Childhood* (1974); Edward Shorter, *The Making of the Modern Family* (1976); and Lawrence Stone, *The Family, Sex and Marriage in England, 1500–1800* (1977). For more on the contribution of these authors to the historiography of childhood and children, see Cunningham, *Children and Childhood.*

129. Ariès, *Centuries of Childhood*, 125.

130. Ariès, *Centuries of Childhood*, 129.

131. N. Lee, *Childhood and Society*, 32.

132. Cunningham, *Children and Childhood.*

133. Cunningham, *Children and Childhood*, 5.

134. James, "Understanding childhood."

135. Brocklehurst, *Who's Afraid of Children?*

136. James and Prout, "New Paradigm."

137. James, "Understanding Childhood."

138. James, "Understanding Childhood."

139. D. T. Cook, "Interrogating Symbolic Childhood."

140. Chin, "Children out of Bounds."

141. James, "Understanding Childhood."

142. D. T. Cook, "Interrogating Symbolic Childhood."

143. Punch, "Negotiating Autonomy," 23–25. Similarly, in order to problematize this hierarchical relationship between children and adults, researchers, within a critical approach to developmental psychology, working at the interface with childhood studies, use the term "adultism" to describe and explain not only children's disadvantaged position within social life but also their positioning within adult-centric research and paternalistic practices produced by this notion of children as human *becomings* who need to follow a certain journey in order to be a rational modern adult (LeFrançois, "Adultism").

144. James, "Understanding Childhood," 34.

145. James and Prout, "New Paradigm," 8.

146. N. Lee, "Challenge of Childhood."
147. Tisdall, "Conceptualising Children."
148. Spyrou, Rosen and Cook, *Reimagining Childhood Studies.*
149. Spyrou, Rosen and Cook, "Introduction," 3.
150. Balagopalan, "Childhood, Culture, History," 38.
151. James and Prout, "New Paradigm"; Jenks, *Childhood.*
152. Jenks, "Journeys into Space," 420.

CHAPTER TWO. HOPE FOR THE FUTURE

1. K. Annan, *We the Children.* The World Summit for Children was a gathering of world leaders to promote the well-being of children. The highpoint of the occasion, held under the auspices of the UN in New York, was the joint signing of a World Declaration on the Survival, Protection and Development of Children and a Plan of Action comprising a detailed set of child-related human development goals for the year 2000. Main conclusions are available at United Nations: Special Session on Children, http://www.unicef.org/specialsession/about /world-summit.htm. The World Fit for Children was the Special Session at the UN and culminated in the official adoption, by some 180 nations, of its outcome document, "A World Fit for Children." It presents the new agenda for the world's children, including twenty-one specific goals and targets for the following decade. See UN General Assembly, World Fit for Children.
2. K. Annan, *We the Children*, preface.
3. K. Annan, *We the Children*, preface.
4. Foucault, *Discipline and Punish.*
5. League of Nations, Geneva Declaration; UN General Assembly, Declaration of the Rights; UN General Assembly, International Year of the Child; UN General Assembly, Convention on the Rights (at the time of writing, there are 140 signatories and 196 parties to the Convention on the Rights of the Child); UN General Assembly, World Declaration; ILO, Convention concerning the Prohibition; UN General Assembly, World Fit for Children; UN General Assembly, Declaration of the Commemorative.
6. UN General Assembly, Universal Declaration of Human Rights; ILO, Convention concerning Minimum Age.
7. Pupavac, "International Children's Rights Regime."
8. UN General Assembly, Plan of Action, ¶36.
9. Foucault, *Security, Territory and Population.*
10. Fowler, *Seeds of Destiny.*
11. Fowler, *Seeds of Destiny*, 3:35.
12. Burman, "Innocents Abroad," 248.
13. Bhabha, "Child."
14. Marshall, "Construction of Children," 138.
15. The twentieth century was first dubbed "the century of the child" by Ellen Key in 1909 (Key, *Century of the Child*).
16. Cunningham, *Children and Childhood.*
17. League of Nations, Geneva Declaration.
18. Wall, "Human Rights," 534.
19. Hendrick, *Child Welfare.*
20. Holzscheiter, *Children's Rights*, 124.
21. James, "Understanding Childhood."
22. Holzscheiter, *Children's Rights.*

23. UN General Assembly, Convention on the Rights.

24. UN General Assembly, Declaration of the Rights, principle 6.

25. UN General Assembly, Convention on the Rights.

26. UN General Assembly, Convention on the Rights, art. 1.

27. Interview 2, UN program officer.

28. Twum-Danso Imoh, "Children's Perceptions."

29. K. Annan, *We the Children*, 5.

30. Archard, *Children*.

31. UN General Assembly, Declaration of the Rights, principle 4.

32. UN General Assembly, Declaration of the Rights, preamble.

33. UN General Assembly, Plan of Action, ¶2.

34. UN General Assembly, Plan of Action, ¶2; emphasis added.

35. UN General Assembly, World Declaration, ¶2; emphasis added.

36. UN General Assembly, World Fit for Children, ¶9.

37. Reynaert, Bouverne-de-Bie, and Vandevelde, "Review of Children's Rights Literature."

38. UN General Assembly, Declaration of the Commemorative, ¶1.

39. UN General Assembly, Declaration of the Rights.

40. Pupavac, "International Children's Rights Regime," 67.

41. Burman, *Deconstructing Developmental Psychology*.

42. Huysmans, "Agency and the Politics of Protection."

43. UN General Assembly, Declaration of the Rights; Simmons, *Mobilizing for Human Rights*; Wall, "Human Rights."

44. UN General Assembly, Plan of Action, ¶5.

45. UN General Assembly, Declaration of the Rights, principle 2.

46. UN General Assembly, Declaration of the Rights, principle 9.

47. ILO, Convention concerning Minimum Age, art. 3.

48. Zelizer, *Pricing the Priceless Child*; ILO, *Worst Forms of Child Labour Convention*.

49. UN General Assembly, Convention concerning the Prohibition; emphasis in the original.

50. UN General Assembly, Convention on the Rights, art. 19.

51. Pupavac, "Misanthropy without Borders."

52. K. Annan, *We the Children*, 101; emphasis added.

53. Rose, *Governing the Soul*.

54. Pupavac, "Misanthropy without Borders," 109.

55. Rasmussen, "Places for Children."

56. Brookfield, *Cold War Comforts*, 111.

57. UNICEF, *Progress of Nations*, 29.

58. UN General Assembly, *Report of the Special Representative*, 30.

59. UN General Assembly, *Report of the Special Representative*, 30.

60. UN General Assembly, *Report of the Special Representative*, 30; UNICEF, *Progress of Nations*.

61. UN General Assembly, Universal Declaration of Human Rights, art. 16(3).

62. UN General Assembly, Declaration of the Rights, principle 6.

63. UN General Assembly, World Declaration, ¶14.

64. UN General Assembly, Plan of Action, ¶18.

65. UN General Assembly, World Fit for Children, ¶15.

66. Bigo, "Protection," 92.

67. Jabri, "Limits of Agency."

68. Freeman, "Introduction." It is worth noting that within the academic debates in the 1970s, authors such as John Holt in *Escape from Childhood* (1974) and Richard Farson in *Birthrights* (1978) brought to the forefront the discussions on children's liberation, focusing on their rights to work, to vote, and to assert their sexual freedom. However, some of these suggestions were considered extreme, and it took another twenty years before this movement made any impact on public policy. See Huynh, D'Costa, and Lee-Koo, *Children and Global Conflict*, 100.

69. UN General Assembly, Convention on the Rights.

70. Schaub, Henck, and Baker, "Globalized 'Whole Child.'"

71. UN General Assembly, World Declaration, ¶22.

72. The Committee on the Rights of the Child is the body of independent experts that monitors implementation of the Convention on the Rights of the Child by its state parties. It also monitors implementation of two optional protocols to the convention, on involvement of children in armed conflict and on the sale of children, child prostitution, and child pornography. This committee was established by the UNCRC, which included its creation, composition, functioning, and role. UNCRC, *General Comment No. 12*, 3.

73. Tisdall, "Conceptualising Children," 61.

74. Freeman, *Rights and Wrongs*, 18.

75. Bhabha, "Independent Children."

76. UN General Assembly, Convention on the Rights, art. 12; emphasis added.

77. UN General Assembly, World Fit for Children, ¶7(9); emphasis added.

78. UN General Assembly, Declaration of the Commemorative, ¶5; emphasis added.

79. Krappman, "Weight of the Child's View," 512.

80. Archard, *Children*, 65.

81. Pupavac, "International Children's Rights Regime."

82. Chin, "Children out of Bounds," 320.

83. Archard, *Children*.

84. Archard, *Children*, 65.

85. UNICEF, *State of the World's Children*, 3.

86. UNICEF, *State of the World's Children*, 3.

87. Hart, "Children's Participation."

88. Hart, "Children's Participation," 411.

89. Cheney, *Pillars of the Nation*.

90. Cheney, *Pillars of the Nation*, 44.

91. Holzscheiter, *Children's Rights*; Wyness, Harrison, and Buchanan, "Childhood, Politics and Ambiguity."

92. Tisdall, "Conceptualising Children," 60.

93. Punch, "Negotiating Autonomy."

94. Oswell, *Agency of Children*, 270.

95. Ruiz-Casares et al., "Children's Rights."

96. Bhabha, "Child."

97. Twum-Danso Imoh, "Children's Perceptions," 484.

98. D. T. Cook, "When a Child."

99. Tabak, Villela, and Trindade Viana, "Youths and Children."

100. Bigo, "Protection," 90.

101. Bhabha, "Child."

102. Bigo, "Protection."

103. UN Dept. of Public Information, "Global Community"; emphasis added.

104. Holzscheiter, *Children's Rights*.

105. K. Annan, *We the Children*, 103.

106. UN General Assembly, World Fit for Children, ¶14.

107. UN General Assembly, International Year of the Child, preamble; emphasis added.

108. UN General Assembly, World Declaration, ¶19.

109. UN General Assembly, Plan of Action, ¶3.

110. UN General Assembly, Plan of Action, ¶3.

111. UNICEF, *Progress of Nations*, i.

112. K. Annan, *We the Children*, 102.

113. Interview 3, UK diplomat.

114. Duffield, "Liberal Way of Development," 57.

115. Duffield, "Development, Territories, and People," 225.

116. UN General Assembly, Declaration of the Commemorative, ¶6.

117. ILO, Convention concerning the Prohibition, art. 3.

118. UN General Assembly, Declaration of the Rights, principle 7.

119. UN General Assembly, International Year of the Child, principle 7.

120. UN General Assembly, International Year of the Child.

121. UN General Assembly, Convention on the Rights, art. 29.

122. UN General Assembly, World Declaration, ¶20.

123. Rose, *Governing the Soul*, 124.

124. The Sustainable Development Goals (SDGs), otherwise known as the Global Goals, are a universal set of goals, targets, and indicators that UN member states will be expected to use to frame their agendas and political policies over the next fifteen years. They are also known as "Transforming Our World: The 2030 Agenda for Sustainable Development" or Agenda 2030. The SDGs follow and expand on the Millennium Development Goals, which were agreed to by governments in 2001, covering a broad range of social and economic development issues.

125. Jenks, *Childhood*, 80.

126. Foucault, *Discipline and Punish*.

127. Foucault, *Discipline and Punish*.

128. Labouisse, "United Nations Children's Fund."

129. Rose, *Governing the Soul*.

130. Nieuwenhuys, "Keep Asking," 295.

CHAPTER THREE. AN INTERNATIONAL EMERGENCY

1. Honwana, "Innocent and Guilty," 33.

2. Invisible Children, *Kony 2012*.

3. Wisnefski, "'Kony 2012' Offers."

4. Burman, *Developments*, 135.

5. Burman, *Developments*, 135.

6. The term "phenomenon" is from Machel, *Promotion and Protection*; see also Singer, *Children at War*.

7. Machel, *Promotion and Protection*, 73; emphasis added.

8. Calhoun, "Imperative to Reduce Suffering," 96.

9. Macmillan, "Child Soldier."

10. Denov, *Child Soldiers*.

11. Nyers, *Rethinking Refugees.*

12. The expression "beast of no nation" refers to Uzodinma Iweala's novel *Beasts of No Nation* (2005), which was made into a movie and distributed by Netflix in 2015.

13. Tabak and Carvalho, "Responsibility to Protect."

14. James and Prout, "New Paradigm."

15. League of Nations, Geneva Declaration; Cunningham, *Children and Childhood.*

16. Watson, "Guardians of the Peace?"

17. For further historical examples of children's involvement in wars, see Marten, *Children and War*; Rosen, *Child Soldiers*; and Rosen, *Armies of the Young.*

18. Macmillan, "Militarized Children."

19. Interview 4, UN program officer.

20. Denov, *Child Soldiers*; Rosen, *Armies of the Young.*

21. Beier, "Everyday Zones of Militarization," 7.

22. ICRC, Additional Protocols; UN General Assembly, Convention on the Rights; UN General Assembly, Rome Statute (at the time of writing, there are 139 signatories and 118 ratifications to the Rome Statute); OAU, African Charter; ILO, Convention concerning the Prohibition; UN General Assembly, Optional Protocol (at the time of writing, there are 129 signatories and 152 parties to the Optional Protocol to the Convention on the Rights of the Child on the involvement of children in armed conflict; the treaty was adopted by Resolution A/RES/54/263 of 25 May 2000 at the fifty-fourth session of the General Assembly of the United Nations and entered into force on February 12, 2002); UNICEF, Cape Town Principles; UNICEF, *Paris Principles.*

23. ICRC, Geneva Convention.

24. As cited in Rosen, *Child Soldiers*, 11; emphasis added.

25. Van Bueren, "International Legal Protection of Children."

26. UN General Assembly, Convention on the Rights, art. 38; OAU, African Charter; UN General Assembly, Optional Protocol.

27. ICRC, Additional Protocol II; UN General Assembly, Optional Protocol, art. 4 (emphasis added).

28. Van Bueren, "International Legal Protection of Children."

29. UN General Assembly, Rome Statute.

30. UN General Assembly, Rome Statute, art. 8.

31. Coomaraswamy, "Optional Protocol to the Convention."

32. ILO, Convention concerning the Prohibition.

33. UNICEF, Cape Town Principles; UNICEF, Paris Principles.

34. UNICEF, Cape Town Principles, 12; emphasis added.

35. UNICEF, Paris Principles.

36. UN General Assembly, Convention on the Rights, art. 38.

37. UN General Assembly, Optional Protocol, preamble; emphasis added. It is worth noting that another important element in the establishment of the Optional Protocol was the appointment of Graça Machel as the United Nations secretary-general's independent expert to undertake a study on "The Impact of Armed Conflict on Children," submitted to the General Assembly in 1996.

38. UN General Assembly, Optional Protocol; emphasis added.

39. Interview 3,UK diplomat.

40. Interview 3, UK diplomat.

41. Child Soldiers International, "United Kingdom."

42. Ministry of Defence, "UK Armed Forces Biannual Diversity Statistics," 1 October 2018, https://assets.publishing.service.gov.uk/government/uploads/system/uploads/attachment _data/file/763676/1_October_2018_Biannual_Diversity_Statistics.pdf.

43. UN General Assembly, Optional Protocol, art. 3.

44. Interview 3,UK diplomat.

45. OAU, African Charter, art. 2; ILO, Convention concerning the Prohibition, art. 2.

46. UNICEF, Cape Town Principles; UNICEF, Paris Principles.

47. UN General Assembly, Rome Statute, art. 8.

48. Beier, "Everyday Zones of Militarization," 6.

49. For the image, see Geneva Call, *Protecting Children in Armed Conflict*. The booklet presents twelve essential rules of behavior for members of armed groups, based on the core provisions of the Deed of Commitment protecting children in armed conflict. See also the Geneva Call website, http://www.genevacall.org/. For the quotation, see Geneva Call, *Protecting Children in Armed Conflict*; emphasis in the original.

50. Drumbl, *Reimagining Child Soldiers*.

51. Coomaraswamy, "Optional Protocol to the Convention," 542.

52. Hockey and James, *Growing Up and Growing Old*.

53. Honwana, *Child Soldiers in Africa*.

54. Coomaraswamy, "Optional Protocol to the Convention," 545.

55. Beah, "Making, and Unmaking."

56. Denov, *Child Soldiers*.

57. Denov, *Child Soldiers*, 2.

58. Beah, "Making, and Unmaking."

59. Beah, "Making, and Unmaking."

60. Beah, *Long Way Gone*, back cover.

61. Nyers, *Rethinking Refugees*.

62. Denov, *Child Soldiers*.

63. Human Rights Watch, "Forgotten Fighters"; Coalition to Stop the Use of Child Soldiers, *Child Soldiers Global Report 2001*.

64. Human Rights Watch, "Forgotten Fighters," 2.

65. Lee-Koo, "Not Suitable For Children."

66. Martins, "Dangers of the Single Story."

67. Ensor, "Participation under Fire."

68. Human Rights Watch, "Forgotten Fighters," 2.

69. Girl soldier recruited at age thirteen in Sri Lanka; Human Rights Watch, "Living in Fear," 27.

70. Dallaire, *They Fight Like Soldiers*, 3, 12, 15, 150.

71. Amnesty International, *Hidden Scandal*, 24.

72. Interview 5, UNICEF adviser.

73. MONUSCO, *Child Recruitment*, front cover.

74. Wyness, *Childhood and Society*.

75. Coomaraswamy, "Optional Protocol to the Convention," 535–36.

76. Lee-Koo, "Not Suitable for Children."

77. Lee-Koo, "Not Suitable for Children," 481.

78. UN General Assembly, *Report of the Special Representative*, 15.

79. Bhabha, "Child."

80. Jamison, "Detention of Juvenile Enemy Combatants"; Coomaraswamy, "Optional Protocol to the Convention," 545.

81. Nyers, *Rethinking Refugees*.

82. Nyers, *Rethinking Refugees*, 7.

83. See the Protocol I to the 1949 Geneva Conventions (1977), art. 43.

84. Interview 2, UN program officer.

85. Human Rights Watch, "How to Fight."

86. Interview 2, UN program officer.

87. Watchlist on Children and Armed Conflict, *Where Are They*, 19.

88. Watchlist on Children and Armed Conflict, *Where Are They*, 19.

89. Drumbl, *Reimagining Child Soldiers*.

90. Singer, *Children at War*, 44.

91. Interview 4, UN program officer.

92. J. Annan and Blattman, "Child Combatants in Northern Uganda."

93. Lee-Koo, "Not Suitable For Children," 483.

94. Denov, *Child Soldiers*.

95. Singer, *Children at War*, 74.

96. Singer, *Children at War*.

97. Dallaire, *They Fight Like Soldiers*, 4.

98. Singer, *Children at War*, 75.

99. "Twin Terrors."

100. "Twin Terrors."

101. Photograph available, for example, at "Myanmar Child Guerrilla Johnny Htoo Surrenders," *China Daily*, 27 July 2006, http://www.chinadaily.com.cn/photo/2006-07/27/content_650620.htm, accessed 19 December 2013; Denov, *Child Soldiers*, 7.

102. "Twin Terrors."

103. Watchlist on Children and Armed Conflict, *Where Are They*, 20.

104. Watchlist on Children and Armed Conflict, *Where Are They*, 21.

105. BBC News, as cited in Denov, *Child Soldiers*, 7.

106. Nolen and Baines, "Making of a Monster?"

107. Nolen and Baines, "Making of a Monster?"

108. Bradshaw, "Justice Dilemma Haunts Uganda."

109. Nolen and Baines, "Making of a Monster?"

110. Nolen and Baines, "Making of a Monster?"

111. Nolen and Baines, "Making of a Monster?"

112. Bradshaw, "Justice Dilemma Haunts Uganda."

113. Nolen and Baines, "Making of a Monster?"

114. Foran, "Interrogating 'Militarized' Images."

115. Friscolanti, "Who Is the Real Omar Khadr?"

116. Friscolanti, "Who Is the Real Omar Khadr?"

117. Puar and Rai, "Monster, Terrorist, Fag," 119.

118. Doyle, "Call to Help."

119. Nyers, *Rethinking Refugees*.

120. Denov, *Child Soldiers*, 9.

121. The picture, drawn from a Playboy magazine edition, is discussed by Denov, *Child Soldiers*, 10.

122. Wessells, *Child Soldiers*, 84.

123. Singer, *Children at War*.

124. Coomaraswamy, "Statement at the Paris International Conference."

125. Coomaraswamy, "Statement at the Event on the Paris Commitments."

126. Lomong, *Running for My Life*.

127. Ellis, "Lopez Lomong."

128. Ensor, "Participation under Fire," 159.

129. Holzscheiter, *Children's Rights*, 100–137.

130. Holzscheiter, *Children's Rights*; Denov, *Child Soldiers*.

131. Walker, *After the Globe*.

132. Walker, "Conclusion."

133. UN General Assembly, *Report of the Special Representative*, 20.

134. K. Annan, *We the Children*, 102.

CHAPTER FOUR. (RE)DRAWING BOUNDARIES
AND RESTORING INTERNATIONAL ORDER

1. Interview 4, UN program officer.

2. UN Security Council, Resolution 1261 (1999).

3. Interview 3, UK diplomat.

4. Some UN Member States have formed the Group of Friends on Children and Armed Conflict, which provides a forum for discussing related issues and advocating the rights of children in support of the Office of the Special Representative for Children and Armed Conflict. Canada has chaired the group since 2006.

5. Interview 6, Liechtenstein diplomat.

6. Interview 9, UN adviser.

7. UN OSRSG for CAAC, *20 Years*, 18.

8. UN Security Council, Resolution 1261 (1999).

9. Interview 4, UN program officer.

10. Interview 2 UN program officer.

11. UN OSRSG for CAAC, *20 Years*, 18.

12. UM Security Council, Resolution 1261 (1999), paragraph 1; emphasis added.

13. UN Security Council, Resolution 1314 (2000).

14. UN Security Council, Resolution 1379 (2001), 5; emphasis added.

15. UN Security Council, Resolutions 1882 (2009), 1998 (2011), 2225 (2015).

16. UN Secretary General, *Children and Armed Conflict* (2010), ¶175.

17. UN Secretary General, *Children and Armed Conflict* (2012), ¶227.

18. Interview 3, UK diplomat.

19. Interview 6, Liechtenstein diplomat.

20. UN Security Council, Resolution 1539 (2004), 3. Resolution 1460, which was passed in 2003, already expressed the Security Council's intention to enter into dialogue with parties to armed conflict in violation of the international obligations applicable to them on the recruitment or use of children in armed conflict, in order to develop clear and time-bound action plans to end this practice. However, it is Resolution 1539 (2004) that clearly establishes the need for parties to develop action plans in a bid to eventually be removed from the "list of shame."

21. UN Security Council, Resolutions 1612 (2005), 1882 (2009).

22. UN Security Council, Resolution 1539 (2004).

23. UN Secretary General, *Children and Armed Conflict* (2005).

24. UN Security Council, Resolution 1612 (2005).

25. Interview 8, UNICEF senior adviser.

26. As cited in UN OSRSG for CAAC, *20 Years*, 23.

27. Interview 7, UNICEF adviser.

28. Interview 7, UNICEF adviser.

29. Interview 7, UNICEF adviser.

30. I interviewed this person in April 2013 in New York, but he or she asked me not to disclose either the name of the NGO or his or her own name.

31. Huynh, D'Costa, and Lee-Koo, *Children and Global Conflict*, 9–34.

32. This argument comes from the interview with the NGO director, April 2013, New York.

33. The Special Court for Sierra Leone was set up jointly by the government of Sierra Leone and the United Nations to try those who bore the greatest responsibility for serious violations of international humanitarian law and Sierra Leonean law committed in the territory of Sierra Leone as of 30 November 1996. For more about this Special Court, see Special Court for Sierra Leone: Residual Special Court for Sierra Leone, http://www.rscsl.org/.

34. UN General Assembly, *Report of the Special Representative*, 5.

35. UN Security Council, Resolution 2068 (2012).

36. Interview 6, Liechtenstein diplomat.

37. Bode, "Reflective Practices."

38. UN Secretary General, *Children and Armed Conflict* (2012), 26, 27–28, 51.

39. Interview 2, UN program officer.

40. UN Security Council, Resolution 2143 (2014).

41. Interview 8, UNICEF senior adviser.

42. Hoffman, "Like Beasts in the Bush," 299.

43. UN Security Council, Resolution 2225 (2015).

44. Lee-Koo, "Not Suitable for Children."

45. Lee-Koo, "'Intolerable Impact of Armed Conflict,'" 64.

46. Lee-Koo, "Not Suitable for Children," 481.

47. Lee-Koo, "'Intolerable Impact of Armed Conflict.'"

48. UN Security Council, Resolution 2427 (2018), 5; emphasis added.

49. Lee-Koo, "'Intolerable Impact of Armed Conflict,'" 59.

50. Interview 3 UK diplomat.

51. Walker, "Lines of Insecurity," 80.

52. UN OSRSG for CAAC, "New Countries Endorse."

53. UN OSRSG for CAAC, "New Countries Endorse"; emphasis in the original. See UNICEF, Paris Principles.

54. Shepler, *Childhood Deployed*.

55. Shepler, *Childhood Deployed*, 79.

56. UN Security Council, Resolution 1261 (1999), 3.

57. "Peace Agreement" (Lomé Peace Agreement), Art. 30.

58. Denov, *Child Soldiers*, 158.

59. According to the Integrated Disarmament Demobilization and Reintegration Standards published by the UN in 2006, the DDR program is geared toward combatants and is constituted of three phases: (1) the disarmament phase, including both the collection of the combatants' small arms and heavy weapons and the development of responsible arms management programs; (2) the demobilization phase, concentrating on the formal and controlled discharge of active combatants from armed groups; and (3) the reintegration phase, a social and economic process by which ex-combatants may acquire civilian status and gain sustainable employment and income. UNICEF, Paris Principles.

60. Cochaired by UNICEF and Save the Children, the Paris Principles Steering Group encourages governments, intergovernmental organizations, and civil society to follow the

Paris Commitments and the Paris Principles and Guidelines in all funding, advocacy, and programming for the protection of children associated with armed forces or armed groups.

61. Interview 1, UNICEF senior adviser.
62. Interview 2, UN program officer.
63. Interview 1, UNICEF senior adviser.
64. UN General Assembly, Convention on the Rights, art. 39; emphasis added.
65. Wessells, *Child Soldiers*, 154.
66. Shepler, *Childhood Deployed*, 80.
67. Wessells, *Child Soldiers*.
68. UNICEF, Paris Principles, 28.
69. Verhey, "Child Soldiers."
70. Interview 1, UNICEF senior adviser.
71. Interview 1, UNICEF senior adviser.
72. Wessells, *Child Soldiers*, 159.
73. Verhey, "Child Soldiers," 12.
74. Interview 1, UNICEF senior adviser.
75. Martins, "Dangers of the Single Story."
76. Verhey, "Child Soldiers," 12.
77. Interview 1, UNICEF senior adviser.
78. Interview 5, UNICEF adviser.
79. Interview 1, UNICEF senior adviser.
80. Interview 1, UNICEF senior adviser.
81. Interview 3, UK diplomat.
82. Twum-Danso, *Africa's Young Soldiers*.
83. Interview 1, UNICEF senior adviser.
84. Ghouri, *Children of Conflict—Congo—Part 1*.
85. Interview 1, UNICEF senior adviser.
86. Interview 1, UNICEF senior adviser.
87. Hanson, "Children's Participation and Agency."
88. "Boy Soldiers."
89. Gislesen, "Childhood Lost?"
90. UNICEF, Paris Principles.
91. Bigo, "Protection."
92. Klasen et al., "Posttraumatic Resilience," 1097.
93. UNICEF, Paris Principles.
94. Wessells, *Child Soldiers*, 160.
95. Interview 8, UNICEF senior adviser.
96. Wessells, *Child Soldiers*, 160.
97. Interview 1, UNICEF senior adviser.
98. Wessells, "Living Wage," 193; emphasis added.
99. War Child, *War*, 7.
100. Mental Health Foundation, cited in Coppock, "Medicalising Children's Behaviour," 151.
101. Pupavac, "Therapeutic Governance."
102. UNICEF, Paris Principles, 38.
103. Betancourt et al., *Psychosocial Adjustment*.
104. UNICEF, Paris Principles, 38.
105. Betancourt et al., *Psychosocial Adjustment*.

106. IASC, *IASC Guidelines on Mental Health*.

107. Interview 2, UN program officer.

108. Betancourt et al., *Psychosocial Adjustment*, 24.

109. Boothby, "When Former Child Soldiers."

110. Boothby, "When Former Child Soldiers," 165.

111. Boothby, "When Former Child Soldiers," 163.

112. Boothby, "When Former Child Soldiers," 164.

113. The Trauma Symptom Checklist for Children is a fifty-four-item self-report measure of posttraumatic stress and related psychological symptomatology in children ages eight to sixteen years who have experienced traumatic events (e.g., physical or sexual abuse, major loss, natural disaster, or witnessing violence).

114. Fassin, "Predicament of Humanitarianism," 46.

115. Summerfield, "Critique of Seven Assumptions," 1452.

116. Coppock, "Medicalising Children's Behaviour," 141.

117. Timimi, "Globalising Mental Health, 154.

118. Boothby, "When Former Child Soldiers," 176.

119. Interview 8, UNICEF senior adviser.

120. Fassin, *Humanitarian Reason*.

121. LeFrançois, "Still Being Psychiatrised," 7.

122. For the image see Save the Children, "Child Soldier."

123. The picture, taken from an issue of *Playboy* magazine, is discussed by Denov in *Child Soldiers*, 10.

124. Walker, *After the Globe*, 257.

CONCLUSION

1. Rosen, *Armies of the Young*, 5.

2. Denov, *Child Soldiers*; Rosen, *Armies of the Young*.

3. T. Cook, "'He Was Determined to Go.'"

4. T. Cook, "'He Was Determined to Go,'" 42.

5. T. Cook, "'He Was Determined to Go,'" 47.

6. John Write, cited in T. Cook, "'He Was Determined to Go,'" 46; emphasis added.

7. J. D. Thomson, cited in T. Cook, "'He Was Determined to Go,'" 54.

8. T. Cook, "'He Was Determined to Go,'" 54.

9. Denov, *Child Soldiers*.

10. Rosen, *Armies of the Young*, 19–56.

11. Rosen, *Armies of the Young*, 20.

12. Misha Melamed, cited in Rosen, *Armies of the Young*, 46–47.

13. Macmillan, "Militarized Children," 73.

14. Lee-Koo, "Horror and Hope," 727.

15. Lee-Koo, "Horror and Hope," 727.

16. Nieuwenhuys, "Keep Asking."

17. The picture appears on Save the Children's twitter account, available at https://twitter.com/savethechildren/status/437617660298559488, accessed 26 February 2018.

18. Postman, *Disappearance of Childhood*.

19. D. T. Cook, "Politics of Becoming," 4.

20. Walker, *After the Globe*, 258.

21. Jenks, "Journeys into Space," 420.

22. Doyle, "Call to Help."

23. D. T. Cook, "Politics of Becoming," 3.

24. Huynh, D'Costa, and Lee-Koo, *Children and Global Conflict*, 50.

25. Beier, "Children, Childhoods, and Security Studies"; Huynh, D'Costa, and Lee-Koo, *Children and Global Conflict*; Foucault, "What Is Enlightenment?," 45.

BIBLIOGRAPHY

Interviews

1. UNICEF senior adviser, Child Protection in Emergencies Unit, August 2012. Interviewer: Jana Tabak. New York, 2012. 1 mp3 file (68 min).
2. Program officer, UN Office of the Special Representative of the Secretary-General for Children and Armed Conflict, August 2012. Interviewer: Jana Tabak. New York, 2012. 1 mp3 file (62 min).
3. Diplomat and member, Permanent Mission of UK to the United Nations, and Security Council Working Group of Children and Armed Conflict, April 2013. Interviewer: Jana Tabak. New York, 2013. 1 mp3 file (42:45 min).
4. Program officer, UN Office of the Special Representative of the Secretary-General for Children and Armed Conflict, April 2013. Interviewer: Jana Tabak. New York, 2013. 1 mp3 file (51:46 min).
5. UNICEF adviser, Child Protection Unit, April 2013. Interviewer: Jana Tabak. New York, 2013. 1 mp3 file (119 min).
6. Diplomat, Permanent Mission of Liechtenstein to the United Nations in New York, and member, "Group of Friends on Children and Armed Conflict," April 2013. Interviewer: Jana Tabak. New York, 2013. 1 mp3 file (35:04 min).
7. UNICEF adviser, Child Protection in Emergencies Unit, April 2013. Interviewer: Jana Tabak. New York, 2013. 1 mp3 file (45:42 min).
8. Senior adviser, UNICEF, June 2017. Interviewer: Jana Tabak. New York, 2017. 1 mp3 file (68:11 min).
9. Adviser, Child Protection Unit, UN Department for Peacekeeping Operations, June 2017. Interviewer: Jana Tabak. New York, 2017. 1 mp3 file (65:10 min).

Published Sources

Amnesty International. *Hidden Scandal, Secret Shame: Torture and Ill-Treatment of Children.* London: Amnesty International, 2000.

Annan, Jeannie, and Chris Blattman. "Child Combatants in Northern Uganda: Reintegration Myths and Realities." In *Security and Post-Conflict Reconstruction: Dealing with Fighters in the Aftermath of War*, edited by Rob Muggah, 103–26. New York: Routledge, 2008.

Annan, Kofi. *We the Children: Meeting the Promises of the World Summit for Children.* New York: UNICEF for the UN, 2001.

Archard, David. *Children: Rights and Childhood.* New York: Routledge, 2004.

Ariès, Philippe. *Centuries of Childhood: A Social History of Family Life.* New York: Alfred A. Knopf, 1962.

Balagopalan, Sarada. "Childhood, Culture, History: Redeploying 'Multiple Childhoods.'" In *Reimagining Childhood Studies*, edited by Spyros Spyrou, Rachel Rosen, and Daniel Thomas Cook, 23–39. London: Bloomsbury Academic, 2019.

Barnett, Errol. "Ex-Child-Soldier: 'Shooting Became Just Like Drinking a Glass of Water.'" CNN, 9 October 2012. http://edition.cnn.com/2012/10/08/world/africa/ishmael-beah-child-soldier.

Bartelson, Jens. *A Genealogy of Sovereignty*. Cambridge: Cambridge University Press, 1995.

Beah, Ishmael. *A Long Way Gone: Memoirs of a Boy Soldier*. Bath: Paragon, 2007.

———. "The Making, and Unmaking, of a Child Soldier." *New York Times Magazine*, 14 January 2007, http://www.nytimes.com/2007/01/14/magazine/14soldier.t.html?pagewanted=all&_r=0.

Beier J. Marshall. *Childhood and the Production of Security*. London: Routledge, 2017.

———. "Children, Childhoods, and Security Studies: An Introduction." *Critical Studies on Security* 3, no. 1 (2015): 1–13.

———. "Everyday Zones of Militarization." In *The Militarization of Childhood: Thinking beyond the Global South*, edited by J. Marshall Beier, 1–16. New York: Palgrave Macmillan, 2011.

Berents, Helen. *Young People and Everyday Peace: Exclusion, Insecurity and Peacebuilding in Colombia*. New York: Routledge, 2018.

Betancourt, Theresa, Ivelina Borisova, Julia Rubin-Smith, Tara Gingerich, Timothy Williams, and Jessica Agnew-Blais. *Psychosocial Adjustment and Social Reintegration of Children Associated with Armed Forces and Armed Groups: The State of the Field and Future Directions*. Cambridge, MA: Psychology beyond Borders and the Francois-Xavier Bagnoud Center for Health and Human Rights/Harvard School of Public Health, 1 May 2008.

Bhabha, Jacqueline. "The Child: What Sort of Human?" *PMLA* 121, no. 5 (2006): 1526–35.

———. "Independent Children, Inconsistent Adults: International Child Migration and the Legal Framework." Innocenti Discussion Paper. Florence: UNICEF Innocenti Research Centre, 2008.

Bigo, Didier. "Protection: Security, Territory and Population." In *The Politics of Protection: Sites of Insecurity and Political Agency*, edited by Jef Huysmans, Andrew Dobson, and Raia Prokhoniv, 84–100. London: Routledge, 2006.

Bode, Ingvild. "Reflective Practices at the Security Council: Children and Armed Conflict and the Three United Nations." *European Journal of International Relations* 24, no. 2 (2017): 1–26.

Boothby, Neil. "Mozambique Life Outcome Study: How Did Child Soldiers Turn Out as Adults?" In *Child Soldiers: From Recruitment to Reintegration*, edited by Alpaslan Ozerdem and Sukanya Podder, 231–46. New York: Palgrave Macmillan, 2011.

———. "When Former Child Soldiers Grow Up: The Keys to Reintegration and Reconciliation." In *A World Turned Upside Down: Social Ecological Approaches to Children in War Zones*, edited by Neil Boothby, Alison Strang, and Michael Wessells, 155–78. Boulder, CO: Kumarian Press, 2006.

Boyden, Jo. "Childhood and the Policy Makers: A Comparative Perspective on the Globalization of Childhood." In *Constructing and Reconstructing Childhood: Contemporary Issues in the Sociological Study of Children*, edited by Allison James and Alan Prout, 187–225. London: Falmer Press, 1991.

Boyden, Jo, and Joana de Berry. Introduction to *Children and Youth on the Front Line: Ethnography, Armed Conflict, and Displacement*, xi–xxvii. Edited by Jo Boyden and Joana de Berry. New York: Berghahn Books, 2004.

"Boy Soldiers." *Newsweek*, 13 August 1995. http://www.newsweek.com/boy-soldiers-182674.

Bradshaw, Steve. "Justice Dilemma Haunts Uganda." BBC News, 8 September 2008, http://news.bbc.co.uk/2/hi/africa/7603939.stm.

Briggs, Jimmie. *Innocents Lost: When Child Soldiers Go to War*. New York: Basic Books, 2005.

Brocklehurst, Helen. "The State of Play: Securities of Childhood—Insecurities of Children." *Critical Studies on Security* 3, no. 1 (2015): 29–46.

———. *Who's Afraid of Children? Children, Conflict and International Relations*. Farnham: Ashgate, 2006.

Brookfield, Tarah. *Cold War Comforts: Canadian Women, Child Safety, and Global Insecurity*. Waterloo, ON: Wilfrid Laurier University Press, 2012.

Burman, Erica. *Deconstructing Developmental Psychology*. New York: Routledge, 2008.

———. "Developmental Psychology and Its Discontents." In *Critical Psychology: An Introduction*, edited by Dennis Fox and Isaac Prilleltensky, 134–49. London: SAGE, 1997.

———. *Developments: Child, Image, Nation*. London: Routledge, 2008.

———. "Innocents Abroad: Western Fantasies of Childhood and the Iconography of Emergencies." *Disasters* 18, no. 3 (1994): 238–53.

Burr, Rachel. *Vietnam's Children in a Changing World*. New Brunswick, NJ: Rutgers University Press, 2006.

Calhoun, Craig. "The Imperative to Reduce Suffering: Charity, Progress, and Emergencies in the Field of Humanitarian Action." In *Humanitarianism in Question: Politics, Power, Ethics*, edited by Michael Barnett and Thomas Weiss, 73–97. Ithaca: Cornell University Press, 2008.

Cheney, Kristen E. *Pillars of the Nation: Child Citizens and Ugandan National Development*. Chicago: University of Chicago Press, 2007.

Child Soldiers International. "United Kingdom." https://www.child-soldiers.org/uk.

Chin, Elizabeth. "Children out of Bounds in Globalising Times." *Postcolonial Studies* 6, no. 3 (2003): 309–25.

Coalition to Stop the Use of Child Soldiers. *Child Soldiers Global Report 2001*. London: Child Soldiers International, 2001.

Commission on Human Security. *Human Security Now*, New York: Commission on Human Security, 2003.

Cook, Daniel Thomas. *The Commodification of Childhood: The Children's Clothing Industry and the Rise of the Child Consumer*. Durham, NC: Duke University Press, 2004.

———. "Interrogating Symbolic Childhood." In *Symbolic Childhood*, edited by Daniel Thomas Cook, 1–14. New York: Peter Lang, 2002.

———. "A Politics of Becoming: When 'Child' Is Not Enough." *Childhood* 22, no. 1 (2015): 3–5.

———. "When a Child Is Not a Child, and Other Conceptual Hazards of Childhood Studies." *Childhood* 16, no. 1 (2009): 5–10.

Cook, Tim. "'He Was Determined to Go': Underage Soldiers in the Canadian Expeditionary Force." *Histoire Sociale/Social History* 41, no. 81 (2008): 41–74.

Coomaraswamy, Radhika. "The Optional Protocol to the Convention on the Rights of the Child on the Involvement of Children in Armed Conflict—Towards Universal Ratification." *International Journal of Children's Rights* 18, no. 4 (2010): 535–49.

Coomaraswamy, Radhika. "Statement at the Event on the Paris Commitments and Paris Principles." Office of the Special Representative of the Secretary-General for Children and Armed Conflict, Paris Principles, 1 October 2007. https://childrenandarmedconflict.un.org/statement/1-oct-2007-paris-principles-new-york/.

———. "Statement at the Paris International Conference 'Free Children from War.'" Office of the Special Representative of the Secretary-General for Children and Armed Conflict, International Conference in Paris, 5 February 2007. https://childrenandarmedconflict.un.org/statement/5-feb-2007-international-conference-in-paris/.

Coppock, Vicky. "Medicalising Children's Behaviour." In *The New Handbook of Children's Rights Comparative Policy and Practice*, edited by Bob Franklin, 139–54. London: Routledge, 2002.

Corsaro, William. *Sociologia da Infância*. Porto Alegre, Brazil: Artmed, 2011.

Cunningham, Hugh. *Children and Childhood in Western Society since 1500*. Harlow, UK: Pearson Education, 2005.

Dallaire, Roméo. *They Fight Like Soldiers, They Die Like Children: The Global Quest to Eradicate the Use of Child Soldiers*. New York: Walker, 2010.

Denov, Myriam S. *Child Soldiers: Sierra Leone's Revolutionary United Front*. Cambridge: Cambridge University Press, 2010.

Doyle, Mark. "Call to Help Liberia's Child Soldiers." BBC, 2 February 2004. http://news.bbc.co.uk/2/hi/africa/3450263.stm.

Drumbl, Mark A. *Reimagining Child Soldiers in International Law and Policy*. Oxford: Oxford University Press, 2012.

Duffield, Mark. "Development, Territories, and People: Consolidating the External Sovereign Frontier." *Alternatives: Global, Local, Political* 32, no. 2 (2007): 225–46.

———. "The Liberal Way of Development and the Development–Security Impasse: Exploring the Global Life-Chance Divide." *Security Dialogue* 41, no. 1 (2010): 53–76.

Ellis, Jessica. "Lopez Lomong: From War Child to U.S. Olympics Star." CNN, 9 August 2012. http://edition.cnn.com/2012/08/06/sport/lopez-lomong-lost-boy/index.html.

Ensor, Marisa O. "Participation under Fire: Dilemmas of Reintegrating Child Soldiers Involved in South Sudan's Armed Conflict." *Global Studies of Childhood* 3, no. 2 (2013): 153–62.

Esteves, Paulo. "Unfolding the International at Late Modernity: International Society and the Humanitarian Space." NUPI Working Paper no. 746. Norwegian Institute of International Affairs, 2008. http://www.css.ethz.ch/en/services/digital-library/publications/publication.html/94408.

Farson, Richard Evans. *Birthrights*. London: Collier Macmillan, 1974.

Fassin, Didier. *Humanitarian Reason: A Moral History of the Present*. Berkeley: University of California Press, 2012.

———. "The Predicament of Humanitarianism." *Qui Parle* 22, no. 1 (2013): 33–48.

Foran, Jessica E. "Interrogating 'Militarized' Images and Disrupting Sovereign Narratives in the Case of Omar Khadr." In *The Militarization of Childhood: Thinking beyond the Global South*, edited by J. Marshall Beier, 195–216. New York: Palgrave Macmillan, 2011.

Foucault, Michel. *Discipline and Punish: The Birth of the Prison*. New York: Vintage Books, 1995.

———. "The Order of Discourse." In *Untying the Text: A Post-Structuralist Reader*, edited by Robert J. C. Young, 50–78. Boston: Routledge, 1981.

———. "Practicing Criticism." In *Politics, Philosophy, Culture: Interviews and Other Writings, 1977–1984*, edited by Lawrence D. Kritzman, 152–56. New York: Routledge, 1988.

———. *Security, Territory and Population: Lectures at the Collège de France, 1977–1978*. New York: Palgrave Macmillan, 2009.

———. "Truth and Power." In *Power/Knowledge: Selected Interviews and Other Writings*, edited by Colin Gordon, 109–33. New York: Prentice Hall, 1980.

———. "What Is Enlightenment?" In *The Foucault Reader*, edited by Paul Rabinow, 32–50. New York: Pantheon Books, 1984.

Fowler, Gene, Jr. *Seeds of Destiny*. US War Department documentary, 19:49. https://archive.org/details/SeedsofDestiny.

Freeman, Michael. "Introduction: Rights, Ideologies and Children." In *The Ideologies of Children's Rights*, edited by Michael Freeman and Philip Veerman. Dordrecht: Martinus Nijhoff, 1992.

———. *The Rights and Wrongs of Children*. London: F. Pinter, 1983.

Friscolanti, Michael. "Who Is the Real Omar Khadr? Murdering Jihadist, Victim of Circumstance or Model-Citizen-in-the-Making?" *Maclean's*, 9 November 2010. http://www.macleans.ca/news/canada/who-is-the-real-omar-khadr/.

Gates, Scott, and Simon Reich, eds. *Child Soldiers in the Age of Fractured States*. Pittsburgh: University of Pittsburgh Press, 2010.

Geneva Call. *Protecting Children in Armed Conflict: Key Rules from Geneva Call's Deed of Commitment*. Geneva: Geneva Call, 2013.

Gislesen, Kirsten. "A Childhood Lost? The Challenges of Successful Disarmament, Demobilisation and Reintegration of Child Soldiers: The Case of West Africa." NUPI Working Paper no. 712. Norwegian Institute of International Affairs, 2006. https://www.files.ethz.ch/isn/27910/712.pdf.

Ghouri, Nadene. *Children of Conflict—Congo—Part 1*. Al Jazeera, video, 12:08, 13 March 2007, http://www.aljazeera.com/programmes/general/2007/02/2008525183938868834.html.

Hansen, Lene. *Security as Practice: Discourse Analysis and the Bosnian War*. Nova York: Routledge, 2006.

Hanson, Karl. "Children's Participation and Agency When They Don't 'Do the Right Thing.'" *Childhood* 23, no. 4 (2016): 471–75.

Hart, Jason. "Children's Participation and International Development: Attending to the Political." *International Journal of Children's Rights* 16, no. 3 (2008): 407–18.

Hendrick, Harry, *Child Welfare: Historical Dimensions, Contemporary Debate*. Bristol: Policy Press, 2003.

Higonnet, Anne. *Pictures of the Innocence: The History and Crisis of Ideal Childhood*. New York: Thames and Hudson, 1998.

Hockey, Jennifer L., and Allison James. *Growing Up and Growing Old: Ageing and Dependency in the Life Course*. London: SAGE, 1993.

Hoffman, Danny. "Like Beasts in the Bush: Synonyms of Childhood and Youth in Sierra Leone." *Postcolonial Studies* 6, no. 3 (2003): 295–308.

Holsti, Kalevi J. *Peace and War: Armed Conflicts and International Order, 1648–1989*. New York: Cambridge University Press, 1991.

———. *The State, War, and the State of War*. New York: Cambridge University Press, 1996.

———. *Taming the Sovereigns: Institutional Change in International Politics*. Cambridge: Cambridge University Press, 2004.

Holt, John. *Escape from Childhood*. Harmondsworth: Penguin, 1975.

Holzscheiter, Anna. *Children's Rights in International Politics: The Transformative Power of Discourse*. New York: Palgrave Macmillan, 2010.

Honwana, Alcinda. *Child Soldiers in Africa*. Philadelphia: University of Pennsylvania Press, 2006.

———. "Innocent and Guilty: Child-Soldiers as Interstitial and Tactical Agents." In *Makers and Breakers: Children and Youth in Postcolonial Africa*, edited by Alcinda Honwana and Filip De Boeck, 31–52. Oxford: James Currey, 2005.

Human Rights Watch. "Forgotten Fighters: Child Soldiers in Angola." *Human Rights Watch* 15, no. 10(A) (April 2003). https://www.hrw.org/reports/2003/angola0403/Angola0403.pdf.

———. "How to Fight, How to Kill: Child Soldiers in Liberia." *Human Rights Watch* 16, no. 2(A) (February 2004). https://www.hrw.org/reports/2004/liberia0204/liberia0204.pdf.

———. "Living in Fear: Child Soldiers and the Tamil Tigers in Sri Lanka." *Human Rights Watch* 16, no. 13(C) (November 2004). https://www.hrw.org/reports/2004/srilanka1104 /srilanka1104.pdf.

———. *"My Gun Was as Tall as Me": Child Soldiers in Burma*. New York: Human Rights Watch, 2002.

———. *The Scars of Death: Children Abducted by the Lord's Resistance Army in Uganda*. New York: Human Rights Watch, 1997.

Human Security Report Project. *Human Security Report 2005: War and Peace in the 21st Century*. Oxford: Oxford University Press, 2006.

Huynh, Kim, Bina D'Costa, and Katrina Lee-Koo. *Children and Global Conflict*. Cambridge: Cambridge University Press, 2015.

Huysmans, Jef. "Agency and the Politics of Protection: Implications for Security Studies." In Huysmans, Dobson, and Prokhovnik, *Politics of Protection*, 1–18.

Huysmans, Jef, Andrew Dobson, and Raia Prokhovnik, eds. *The Politics of Protection: Sites of Insecurity and Political Agency*. New York: Routledge, 2006.

Images Asia. *No Childhood at All: Child soldiers in Burma*. Chiangmai, Thailand: Nopburee Press, 1997.

Inter-Agency Standard Committee (IASC). *IASC Guidelines on Mental Health and Psychosocial Support in Emergency Settings*. Geneva: IASC, 2007.

International Commission on Intervention and State Sovereignty (ICISS). *The Responsibility to Protect: Report of the International Commission on Intervention and State Sovereignty*. Ottawa: International Development Research Centre, 2001.

International Committee of the Red Cross (ICRC). "Additional Protocols to the Geneva Conventions of 12 August 1949." 8 June 1977. http://www.icrc.org/eng/war-and-law/treaties -customary-law/geneva-conventions/.

———. "Geneva Convention Relative to the Protection of Civilian Persons in Time of War (Fourth Geneva Convention)." 12 August 1949, 75 UNTS 287. http://www.refworld.org /docid/3ae6b36d2.html.

International Labour Organization (ILO). *Convention concerning Minimum Age for Admission to Employment*, C138, 19 June 1976, http://www.ilo.org/dyn/normlex/en/f?p= NORMLEXPUB:12100:0::NO::P12100_ILO_CODE:C138

———. "Convention concerning the Prohibition and Immediate Action for the Elimination of the Worst Forms of Child Labour." C182, Geneva, 17 June 1999. http://www.ilo.org/dyn /normlex/en/f?p=NORMLEXPUB:12100:0::NO::P12100_ILO_CODE:C182

———. *Wounded Childhood: The Use of Children in Armed Conflict in Central Africa*. Geneva: International Labour Office, 2003.

Invisible Children. *Kony 2012*, video, 29:58, posted by Invisible Children, 5 March 2012. https:// www.youtube.com/watch?v=Y4MnpzG5Sqc

Iweala, Uzodinma. *Beasts of No Nation*. New York: HarperCollins Books, 2005.

Jabri, Vivienne. "The Limits of Agency in Times of Emergency." In Huysmans, Dobson, and Prokhovnik, *Politics of Protection*, 136–53.

———. *War and the Transformation of Global Politics*. New York: Palgrave Macmillan, 2007.

Jacob, Cecilia. *Child Security in Asia: The Impact of Armed Conflict in Cambodia and Myanmar*. London: Routledge, 2014.

———. "'Children and Armed Conflict' and the Field of Security Studies." *Critical Studies on Security* 3, no. 1 (2015): 14–28.

James, Allison. "Understanding Childhood from an Interdisciplinary Perspective." In *Rethinking Childhood*, edited by Peter B. Pufall and Richard P. Unsworth, 25–37. New Brunswick: Rutgers University Press, 2004.

James, Allison, and Alan Prout. "A New Paradigm for the Sociology of Childhood? Provenance, Promise and Problems." In *Constructing and Reconstructing Childhood: Contemporary Issues in the Sociological Study of Children*, edited by Allison James and Alan Prout, 7–34. London: Falmer Press, 1991.

James, Allison, and Chris Jenks. "Public Perceptions of Childhood Criminality." *British Journal of Sociology* 47, no. 2 (1996): 315–31.

James, Allison, Chris Jenks, and Alan Prout. *Theorizing Childhood*. Cambridge: Polity Press, 1998.

Jamison, Melissa A. "Detention of Juvenile Enemy Combatants at Guantanamo Bay: The Special Concerns of the Children." *U.C. Davis Journal of Juvenile Law & Policy*, 127 (2005): 139–41.

Jenks, Chris. *Childhood*. London: Routledge, 2005.

———. "Journeys into Space." *Childhood* 12, no. 4 (2005): 419–24.

Linde, Robyn. "The Globalization of Childhood: The International Diffusion of Norms and Law against the Child Death Penalty." *European Journal of International Relations* 20, no. 2 (2014): 544–68.

Kaldor, Mary. *New and Old Wars: Organized Violence in a Global Era*. Stanford, CA: Stanford University Press, 1999.

Key, Ellen. *The Century of the Child*. New York: G.P. Putnam's Sons, 1909.

Klasen, Fionna, Gabriele Oettingen, Judith Daniels, Manuela Post, Catrin Hoyer, and Hubertus Adam. "Posttraumatic Resilience in Former Ugandan Child Soldiers." *Child Development* 81, no. 4 (2010): 1096–113.

Krappmann, Lothar. "The Weight of the Child's View (Article 12 of the Convention on the Rights of the Child)." *International Journal of Children's Rights* 18, no. 4 (2010): 501–13.

Labouisse, Henry R. "United Nations Children's Fund—Acceptance Speech." On the occasion of the award of the Nobel Peace Prize in Oslo, December 10, 1965. https://www.nobelprize.org/prizes/peace/1965/unicef/acceptance-speech/.

League of Nations. "Geneva Declaration of the Rights of the Child." 26 September 1924. http://www.un-documents.net/gdrc1924.htm.

Lee, Ah-Jung. "Understanding and Addressing the Phenomenon of 'Child Soldiers': The Gap between the Global Humanitarian Discourse and the Local Understandings and Experiences of Young People's Military Recruitment." Refugee Studies Centre, Working Paper Series, no. 52. Oxford: Refugee Studies Centre, January 2009.

Lee, Nick. "The Challenge of Childhood: The Distribution of Childhood's Ambiguity in Adult Institutions." *Childhood* 6, no. 4 (1999): 455–74.

———. *Childhood and Society: Growing Up in an Age of Uncertainty*. Buckingham, UK: Open University Press, 2001.

Lee-Koo, Katrina. "Horror and Hope: (Re)presenting Militarised Children in Global North–South Relations." *Third World Quarterly* 32, no. 4 (2011): 725–42.

———. "'The Intolerable Impact of Armed Conflict on Children': The United Nations Security Council and the Protection of Children in Armed Conflict." *Global Responsibility to Protect* 10 (2018): 57–74.

———. "Not Suitable for Children: The Politicisation of Conflict-Affected Children in Post-2001 Afghanistan." *Australian Journal of International Affairs* 67, no. 4 (2013): 475–90.

LeFrançois, Brenda A. "Adultism." In *The Encyclopedia of Critical Psychology*, edited by Thomas Teo, chapter 6. Berlin: Springer Verlag, 2013.

———. "And We Are Still Being Psychiatrised." *Asylum* 19, no. 1 (2012): 7–8.

Lomong, Lopez. *Running for My Life: One Lost Boy's Journey from the Killing Fields of Sudan to the Olympic Game.*, Nashville, TN: Thomas Nelson, 2012.

Lorey, Mark. *Child Soldiers: Care & Protection of Children in Emergencies: A Field Guide.* London: Save the Children Fund, 2001.

Machel, Graça. *The Impact of War on Children: A Review of Progress since the 1996 United Nations Report on the Impact of Armed Conflict on Children.* London: Hurst, 2001.

———. *Promotion and Protection of the Rights of Children: Impact of Armed Conflict on Children.* Report of Graça Machel, expert appointed by the Secretary General of the United Nations, New York, A/50/60, 1996.

Macmillan, Lorraine. "The Child Soldier in North–South Relations." *International Political Sociology* 3, no. 1 (2009): 36–52.

———. "Militarized Children and Sovereign Power." In *The Militarization of Childhood: Thinking beyond the Global South*, edited by J. Marshall Beier, 61–76. New York: Palgrave Macmillan, 2011.

MacVeigh, Joahanna, Sarah Maguire, and Joanna Wedge. *Stolen Futures: The Reintegration of Children Affected by Armed Conflict.* London: Save the Children, 2007.

Malesevic, Sinisa. "The Sociology of New Wars? Assessing the Causes and Objectives of Contemporary Violent Conflicts." *International Political Sociology* 2, no. 2 (2008): 97–112.

Malkki, Liisa. "Children, Humanity and the Infantilization of Peace." In *In the Name of Humanity: The Government of Threat and Care*, edited by Ilana Feldman and Miriam Ticktin, 58–85. Durham, NC: Duke University Press, 2010.

Marshall, Dominique. "The Construction of Children as an Object of International Relations: The Declaration of Children's Rights and the Child Welfare Committee of League of Nations, 1900–1924." *International Journal of Children's Rights* 7 (1999): 103–47.

Marten, James. *Children and War: A Historical Anthology.* New York: New York University Press, 2002.

Martins, Catarina. "The Dangers of the Single Story: Child-Soldiers in Literary Fiction and Film." *Childhood* 18, no. 4 (2011): 434–46.

McGregor, Ewan. "Ewan McGregor: With Your Help, UNICEF Can Give Child Soldiers Another Chance at Childhood." *Independent* (London), 9 December 2012. http://www.independent.co.uk/voices/comment/ewan-mcgregor-with-your-help-unicef-can-give-child-soldiers-another-chance-at-childhood-8393283.html.

Mills, China. "'Special' Treatment, 'Special' Rights: Children Who Hear Voices as Doubly Diminished Identities." In *Law and Childhood Studies*, edited by Michael Freeman, 438–55. Oxford: Oxford University Press, 2012.

Moeller, Susan D. "A Hierarchy of Innocence: The Media's Use of Children in the Telling of International News." *Harvard International Journal of Press/Politics* 7, no. 1 (2002): 36–56.

Münkler, Herfried. *The New Wars.* Cambridge: Polity Press, 2005.

Newman, Edward. "The 'New Wars' Debate: A Historical Perspective Is Needed." *Security Dialogue* 35, no. 2 (2004): 173–89.

Nolen, Stephanie, and Erin Baines. "The Making of a Monster?" *Globe and Mail*, 25 October 2008. Canadian Children's Rights Council. https://canadiancrc.com/newspaper_articles/Globe_and_Mail_The_Making_of_a_Monster_child_soldier_25OCT08.aspx.

Nieuwenhuys, Olga. "Global Childhood and the Politics of Contempt." *Alternatives: Global, Local, Political* 23, no. 3 (1998) 267–89.

———. "Keep Asking: Why Childhood? Why Children? Why Global?" *Childhood* 17, no. 3 (2010): 291–96.

Nyers, Peter. *Rethinking Refugees: Beyond States of Emergency.* New York: Routledge, 2006.

Organization of African Unity (OAU). "African Charter on the Rights and Welfare of the Child." 11 July 1990, CAB/LEG/24.9/49 (1990). https://www.unicef.org/esaro/African_Charter_articles_in_full.pdf.

Oswell, David. *The Agency of Children: From Family to Global Human Rights*. New York: Cambridge University Press, 2013.

"Peace Agreement between the Government of Sierra Leone and the Revolutionary United Front of Sierra Leone" (Lomé Peace Agreement) . Lomé, 7 July 1999. https://peacemaker.un.org/sites/peacemaker.un.org/files/SL_990707_LomePeaceAgreement.pdf.

Postman, Neil. *The Disappearance of Childhood*. New York: Vintage Books, 1982.

Pruitt, Lesley. "Fixing the Girls." *International Feminist Journal of Politics* 15, no. 1 (2013): 58–76.

Puar, Jasbir K., and Amit S. Rai. "Monster, Terrorist, Fag: The War on Terrorism and the Production of Docile Patriots." *Social Text* 20, no. 372 (2002): 117–48.

Punch, Samantha. "Negotiating Autonomy: Childhoods in Rural Bolivia." In *Conceptualizing Adult-Child Relations*, edited by Leena Alanen and Berry Mayall, 23–36. London: Routledge, 2001.

Pupavac, Vanessa. "The International Children's Rights Regime." In *Rethinking Human Rights: Critical Approaches to International Politics*, edited by David Chandler. New York: Palgrave Macmillan, 2002.

———. "Misanthropy without Borders: The International Children's Rights Regime." *Disasters* 25, no. 2 (2001): 95–112.

Pupavac, Vanessa. "Therapeutic Governance: Psycho-social Intervention and Trauma Risk Management." *Disasters* 25, no. 4 (2001): 358–72.

Qvortrup, Jens. "Childhood as a Structural Form." In *The Palgrave Handbook of Childhood Studies*, edited by Jens Qvortrup, William A. Corsaro, and Michael-Sebastian Honig, 21–33. Houndmills: Palgrave Macmillan, 2011.

———. "Varieties of Childhood." In *Studies in Modern Childhood: Society, Agency, Culture*, edited by Jens Qvortrup, 1–20. New York: Palgrave Macmillan, 2005.

Qvortrup, Jens. "The Waiting Child." *Childhood* 11, no. 3 (2004): 267–73.

Rasmussen, Kim. "Places for Children—Children's Places." *Childhood* 11, no. 2 (2004): 155–73.

Reynaert, Didier, Maria Bouverne-de-Bie, and Stijn Vandevelde. "A Review of Children's Rights Literature since the Adoption of the United Nations Convention on the Rights of the Child." *Childhood* 16, no. 4 (2009): 518–34.

Rose, Nikolas. *Governing the Soul: The Shaping of the Private Self*. London: Free Association Books, 1999.

Rosen, David. *Armies of the Young: Child Soldiers in War and Terrorism*. New Brunswick, NJ: Rutgers University Press, 2005.

———. *Child Soldiers: A Reference Book*. Santa Barbara, CA: ABC-CLIO, 2012.

———. *Child Soldiers in the Western Imagination: From Patriots to Victims*. New Brunswick, NJ: Rutgers University Press, 2015.

Ruiz-Casares, Mónica, Tara M. Collins, E. Kay M. Tisdall, and Sonja Grover. "Children's Rights to Participation and Protection in International Development and Humanitarian Interventions: Nurturing a Dialogue." *International Journal of Human Rights* 21, no. 1 (2017): 1–13.

Ryan, Patrick. "How New Is the 'New' Social Study of Childhood? The Myth of a Paradigm Shift." *Journal of Interdisciplinary History* 38, no. 4 (2008): 553–76.

Save the Children. "Child Soldier." Advertising campaign, Ads of the World, 20 October 2009. https://www.adsoftheworld.com/media/outdoor/save_the_children_child_soldier.

Schaub, Maryellen, Adrienne Henck, and David P. Baker. "The Globalized 'Whole Child': Cultural Understandings of Children and Childhood in Multilateral Aid Development Policy, 1946–2010." *Comparative Education Review* 61, no. 2 (May 2017): 298–326.

Seuss, Dr. *Happy Birthday to You!* New York: Random House Books for Young Readers, 1959.

Shapiro, Michael J. *Reading Postmodern Polity: Political Theory as Textual Practice*. Minneapolis: University of Minnesota Press, 1992.

Shepler, Susan. *Childhood Deployed: Remaking Child Soldiers in Sierra Leone*. New York: New York University Press, 2014.

Simmons, Beth. *Mobilizing for Human Rights: International Law in Domestic Politics*. New York: Cambridge University Press, 2009.

Singer, Peter. W. *Children at War*. Berkeley: University of California Press, 2006.

Small Arms Survey. *Small Arms Survey 2008: Risk and Resilience*. Geneva: Small Arms Survey, 2008.

Spyrou, Spyros, Rachel Rosen, and Daniel Thomas Cook. *Reimagining Childhood Studies*. London: Bloomsbury Academic, 2019.

———. "Introduction: Connectivities . . . Relationalities . . . Linkages . . ." In *Reimagining Childhood Studies*, edited by Spyros Spyrou, Rachel Rosen, and Daniel Thomas Cook. London: Bloomsbury Academic, 2019.

Stephens, Sharon. Introduction to *Children and the Politics of Culture*, edited by Sharon Stephens, 3–48. Princeton, NJ: Princeton University Press, 1995.

Summerfield, Derek. "A Critique of Seven Assumptions behind Psychological Trauma Programmes in War-Affected Areas." *Social Science & Medicine* 48, no. 10 (1999): 1449–62.

Tabak, Jana, and Leticia Carvalho. "Responsibility to Protect the Future: Children on the Move and the Politics of Becoming." *Global Responsibility to Protect* 10, no. 1–2 (2018): 121–44.

Tabak, Jana, Luiza Villela, and Manuela Trindade Viana. "Youths and Children between Borders: Critical Reflections on the (Im)Possibilities of Former Child-Soldiers as Peacebuilders in the Colombian Peace Process." Paper presented at the Third Academic Conference on International Mediation, Rio de Janeiro, Brazil, July 2017.

Timimi, Sami. "Globalising Mental Health: A Neo-liberal Project." *Ethnicity and Inequalities in Health and Social Care* 4, no. 3 (2012): 155–60.

Tisdall, E. Kay. "Conceptualising Children and Young People's Participation: Examining Vulnerability, Social Accountability and Co-production." *International Journal of Human Rights* 21, no. 1 (2017), 59–75.

"The Twin Terrors." *Time*, 7 February 2000. http://content.time.com/time/world/article/0,8599,2054474,00.html.

Twum-Danso, Afua. *Africa's Young Soldiers: The Co-option of Childhood*. Pretoria: Institute for Security Studies, 2003.

Twum-Danso Imoh, Afua. "Children's Perceptions of Physical Punishment in Ghana and the Implications for Children's Rights." *Childhood* 20, no. 4 (2013): 472–86.

United Nations Children's Fund (UNICEF). Cape Town Principles and Best Practices. Adopted at the Symposium on the Prevention of Recruitment of Children into the Armed Forces and on Demobilization and Social Reintegration of Child Soldiers in Africa, Cape Town, 27–30 April 1997. http://www.unicef.org/emerg/files/Cape_Town_Principles(1).pdf.

———. *The Paris Principles: Principles and Guidelines on Children Associated with Armed Forces or Armed Groups*. Paris: UNICEF, 2007. https://www.unicef.org/protection/files/Paris_Principles_EN.pdf.

———. *The Progress of Nations*. New York: UNICEF, 2000.

———. *The State of the World's Children*. New York: UNICEF, 2003.

———. *Will You Listen? Young Voices from the Conflict Zone*. Geneva: UNICEF, 2007.

United Nations Committee on the Rights of the Child (UNCRC). *General Comment No. 12 (2009): The Right of the Child to Be Heard*. 20 July 2009. CRC/C/GC/12. https://www.refworld.org/docid/4ae562c52.html.

United Nations Department of Public Information. "Global Community Cannot Continue Failing Children, Says Secretary-General in Observance Remarks, Stressing 'This Is Completely Unacceptable.'" Press release, SG/SM/18790-ICEF/1892-OBV/1753, 20 November 2017. https://www.un.org/press/en/2017/sgsm18790.doc.htm.

United Nations Development Programme (UNDP). *Human Development Report, 1994*, New York: Oxford University Press, 1994, http://hdr.undp.org/sites/default/files/reports/255/hdr _1994_en_complete_nostats.pdf.

United Nations General Assembly. Convention on the Rights of the Child. 20 November 1989. United Nations, Treaty Series, vol. 1577: 3. http://www.refworld.org/docid/3ae6b38f0.html.

United Nations General Assembly. Declaration of the Commemorative High-Level Plenary Meeting Devoted to the Follow-up to the Outcome of the Special Session on Children. A/ RES/62/88, 25 January 2008. https://www.refworld.org/docid/5290a9da6.html.

United Nations General Assembly. Declaration of the Rights of the Child. 10 December 1959, A/RES/1386 (XIV). https://www.refworld.org/docid/3ae6b38e3.html.

United Nations General Assembly. International Year of the Child. 18 October 1979, A/ RES/34/4. http://www.refworld.org/docid/3b00f1b462.html.

United Nations General Assembly. Optional Protocol to the Convention on the Rights of the Child on the Involvement of Children in Armed Conflict. 25 May 2000. http://www .refworld.org/docid/47fdfb180.html.

United Nations General Assembly. Plan of Action for Implementing the World Declaration on the Survival, Protection and Development of Children in the 1990s. World Summit for Children, New York, 30 September 1990. http://www.un-documents.net/wsc-plan .htm.

United Nations General Assembly. *Report of the Special Representative of the Secretary-General for Children and Armed Conflict.* A/62/228, 13 August 2007. http://www.refworld.org/docid /47316f602.html.

United Nations General Assembly. Rome Statute of the International Criminal Court. 17 July 1998. http://www.refworld.org/docid/3ae6b3a84.html.

United Nations General Assembly. Universal Declaration of Human Rights. 10 December 1948, 217 A (III). http://www.refworld.org/docid/3ae6b3712c.html.

United Nations General Assembly. World Declaration on the Survival, Protection and Development of Children. 30 September 1990. http://www.unicef.org/wsc/declare.htm.

United Nations General Assembly. A World Fit for Children. Resolution adopted by the General Assembly, 11 October 2002. http://www.refworld.org/docid/5290a8624.html.

United Nations General Assembly. "World Summit for Children." 30 September 1990. https:// www.unicef.org/wsc/declare.htm.

United Nations Office of the Special Representative of the Secretary-General for Children and Armed Conflict (UN OSRSG for CAAC). "New Countries Endorse the Paris Commitments to End the Use of Child Combatants." Press release, 28 September 2010. https:// childrenandarmedconflict.un.org/press-release/28Sep10/.

United Nations Office of the Special Representative of the Secretary-General for Children and Armed Conflict (UN OSRSG for CAAC). *20 Years to Better Protect Children Affected by Conflict.* United Nations, December 2016. https://childrenandarmedconflict.un.org/wp -content/uploads/2017/06/Twenty-Years-of-Work-Updated-Booklet_web.pdf.

United Nations Organization Stabilization Mission in the Democratic Republic of the Congo (MONUSCO). *Child Recruitment by Armed Groups in DRC: From January 2012 to August 2013.* MONUSCO, October 2013. https://monusco.unmissions.org/sites/default/files /131024_monusco_cps_public_report_on_armed_group_recruitment_2012-2013.pdf.

United Nations Secretary General. *Children and Armed Conflict: Report of the Secretary-General (2005)*. A/59/695–S/2005/72, 9 February 2005. http://undocs.org/S/2005/72.

———. *Children and Armed Conflict: Report of the Secretary-General (2010)*. A/64/742–S/2010/181, 13 April 2010. http://undocs.org/S/2010/181.

———. *Children and Armed Conflict: Report of the Secretary-General (2012)*. A/66/782–S/2012/261, 26 April 2012. http://undocs.org/S/2012/261.

United Nations Secretary General. *Children and Armed Conflict: Report of the Secretary-General (2013)*. A/67/845–S/2013/245, 15 May 2013. https://undocs.org/en/A/67/845.

United Nations Security Council. Resolution 1261 (1999) (children in armed conflicts). 30 August 1999, S/RES/1261(1999). https://undocs.org/S/RES/1261(1999).

United Nations Security Council. Resolution 1314 (2000) (children in armed conflicts). 11 August 2000, S/RES/1314(2000). https://undocs.org/S/RES/1314(2000).

United Nations Security Council. Resolution 1379 (2001) (children in armed conflicts). 20 November 2001, S/RES/1379(2001). https://undocs.org/S/RES/1379(2001).

United Nations Security Council. Resolution 1460 (2003) (children in armed conflicts). 30 January 2003, S/RES/1460(2003). https://undocs.org/S/RES/1460(2003).

United Nations Security Council, Resolution 1539 (2004) (children in armed conflicts). 22 April 2004, S/RES/1539(2004). https://undocs.org/S/RES/1539(2004).

United Nations Security Council. Resolution 1612 (2005) (children in armed conflicts). 26 July 2005, S/RES/1612(2005). https://undocs.org/S/RES/1612(2005).

United Nations Security Council. Resolution 1882 (2009) (children in armed conflicts). 04 August 2009, S/RES/1882(2009). https://undocs.org/S/RES/1882(2009).

United Nations Security Council. Resolution 1998 (2011) (children in armed conflicts). 12 July 2011, S/RES/1998(2011). https://undocs.org/S/RES/1998(2011).

United Nations Security Council. Resolution 2068 (2012) (children in armed conflicts). 19 September 2012, S/RES/2068(2012). https://undocs.org/S/RES/2068(2012).

United Nations Security Council. Resolution 2143 (2014) (children in armed conflicts). 7 March 2014, S/RES/2143(2014). https://undocs.org/S/RES/2143(2014).

United Nations Security Council. Resolution 2225 (2015) (children in armed conflicts). 18 June 2015, S/RES/2225(2015). https://undocs.org/S/RES/2225(2015).

United Nations Security Council. Resolution 2427 (2018) (children in armed conflicts). 9 July 2018, S/RES/2427(2018). https://undocs.org/S/RES/2427(2018).

Vallely, Paul. "A Childhood Violated: Why We Are Launching This Campaign with Unicef to Help Africa's Child Soldiers." *Independent* (London), 9 December 2012.

Van Bueren, Geraldine. "The International Legal Protection of Children in Armed Conflicts." *International and Comparative Law Quarterly* 43, no. 4 (1994): 809–26.

Verhey, Beth. "Child Soldiers: Preventing, Demobilizing and Reintegrating." Africa Region Working Paper, series 23. Washington, DC: World Bank, 2001.

Wagnsson, Charlotte, Maria Hellman, and Arita Holmberg. "The Centrality of Non-Traditional Groups for Security in the Globalized Era." *International Political Sociology* 4, no. 1 (2010): 1–14.

Walker, R. B. J. *After the Globe, before the World*. New York: Routledge, 2010.

———. "Conclusion: Sovereignties, Exceptions, Worlds." In *Sovereign Lives: Power in Global Politics*, edited by Jenny Edkins, Véronique Pin-Fat, and Michael Shapiro, 239–50. New York: Routledge, 2004.

———. "The Double Outside of the Modern International." *Ephemera: Theory & Politics in Organization* 6, no. 1 (2006): 56–69.

———. *Inside/Outside: International Relations as Political Theory*. New York: Cambridge University Press, 1993.

———. "Lines of Insecurity: International, Imperial, Exceptional." *Security Dialogue* 37, no. 1 (2006): 65–82.

Wall, John. "Human Rights in Light of Childhood." *International Journal of Children's Rights* 16, no. 4 (2008): 523–54.

War Child. *War: The Next Generation*. London: War Child, 2013.

Watchlist on Children and Armed Conflict. *Where Are They . . . ? The Situation of Children and Armed Conflict in Mali*. New York: Watchlist on Children and Armed Conflict, 2013

Watson, Alison M. S. "Can There Be a 'Kindered' Peace?" *Ethics and International Affairs* 22, no. 1 (2008): 35–42.

———. *The Child in International Political Economy: A Place at the Table*. London: Routledge, 2009.

———. "Children and International Relations: A New Site of Knowledge?" *Review of International Studies* 32 (2006): 237–50.

———. "Guardians of the Peace? The Significance of Children to Continued Militarism." In *The Militarization of Childhood: Thinking beyond the Global South*, edited by J. Marshall Beier, 43–60. New York: Palgrave Macmillan, 2011.

Wessells, Michael. *Child Soldiers: From Violence to Protection*. Cambridge, MA: Harvard University Press, 2006.

———. "A Living Wage: The Importance of Livelihood in Reintegrating Former Child Soldiers." In *A World Turned Upside Down: Social Ecological Approaches to Children in War Zones*, edited by Neil Boothby, Alison Strang, and Michael Wessells, 179–97. West Hartford, CT: Kumarian Press, 2006.

Wille, Christina. "Children Associated with Fighting Forces (CAFF) and Small Arms in the Mano River Union (MRU)." In *Armed and Aimless: Armed Groups, Guns, and Human Security in the Ecowas Region*, edited by Eric G. Beran and Nicolas Florquin, 181–221. Geneva: Small Arms Survey, 2005.

Wisnefski, Kenneth C. "'Kony 2012' Offers Businesses Lessons on Viral Marketing." *Washington Post*, 10 March 2012. https://www.washingtonpost.com/business/on-small-business/kony-2012-offers-businesses-lessons-on-viral-marketing/2012/03/09/gIQAGBsh1R_story.html?utm_term=.737b2ac7d1e2.

Woodhead, Martin. "Child Development and the Development of Childhood." In *The Palgrave Handbook of Childhood Studies*, edited by Jens Qvortrup, William A. Corsaro, and Michael-Sebastian Honig, 46–61. Houndmills, UK: Palgrave Macmillan, 2011.

———. "Psychology and the Cultural Construction of Children's Needs." In *Constructing and Reconstructing Childhood: Contemporary Issues in the Sociological Study of Children*, edited by Allison James and Alan Prout, 61–81. London: Falmer Press, 1991.

Wyness, Michael. *Childhood and Society: An Introduction to the Sociology of Childhood*. New York: Palgrave Macmillan, 2006.

Wyness, Michael, Lisa Harrison, and Ian Buchanan. "Childhood, Politics and Ambiguity." *Sociology* 38, no. 1 (2004): 81–99.

Zelizer, Viviana A. *Pricing the Priceless Child: The Changing Social Value of Children*. Princeton, NJ: Princeton University Press, 1994.

INDEX